W9-CIG-576

WITHDRAWN

Malraux's Heroes and History

MALRAUX'S HEROES AND HISTORY

JAMES W. GREENLEE

NORTHERN ILLINOIS UNIVERSITY PRESS
DeKalb

The photograph of André Malraux is reproduced with the permission of *le Service Expositions de l'Ambassade de France,* New York, N.Y.

Library of Congress Cataloging in Publication Data
Greenlee, James W   1933–
    Malraux's heroes and history.
    Bibliography: p.
    Includes index.
    1. Malraux, André, 1901–   —Knowledge—History.
2. History in literature. I. Title. PQ2625.A716Z674 1975   843'.9'12   74–
    12819 ISBN 0-87580-051-3

Copyright © 1975 by Northern Illinois University Press
Published by the Northern Illinois University Press,
DeKalb, Illinois 60115
Manufactured in the United States of America
All rights reserved
Designed by Gary Gore

For Nancy Pool Greenlee

CONTENTS

PREFACE

$\mathcal{T}$HIS study of Malraux's heroes and history began several years ago as an introduction to a broader study of the novels and plays of those politically committed writers who emerged in France after World War II. With the aid of a grant from the National Endowment for the Humanities, I set out to determine how such writers as Simone de Beauvoir, Camus, Sartre, Roger Vailland, and Vercors looked at history and, more specifically, how they appraised the individual's role in the historical evolution of mankind. The introduction on Malraux was to have summarized the legacy of the novelist who, long before World War II spread its pall over Europe and the Orient, was already depicting the adventures of characters driven by a metaphysical absurdity to seek a justification for their lives through political activism. I soon discovered that I could not do justice to the evolution of Malraux's views in the limited space of an introduction, and I set aside my original project in order to give full attention to the thought of the author whom I came to admire above those writers who inherited his activist commitment.

Malraux's Heroes and History retains much of the perspective that I had originally intended to give my introduction: it remains essentially an investigation of the changing views of history that underlie Malraux's novels. Beyond that, it presents an interpretation of the particular understanding of history that the novelist assigned to his principal characters. Although the importance of history is regularly mentioned in studies of Malraux's fiction, his novels have not yet been investigated with the aim of establishing the historical concept on which they are based. Because a historical perspective clarifies certain obscure aspects of Malraux's fiction, I hope that this study will supplement and, with good fortune, correct earlier readings of Malraux's novels.

Preface

In composing this book, my aim has been to limit my investigations to Malraux's changing concepts of history, rather than attempt an exhaustive study of his works, much of which would necessarily repeat research already published. In pursuit of my goal, I have, for instance, given but scant attention to Malraux's early *farfelus*, the fantasies that reveal too little of their author's historical consciousness to clarify his views on man's place in the historical process. Likewise, I have referred only collaterally to the rich art studies begun in the 1930s but published only after World War II, when Malraux had ceased writing fiction. Where they illuminate the obscure areas of his thought—as they certainly do for the last two novels—I have not hesitated to draw on them, but I have not made them a major object of my research. This limited scope of *Malraux's Heroes and History* may disappoint some students of Malraux, but I hope that the patient reader will see how the appreciation of his novels gains from an understanding of the history that underlies them.

Without the year's research financed by a grant from the National Endowment for the Humanities, it is unlikely that this project would ever have found its beginning. I take this opportunity, first, to thank the Endowment for its assistance and, second, to express the hope that the federal government will find the resources to encourage more scholarship in the Humanities.

When the scope of my project changed from the post-World War II writers to Malraux, considerable research still remained to be done. The Humanities Division of the California Institute of Technology generously contributed its support. My gratitude goes out to Hallett Smith and his successor as Chairman of the Caltech Humanities Division, Robert Huttenback, for the material assistance they made available to me. But more important to the completion of *Malraux's Heroes and History* has been the advice and information furnished by my former colleagues at Caltech, particularly the historians and philosophers—true humanists in the finest sense of the word. And for the encouragement and help of Caltech's medieval historian, John Benton, I would like to give special thanks: without the confidence that he showed in my

Preface

project and in my ability to carry it out, I am sure that it would never have been completed.

I wish to thank, too, W. M. Frohock of Harvard University, Walter Langlois of the University of Wyoming, Robert Champigny of Indiana University, and Stanley Gray of the University of Illinois who read my manuscript at different phases of preparation: with the aid of their insight and expertise, I believe that I have been able to avoid many of the pitfalls of Malraux scholarship. But undoubtedly the greatest assistance came from my wife Nancy. During the whole period of composition, she gave more of herself in typing, checking out information, and proofreading than a husband can reasonably expect. It is to her that I address this book, with the hope that it holds as much meaning for informed general readers like her as for professional scholars.

Malraux's Heroes and History

1 INTRODUCTION

The European thinks of himself acting in a world
. . . where destiny is history.

Antimémoires

FOR an indication of André Malraux's im-
portance in contemporary history the modern reader need only
consult his daily newspapers. Rarely does much time go by without his name making the news. And this celebrity dates from as
far back as 1924 when his exploits in Indochina were first being
reported in European and American papers. Nevertheless, until
Malraux chooses to reveal more about his past, the extent of his
participation in the Resistance, the Communist movement, and
French politics will remain in doubt. Still there is ample documentation on his role in Indochinese anticolonialism, European
antifascism, the Spanish Civil War, the liberation of France, and
two Gaullist governments. For several years he has been reported
in the press as a candidate for the Nobel Prize in literature, and
most recently he amazed the world by publicly offering his services to Bangladesh during its struggle for independence. Even
without his declaration, it is evident that Malraux must believe he
has played an important role in world politics. But, because he
is so cautious about explaining his motives, even his most thor-
ough biographers have had difficulty in assessing them and interpreting his ideas on his own place in history.

Malraux has, so it seems, retreated behind the legend that has
grown up about him, leaving his novels and essays to speak on
his behalf. To be sure, they contain little that explains his own
life, but they constitute a rich source for his views on the individual's place in the historical process. In his fictional works
especially there can be found a constant reevaluation of history,
that process which, for the purpose of understanding its repre-

sentation in his novels, can be taken as social evolution and the political events that provide its direction. A specific attitude towards history can be identified in each of his protagonists, be they the European adventurers projected into the chaotic Orient of the 1920s, the revolutionaries in Germany and Spain of the 1930s, or the French tank commander of World War II. Out of their dramas emerges Malraux's criticism or appreciation of the historical view they incarnate. But no single novel can explain his complex and changing view: what conclusions on history can be drawn from the Oriental subjects conflict with those of the stories set in Europe. And Malraux's last novel, written after the French capitulation of 1940, introduces an altogether different notion of history, one which underlies the art studies he composed after the Liberation, but one which he may repudiate in the memoirs now being prepared.

Malraux's reinterpretation of history is one of the strengths of his fiction. Its importance has been largely overlooked by those scholars who find in his novels a continuing elaboration of the basic tragedy of mankind abandoned in a hostile universe. Their studies have the merit of explaining the totalitarian bent of Malraux's thought: they have shown how his fiction as well as the following art studies and autobiographical essays testify to his search for a single justification for all human endeavor or, conversely, a single concept of action that confers meaning on an individual's entire life. But in concentrating on the unity of Malraux's thought, they have failed to explain how each of the successive views of history presented in the novels can restore the sense of communion with the universe, the spiritual communion lost, according to the novelist, with the death of God.

In sharp contrast to these existentialistic interpretations are those of the more politically inclined critics, Lucien Goldmann in France and David Wilkinson in the United States. The Marxist critic Goldmann analyzed Malraux's changing views of history in *The Sociology of the Novel (Pour une sociologie du roman)*. There he associated the three stages of the writer's thought with a general evolution of the novel as literary translation of the quest for authentic social values. According to this interpretation, each stage of the evolution was focused in a "problematic" hero. Like-

Introduction

wise, Wilkinson found that Malraux's changing politics was reflected in three types of protagonists. Departing from the most divergent views, the two scholars arrive at surprisingly similar views on the politics in Malraux's novels. But their interpretations fail to sound the depths of the writer's changing views on the individual's relation to history: neither Goldmann nor Wilkinson have explained why Malraux's adventurers and revolutionaries have turned to political activism. They have excluded from their analyses the metaphysical considerations that the previous scholars rightly saw as a fundamental aspect of Malraux's fiction.

A comprehensive view of the politics of his novels must add a metaphysical dimension to any interpretation of the political motives of his characters. Then his changing view of history and politics can be seen to testify to his changing views on the individual's struggle to wrest a religious meaning for his life out of the chaos of the universe. His characters' search for that meaning in the activism that makes history happen is the subject of this study of history and Malraux's heroes.

It is in the novels Malraux published after 1933 that politics functions as surrogate religion. But before exploring the later novels, it is necessary to review, as did Malraux, what many European intellectuals saw as the legacy of a defunct Christianity. Such a review repeats much that his earliest critics have already observed. But the repetition is necessary if one is to appreciate the tragic view of history that Malraux associated early in his career with the human condition.

In 1925, some twenty years before the inhumanities and atomic destruction of World War II conditioned the Western world to appreciate Albert Camus's definition of the absurd, Malraux wrote of it in *The Temptation of the West (La tentation de l'Occident)*. In this, his first long work of fiction, he identified the moral and metaphysical problems of the modern European, the problems to which he devoted the remainder of his literary career. It stands as his first contribution to the polemics provoked in Europe by Oswald Spengler's dire prediction of the decline of the West. While Malraux could not endorse the Spenglerian concept of an evolution leading inevitably to the senescence and death of Europe, he did agree that Western traditions rooted in a remote past no longer supported a vigorous civilization.

The Greeks, Malraux observed in accordance with most Hellenists, bequeathed to Europe the humanistic concept that man himself is the source of all values. For whatever satisfaction this notion provided, it also carried with it a sense of cosmic isolation. As the chapter on this work will show in more detail, Malraux saw that Christianity temporarily restored the individual's link with the divine forces of creation and offered the comfort provided by Oriental religions—a sense of communion with the universe. Furthermore, it promised immortality, preserving individual lives from the annihilation that death represents for Malraux. But, following the Nietzschean death of God, the Christian concept of man and his immortal soul also died, according to Malraux. The modern European was then left with nothing more than a heightened sense of the futility of existence and of his own isolation in the universe—what Malraux, long before Camus, called "the absurd."

In "On European Youth" ("D'une jeunesse europééne"), his 1927 essay, which can be taken conveniently as the literary manifesto of the post-Dada generation of absurdists, Malraux proposed that art should be the laboratory where solutions to the absurd are tested. Had he followed his own precepts, his first novels would have investigated alternatives to the humanistic individualism that temporarily filled the void left by the disappearance of Christian values. His 1928 novel *The Conquerors (Les conquérants)* and the 1930 novel *The Royal Way (La voie royale)* illustrate instead the futility of searching for a solution to the absurd in politics, the day-to-day expression of history. These novels of Oriental revolution and intrigue elaborate, through fictional characters, what Malraux only sketched in *The Temptation of the West* as the tragedy of the European adventurer. Rather than provide a solution to the absurd, history is the domain of tragedy, where an inevitable defeat only confirms the absurdity of life.

It is only with his third novel, *Man's Fate (La condition humaine*, 1933), that Malraux begins his search for solution. But, as depicted in this, his most successful book, history remains hostile. Only because they do not need victory to justify their lives do

Introduction

Malraux's first exemplary heroes cheat the absurd. They place their goals outside of history and are able to find a personal satisfaction in the "virile fraternity" of revolutionary activism, even though they are unable to improve the lot of the exploited Chinese laborers.

While this evolution is a logical development of Malraux's thought, it is inconsistent with the representation of his heroes as Communists: who more than a Communist, be he a Stalinist, Trotskyist, or Maoist, should appreciate the need for political victories in order to effect the social reforms that are the party goals? But, as of 1933 when *Man's Fate* was published, Malraux's fiction still presented history as the domain of the absurd. He refused to look for a redemption from the absurd in historical success, but he retained the hope that the Oriental aspiration for identification with the cosmos could be wedded to the Western faith in creative action. And, after criticizing communism in this novel, he went on in the next to show how Marxism could redeem the individual's tragic destiny.

Published in 1935, *Days of Wrath (Le temps du mépris)* marks the transition from despair over the effects of history to the hope that history can afford a salvation. It is a pivotal work in Malraux's career but not a novel he was proud of: he authorized only two new editions and excluded it from the last collected edition of his works. Perhaps the unconcealed communist bias of this, his shortest novel, explains his dissatisfaction. In it, Malraux illustrates how it is possible for man to escape the absurd, not by participating in the events of history alone, but by espousing the dialectical movement of history: his redemption comes through participation in history at the "metaphysical" level where the events are caused.

While Christian theologians, such as St. Augustine, argued for a direction to history which prepared for the second coming of Christ, credit for interpreting the meaning of history in secular terms goes to the nineteenth-century German philosopher Hegel. He saw history evolving according to a predetermined "dialectical" pattern from which derived the social conditions under which men live. A few decades later, Karl Marx reinterpreted the dialectic in order, in his words, "to stand it on its feet." For the

Malraux's Heroes and History

author of *Capital,* social and economic conditions did not derive from the dialectic. To the contrary, they gave history its direction, one which would carry the working man to victory over the capitalist.

Although Malraux must have first learned of the dialectical view of history through Marxism, his thought was most akin to Hegel's. He acknowledged an abstract ideal of brotherhood and social democracy, but he also discovered in the Marxist dialectic what was inherent in Hegel—a secular religion that afforded the activist the metaphysical comforts of participation in the universal course of history. This discovery is sketched at the conclusion of *Days of Wrath* where it is punctuated by the exaltation characteristic of a divine revelation.

The same faith in history inspires the main characters of *Man's Hope (L'espoir),* the novel generally acclaimed to rank just behind *Man's Fate* as Malraux's best. This fictional representation of the Spanish Civil War borrows much from the author's role in forming and commanding an air squadron composed of foreign volunteers. As literary traditions illustrate, a person closely involved in a limited phase of war has difficulty presenting a cohesive account of the campaigns, and Malraux is no exception. What his account does provide is an amorphic succession of battle scenes, bound together by a singularly communistic motif—the evolution of the war from a heroic anarchist rebellion to an organized communist revolution. At the same time, the novel criticizes the historical pessimism of the communist revolutionaries in *Man's Fate.* For those who perceive a dialectical movement in history, Malraux indicates, history ceases to destroy man and becomes the instrument for his integration with the universe. For them, it ceases to be an element of man's tragic destiny and serves as a religious link with eternity—not the sempiternity of endless time, but the more restricted eternity that encompasses the existence of mankind. Although it offers no immortality, the dialectical view of history does permit the individual to inscribe his life in the vast continuum of the human race.

Understanding Malraux's concept of "antidestiny" requires a closer study of the novels than is appropriate to an introduction. It should be nonetheless evident that he was more interested in

8

Introduction

the metaphysics of the Spanish Civil War than its political objectives. While *Man's Hope* confirms such an interpretation, documentation of his activities testifies to a deep commitment to the Republican cause. His commitment may have slackened, however, for he devoted the last months of the war to filming one of the final episodes of his novel. Franco's victory in 1939 must have led Malraux to question whether or not historical dialectic could ever offer a redemption from the absurd: it certainly appeared to be less than an infallible explanation of history, and no future Malraux protagonists would find an antidestiny in Communist party activism.

The events leading up to World War II could only have further eroded his faith in Marxist metahistory. While England and France were offering Czechoslovakia up to Hitler from the West, Russia and Germany were parceling up Poland. And shortly afterwards, Europe's first communist state began its expansion into Finland and the Baltic states. In case that were not enough to erode his Marxist predilections, the French Communist party's collaboration with the occupying German army surely must have been. By the time Germany invaded Russia in June 1941, Malraux had ceased to lend any support to communism. And when he finally joined the Resistance, he chose the Gaullist Forces Françaises de l'Intérieur in preference to the Communist Francs-Tireurs et Partisans Français. But that did not occur until after the publication of his last novel, *The Walnut Trees of Altenburg (Les noyers de l'Altenburg)*, in 1943.

That discursive and abstract work carries Malraux's repudiation of Marxism—not directly, but by implication—and, at the same time, proposes a final basis for redemption from the absurd. If Malraux's ten-year flirtation with communism is to be considered, as some biographers think, as a deviation from an otherwise unified thought, the secular religion presented in *The Walnut Trees of Altenburg* likewise departs from the view of history introduced in *The Temptation of the West* and repeated in the three novels set in the Orient. In one letter to his fictional French correspondent, Ling identifies as one of the sources of Western anxiety the absence of any single permanent human quality. It was principally for the lack of a common human ingredient that

9

Malraux's Heroes and History

history failed to offer the response to the absurd which makes it an antidestiny. Marxism, however, provided the basis of that coherence. It lay in the economic determinism that Malraux was unable to accept entirely. But when he rejected Marxism, he retained his confidence in a historical coherence and made the search for its base the main theme of his last novel. Through the protagonist, Berger, whose name he took in the Resistance, Malraux reveals how all human endeavors are elicited by the instincts of brotherhood and horror of death. The conditions for action then never change, nor is there any real progress—death cannot be overcome, and brotherhood cannot be realized once and for all. Therefore, there is no historical progress. In this final novel Malraux takes his two principal characters out of the realm of historical change and places them in a domain of static "antihistory," where the passage of time is no longer important and where politics offers no metaphysical satisfactions.

In such a domain individual acts can be inscribed in the eternity of mankind. The individual who appreciates antihistory thus satisfies the first of the two conditions Malraux posed in his first work of fiction as essential if man were to be spared the torments of the absurd and recover a sense of integration with the universe. But since no progress is conceivable, few would feel solicited to act. The possibility of satisfying Malraux's second condition—that will and action retain their value—is restricted to an elite who are able to find some reason to act. In the final pages of *The Walnut Trees of Altenburg*, effective action becomes the privilege of the artist who is able to represent man's eternal struggle to wrest some meaning out of the absurd.

After World War II, Malraux was able to investigate his concept of art as an antidestiny in his studies on painting and sculpture. Somewhat later, in 1967, he published the first part of his *Antimemoirs (Antimémoires)*, which annexes large segments of his last work of fiction to his political life. If Malraux's autobiography is read with reference to his fiction, it is possible to see that politics—or perhaps the expression "statesmanship" is more appropriate—can likewise provide the raw stuff of an antidestiny. Like the first volume of *Antimemoirs*, those which he has already added disclose an intelligence constantly seeking what is timeless

Introduction

in the endeavors of men, and seeking thereby to free itself from identification with a single historical period. They appear to belong to the cycle initiated by the last novel. Perhaps publication of future *Antimemoirs* or future installments of *The Mirror of Limbo* (*Le miroir des Limbes*), as Malraux has renamed the collection of his autobiographical essays, will confirm whether or not the evolution of the historical view recorded in his fiction corresponds to his concept of his own place in history.

This evolution has been more irregular than many previous studies have shown. Its irregularity becomes apparent when Malraux's fiction is viewed from the standpoint of the historical role he has assigned to his characters. History may not be the only key to Malraux's complexity, but it is the key to understanding how his thought was modified during the course of his literary career. The evolution only begins with Malraux's discovery of the Orient during his two prolonged visits to Indochina. The remaining steps can be reconstructed by a chronological study of his fictional works—all of them, not only those by which he hopes to be remembered in the antihistory of literature.

2 THE TEMPTATION
OF THE ORIENT

$\mathcal{L}$ ITTLE in André Malraux's earliest publications suggests the directions his later fiction was to take. They stand principally as testimony to his efforts to overcome the disadvantages of his childhood and establish a career in a profession normally reserved, in France, to the more comfortable bourgeoisie. So ashamed was Malraux of his origins that it took Clara Goldschmidt, his first wife, several months of marriage to learn of them—at least so she reports in her autobiography.[1]

Always a good student, young André devoted his adolescence to qualifying for admission to the prestigious Lycée Condorcet in Paris. No sooner had he qualified, according to one biographer, than he ceased attending classes.[2] No grades were recorded for him in school records; he never passed his baccalaureate and never attended the Paris Institute of Oriental Languages—contrary to a legend he allowed to develop. His early manhood was certainly legendary, but not for the reasons that he has allowed to circulate.

Malraux's literary training came through his own independent efforts. His talents soon earned him the admiration of the poet Max Jacob and of a minor literary figure, Daniel-Henry Kahnweiler, who published the adolescent writer's work. When Malraux was but nineteen, Kahnweiler prepared a sumptuous edition of the short *Paper Moons,*[3] written two years earlier. Like a character from an André Gide satire on fin de siècle literary salons, young Malraux had adapted post-symbolist fantasy into an allegory on the fear of death. Although it was abundantly illustrated by Fernand Léger, it received scant notice. Recent literary scholars, combing its thirty pages for the first evidence of Malraux's genius, have given it far more attention.

13

Malraux's Heroes and History

Malraux has authorized republication of *Paper Moons* in the 1945 and 1970 collective editions of his works.[4] A series of accounts of an imaginary "Puppet Fireman" was not so fortunate, nor were the tales entitled "Written for an Idol with a Trunk" and "Written for a Plush Bear," which survive at the Paris Bibliothèque Nationale in forgotten literary journals.[5] The last of Malraux's fantasies, *The Farfelu Kingdom*, has undergone several revisions since it was first written in 1920. The definitive version, published in 1928,[6] has also been reprinted in the two collections. In this revised form, it shows the maturity the author acquired through his experience in Indochina.

The early fantasies, Malraux's *farfelus*, present something of a puzzle to the student of Malraux. Although they lack real literary merit, they nonetheless announce many of the themes to which the mature novelist constantly returns. Their grotesqueness, for instance, can be interpreted as a predilection to the irony that abounds in the later fiction. But this interpretation rests on an appreciation of the more serious novels. Readers interested in understanding Malraux's views of history can disregard these youthful efforts and begin with the works that grew directly out of his first two trips to the Orient in 1923 and 1925. It is as though he had to leave the atmosphere of the Paris literary salons to find his true literary vocation. But it can hardly be claimed that a search for literary subjects brought about the first trip: far more materialistic and, in fact, ignominious motives lay behind it. Malraux, his young wife Clara, and his childhood companion Louis Chevasson set off in October 1923 to improve their fortunes by stealing Khmer statues, which they hoped to sell to British and American collectors. This escapade brought the youthful adventurers face to face with the French colonial authorities in Indochina. While the corruptible functionaries frequently cast a blind eye on the piracy of statues, they showed no such indulgence to the three youths.

Returning to the Cambodian capital of Phnom Penh with their loot, Malraux and his companions were arrested. The men were tried for theft, the only charge that could be brought against them. Malraux was sentenced to three years' imprisonment and Chevasson to eighteen months. Clara, whose health was severely

14

The Temptation of the Orient

threatened by dysentery contracted in the jungle, was permitted to return to France. Once she reached the Paris intellectual circles, she mounted a campaign for the release of the two young men, still detained in Cambodia. Her efforts of two hectic months rallied Paris artists and writers behind the cause of the two adventurers, but this likely had little effect on their appeal. Malraux and Chevasson were again found guilty. But this time they received suspended sentences and immediately left Indochina.

While Malraux's actions were at least as colonialistic as those of the most venal officials in Saigon, his imprisonment turned him into an anticolonial activist. No sooner had he returned to France than he began preparations for a second trip to Indochina, but now his intentions were clearly political. What proportions of revenge and of political zeal conditioned his decision to return to Saigon in January 1925 would be difficult to determine, though his activities on behalf of Indochinese anticolonialism have been well documented. He has been shown to have confined his efforts principally to journalism: aging issues of his newspapers, *Indochine* and *Indochine enchaînée,* are still on file at the Bibliothèque Nationale. In addition, he was an active supporter, if not an organizer, of the nationalistic Young Annam movement in Saigon, and shortly before his departure in January 1926, he became a member of the Cholon Section of the Kuomintang.

His support of Vietnamese nationalism proved futile, and after a year in Saigon, he must have had some doubts about an individual's ability to influence the course of history. He and Clara returned to France, although hardly to bring their anticolonial message to the French people—the explanation given by admiring biographers.[7] He immediately resumed his suspended literary career: Clara's efforts to win his freedom apparently brought him the notoriety required to launch it successfully. His first mature work, *The Temptation of the West,* appeared a few months after his return, and he founded a publishing house of his own, the now defunct Editions à la Sphère. The next year he joined the editorial staff of the prestigious publisher Gallimard, and from 1927 until 1933, he devoted most of his efforts to writing. In 1927 he published an important essay on the artist's role as a moralist, entitled "On European Youth."[8] The next year he published his

Malraux's Heroes and History

first novel, *The Conquerors*, and his second novel, *The Royal Way*, appeared two years later, in 1930. Also in that year there appeared *The Life of Napoleon* (*La Vie de Napoléon*), the first of the anonymous biographies he compiled for Gallimard—even distinguished Parisian publishers have to produce sure money-makers sometimes—and the first of Malraux's art studies, a brief pamphlet entitled *The Gothic Buddhist Works of Pamir.*

His interest in Oriental art had twice taken him to the Middle East, and in 1931 he returned there as part of a protracted, round-the-world trip with Clara. It was during this trip that Malraux visited mainland China for the first time. Brief as the visit must have been, it afforded him valuable insight into the Chinese Nationalist repression of communism in China, the theme of *Man's Fate.* The year 1932 was devoted largely to the composition of this novel, which appeared serially in the *Nouvelle Revue Francaise* between January and June of 1933.

Malraux's literary activity from the time of his return to France early in 1927 to the publication of his prize-winning novel in 1933 seems to have left him with little time for politics. But it cannot be overlooked that the novels he composed during this period reveal a pessimism about the individual's role in history. Whether the withdrawal from politics was the cause or the effect of this view can only be a matter of conjecture until Malraux chooses to clarify this period of his life. The return to Paris literary circles marks, nonetheless, a change in Malraux's priorities: literary creation replaced militancy at the center of his personal values. Politics became for him the domain of futility; and to a certain degree, Malraux's first novels stand as an explanation for his renunciation of politics.

Withdrawal from politics was signaled in advance of the novels by Malraux's first long work, *The Temptation of the West.* This plotless work is a fictional correspondence between a Chinese intellectual traveling in Europe and his European acquaintance living in China. The letters of Ling, who writes from a Confucianist perspective, carry the bulk of the message. Through his bemused Chinese visitor, Malraux presents an attack on Western values reminiscent of the one Nietzsche earlier attributed to the Persian Zarathustra. The European correspondent, identified

The Temptation of the Orient

only as "A.D.," confirms Ling's observations but finally rejects the Oriental alternatives to Western individualism. The last letters he writes from China carry a rejection of the traditional Chinese view of man and leave unanswered the problem of man's place in the world.

While it is very likely that this work dates principally from 1925 and 1926, Malraux gives the years 1921 to 1925 as the period of composition. There is some justification, however, for the earlier dates. Before conceiving his art piracy scheme, Malraux conducted his own independent but extensive study of Oriental art. This knowledge of Eastern culture greatly nourished the work that was intended to criticize the foundations of Western individualism, but no more than his own experiences in Indochina.

Malraux must have discovered during the time he spent among the Chinese of the Cholon district in Saigon the opposition between Confucianist resignation to an immutable world order and the Oriental political activist's hope to improve man's lot. Since the work develops a conclusion based on this opposition, it is very likely the product of that frustrating year of political activism. But dating is only of secondary importance: it is far more important to note how the time spent in study and travel was essential to the maturation of Malraux's thought. It permitted him to weigh the East against the West and arrive at his own understanding of the existential problems of Western man.

The informed reader of 1926 might also have interpreted *The Temptation of the West* in the larger context of the European malaise that followed World War I and the Russian Revolution. And, to a large extent, the work does bear the stamp of its time. Malraux did not hesitate to attach his first important work of fiction to the reappraisal of European values fueled by the publication of Oswald Spengler's *The Decline of the West* in 1923. While he did not align himself with the doomsayers who anticipated the degeneration of Europe or those who raised ominous cries about the "yellow menace" from the Orient, he did contest the defenses of Western culture offered up by Christian essayists like Henri Massis in France and G. K. Chesterton in England.[9] His conclusions were, however, neither Spenglerian nor Christian; rather they contained the challenge to reassess the value of an indi-

17

Malraux's Heroes and History

vidual's will and action. Starting with *The Temptation of the West* but continuing well beyond the time that gave birth to it, this challenge was to inspire all his writing—fiction, art history, and biography. This fictional correspondence thus constitutes a valuable introduction to the novels in which the individual's relation to history is represented first as the source of existential anguish, then as a solution to it.

Ling opens the correspondence by observing how little life in Europe resembles the image transmitted by European works of art. He does not elaborate on this observation, but reports that the highest achievements of Western intelligence have had scant effect on European society. Aside from the geometrical gardens of France and the precisely constructed temples of the Acropolis, Ling finds little evidence of the European's success in imposing his will on the world. He finds only reasons for discrediting the products of the European mind and readily earns the endorsement of his French correspondent, equally critical of his own cultural heritage.

Throughout the work, an Oriental ideal of an integration with the cosmos is contrasted with the modern European ideal of heroism inherited from classical Greek and Christian traditions. Malraux's development of these oppositions is most discursive, if not simply fragmented. The device of a fictional correspondence gives him a license to explore in a random way ideas that could be expressed more cohesively in an essay. Appreciation of Malraux's thought requires a rearrangement of his presentation. Such a deformation may make the book more comprehensible, but it deprives it of the lyricism in which Malraux already casts the tragedy of Western man. While his meaning may be somewhat obscured by his discursive style, he has successfully given his ideas an affective dimension by attributing them to characters who do not suppress their feelings when writing about their observations.

Encouraged by the approval of his French acquaintance, Ling continues by observing that ancient Greeks set the individual apart from his world and even apart from other men. Malraux's Chinese character seems to discover for himself the legacy of the ancient Greeks, the notion that man is the source of human values. Even Greek statuary conveys to him the message Europeans have come to call humanism. He writes, "A few moments ago, when I was referring to that humble museum . . . , the head of a young man with open eyes struck me as an allegory of the Greek genius, with its profound insinuation: measure all values against the length and intensity of one human life."[10] The Greeks, Ling notes, have conferred a dignity on the individual, and the passion of the Greeks became their defiance of a divine order that destroyed individual worth. Malraux represents the Greeks as having searched for no definition of man in eternity; they sought no link with the world and prized above all their opposition to it. Rather, in Malraux's view, they claimed for man that prerogative that their predecessors were all too ready to cede to the gods: the ability to impose the stamp of their personality on the world. As Malraux interprets Greek thought, the human will was more highly honored than the integration into the cosmos. Even though the ancient Greeks lost the comforts of religion, they discovered in their independence from the gods the satisfactions of personal accomplishment.[11]

In making the individual the source of values, the ancient Greeks deprived human life of any metaphysical meaning. While they gave man a personal dignity and independence from the gods, they also condemned him to the cosmic isolation of the absurd. It is paradoxical, then, that Malraux's Chinese observer conjectures that Greek thought laid a foundation for the conversion of Europe to Christianity. The new religion wedded the Greek respect for the personality with an Oriental sense of integration with the universe. It was able to provide the metaphysical comfort that the primitive individualism of ancient Greece could not. It offered Christians an eternal bond to God and provided a direction for what Malraux presents as Western man's egocentric passion to wrest his existence from the annihilation of death —or, in positive terms, to give his life some permanence.

The key to the integration of the individual into the universe is the Christian concept of the soul. Since death does not destroy the soul, life is everlasting. Then, too, the God who created the soul of each individual continues to communicate with him through it. It thus constitutes a link between man and the divine forces of the universe. Malraux's characters do not specifically mention it in their letters, but the soul evidently is the contribution of Christianity that explains the permanence of the personality and, at the same time, rescues the individual from metaphysical isolation.

During the centuries of its ascendancy, Christianity offered a perfect marriage of the individual and the universe. So well did it suit Malraux's concept of the existential aspirations of Western man that one very reliable American critic saw in his praise the basis for an eventual return to the Church.[12] It is unlikely that this prediction will ever be realized, for Malraux's works show that the notion of a personal God fails to satisfy him. He places himself firmly in the tradition of Western agnostic thought. For him, as for many other Europeans, the tenuous link between the individual and the universe has disintegrated and, with it, the principles which directed life. Elaborating on Nietzsche, Ling writes aphoristically to A.D., "For you, absolute reality was God, then man, but *man died* (Malraux's emphasis) after God and, in anguish, you search for a divinity to whom you could entrust his strange heritage" (pp. 174–75).

The death of Christianity leaves a double legacy: a heightened awareness of the self and an absence of any direction to human life. Modern Western individualism is interpreted by Malraux's two fictional correspondents as a blind passion, a will with no object and a sense of disharmony with the world. Two decades before the public discovered the notion in Camus's *The Myth of Sisyphus,* Malraux was already describing the legacy of Christianity as "the essential absurdity at the center of European men" (p. 78). Because the notion of the absurd is interpreted as coming from the loss of an individualistic religion, it is unique to the West —or, as Malraux prefers, to Western agnosticism. This loss reduces all individual effort to futile gesture and leaves the European again with the torment of cosmic isolation. It is for his futility and isolation that he becomes tragic: not, as the ancient Greeks would have it, for his hubristic defiance of destiny.

In making the Greeks responsible for our absurd heritage, Malraux gives them too much credit. The funeral art of ancient

The Temptation of the Orient

Egypt and the history of the ancient civilizations of the Middle East reflect metaphysical concerns similar to the Hellenistic sense of cosmic alienation. With the publication of the first fragments of *The Psychology of Art* in December 1937,[13] Malraux corrected his oversight, but the initial error stands as a testimony to his concept of the special role of the European. He sees himself and other Westerners as singled out by their historical destiny to wrest a meaning for human life out of a universe where no meaning is given. His French character writes that, with the death of God and of the Christian notion of the soul, the European is left with the freedom to act and with the vain hope that his actions will produce a justification for his life. Some years later, Malraux's characters will observe, more aphoristically, that man is defined by what he does. Jean-Paul Sartre uses the same definition of man based on a comparable concept of freedom, but in his *Being and Nothingness,* he describes as agony man's fundamental freedom and his "condemnation" to act without guidelines. Malraux's protagonists are rarely so tormented: they are able to face the absurd with the confidence that only Orestes among Sartre's heroes attains in the play *The Flies.*

Malraux evidently has little interest in the individual who refuses to come to grips with the absurd—far less than Sartre, Camus, and writers in their train who gave so much attention to the problems of accepting Western man's tragic fate. He is no more able to resign himself than they are, but he directs his efforts toward transcending it. Still, characters capable of overcoming the absurd appear only in Malraux's later works. It is through characters such as Ling and A.D. that he defines the problem of the European. It is not just the problem of recognizing man's isolation in the universe, Ling explains on behalf of Malraux, but more of giving reality to one's life through action. The necessity to act has created an atmosphere of movement, of historical change; the individual gives his personality reality by changing the world about him, by imposing his will upon it. Any reality, then, that a personality acquires is condemned to disappear through the process of change, and any attempt to defend this acquired reality against erosion by change must lead to a conflict between individuals. When Ling's observations are pur-

Malraux's Heroes and History

sued to their logical consequences, Western individualism is seen to have spawned a climate of hostility. In it, man is pitted against man in a struggle to impose the stamp of one's own personality on history. To illustrate the futility of this struggle, Ling offers this description of Europeans: "Race subjected to the test of action and promised thereby the bloodiest of destinies" (p. 104). He does not conceal his preference for the static calm of the Orient, which affords him the satisfaction of belonging to a stable world. Nor does he regret that his view of the world deprives his own life of any importance.

Beneath comments such as these lies the author's wish that human will and action can retain their importance. But so long as the European remains confined to the domain of historical flux, Malraux's Chinese spokesman reports, he can enjoy nothing more than passing "erotic" pleasures. It is by this adjective, selected for its derogatory connotations, that Ling characterizes the individual's efforts to assert his will over another person. They yield only the fleeting satisfactions akin to those enjoyed by the male dominating his submissive female partner.

This assimilation of personal achievement to the sex act can be misunderstood. Malraux does not intend that women be seen as objects of carnal pleasure, but as objects to be dominated. They represent the most convenient conquest for the virile European who derives a perverse personal satisfaction from subordinating others to his will. But bringing others under his domination is only the first step of a quest for self-understanding. What he seeks above all is a confirmation of his place in the world. It can come only after his domination is acknowledged by a victim. Through his victim's act of submission he perceives his own importance. This self-perception is the goal that Malraux's character associates with eroticism, but which might more precisely be called sadism.

According to Ling, the need for such psychological satisfaction takes the European out of the bedroom and into the political arena, where he finds greater challenge and greater reward. It impels him to victories that far outweigh any sexual conquests. Like Freud's concept of sublimation, Malraux's eroticism becomes the mainspring of personal achievement. So great is the

The Temptation of the Orient

resemblance of these views of human sexuality that a contrast of the two is useful.

Although Freud had been popularized in France by the time Malraux was composing *The Temptation of the West,* his psychology appears to have had little influence on the ideas attributed to Ling. The Viennese psychoanalyst viewed sexuality as a motivation that could be sublimated or diverted, for reasons of propriety, from a sexual object to a socially approved goal: accomplishment is thus the result of a correction of innate animal impulses. For Malraux it is quite the contrary, for he believes that personal accomplishment comes from an intelligent, conscious redirection of sexual energy, the opposite of the subconscious process of sublimation. Both agree that the basis of personal achievement is sexual, but Malraux represents sexual energy as a valuable psychological resource, no matter what direction it assumes. He does not decry the pleasures of a sexual conquest, but indicates that the erotic force can be more profitably directed toward other goals. In *The Royal Way* particularly, eroticism drives the protagonist forward in the metaphysical struggle to wrest from death a meaning for his life. And already in *The Temptation of the West* it is presented as the source of the only spiritual satisfactions available to the Westerner cut off from the comforts of religion by his Greek heritage. Whatever victories he may earn, the Chinese character relates, are the results of an intelligently directed sexual drive and not, as Freud has it, the byproducts of social taboos. But Freud, it must be said, studied sex in the light of social restraints, whereas Malraux's views reflect his metaphysical bias. Their different perspectives yield different interpretations of the function of sexuality.

Sharing the novelist's lofty perspective, the fictional correspondents of *The Temptation of the West* never lose sight of the limits of sexuality. They agree that it may offer the European a temporary distraction from his metaphysical problems, but certainly it is no solution to them. As A.D. writes his endorsement of Ling's, and presumably the author's, observations on eroticism, he adds his own commentaries on European eroticism. He defines as an "erotic game" the attempt to impose one's own will and read a confirmation of others' acceptance of it: "The whole

23

erotic game lies in this: to be one's self and *the other;* to feel one's own sensations and those of the partner" (p. 102). He goes on to explain that the European discovered the female body because, he implies, it was through his subjugation of a woman that he was able to find individualistic satisfactions at their most rudimentary level.

As Malraux represents it, this competition imparts a sense of social isolation that accompanies the metaphysical isolation of the absurd. Others are seen only as adversaries, possible victims devoid of any human dignity or, more ominously, possible conquerors. But defeat is to be avoided at all costs. It entails the destruction of the personality—the fate of women so unfortunate as to fall in love. It should be evident that erotic domination is not proposed as an ideal. Malraux suggests through his characters, however, that it provides the only satisfaction in a world where personal accomplishments are so rapidly obliterated by history. Later, in the 1933 novel *Man's Fate,* Malraux's spokesman describes eroticism in even more inflated terms. In apparent contrast to the alternative to eroticism illustrated in the novel, Gisors represents it as the means of realizing the ideal of a God ("to become man knowing that he will recover his divine powers") and, at the same time, the ideal of man ("to become God without losing his personality"). In *The Temptation of the West,* however, it is presented more modestly as the only comfort open to the individualist unable to find his satisfactions in religion or social action.

Malraux's seeming identification of eroticism with the West is as inaccurate as his identification of the absurd with Ancient Greece. His study and travels undoubtedly brought him into contact with the erotic statuary of the Orient. He must have observed the differences between the eroticism of Eastern art and that which underlies the European urge for domination. He has made no effort to extend his interpretation to Oriental religious art and, instead, restricts eroticism to the West. For him, it remains a distinctive characteristic of the modern European: among the peoples of the world, the Westerner alone seems to face the menace of death that renders all human enterprise futile; he alone recognizes how death confines his activity to a few moments in eternity. After his moments of glory, his entire existence is effaced. And, adds Ling, the European who is conscious of the futility of his efforts cannot avoid being tormented by the prospect of death: "Total awareness of the world is death, and you understood it well" (p. 175). This is what Malraux sees as the source of man's anguish, not the existential agony of decision that Sartre emphasized.

Through Ling, he suggests that art may constitute a domain where an individual's actions may be spared the erosion of historical change. So important is art in *The Temptation of the West* that it must be considered one of the principal themes. It serves to focus the difference between Malraux's interpretation of the Oriental and Occidental world views, a difference observed, however, only from the Oriental perspective of Ling.

Malraux attributes to his character a preference for the suggestive stylization of Eastern art and does not allow him to see how the Western art of a Goya or a de la Tour can also aspire to permanence. Ling's attention is arrested instead by more contemporary artists, innovators concerned with developing a novel, personal view of the world. These artists seem only to be translating into an esthetics the individualist's desire for conquest. Consequently, Ling dismisses recent European efforts to perfect a personal style. For him, it is more important for an artist to understand what is permanent in humanity, what is unaffected by passing time. These insights cannot come from simple observation, for the models the artists see do not reveal their permanence. They require a penetration to the very marrow of life. Only then can the artist apply the techniques of his craft to represent what is permanent in the flux of human existence. Ling writes: "Understanding the world of successive existences is first of all understanding [the nature of the human species]; and it is through it that the artist's craft reveals the world" (pp. 121–22). Ling reveals an Oriental outlook when he insists that art acquires its value only when it captures aspects of the world that are free from change, but it is a view that Malraux no doubt shared with his character, since it is expressed again later in the art studies published after the war. Confirmation, however, must await publication of those studies after World War II. Here he is only interested in criticizing the narrowness of Western art, and his praise for Eastern art is intended principally to highlight the contrasts between the two.

By way of confirmation, A.D. writes back to elaborate Ling's observations.[14] The Frenchman's response conveys the rather exclusive view, perhaps understandable coming from a spokesman for a creative artist, that art alone concerns itself with the study of man. He sees the rapid evolution of artistic styles as the evidence of the incompatibility of the European world view with the reality of the world. The desire to adjust art to this reality has become, according to Ling, one of "the temptations facing the West." The goal of the Western spirit is not, unfortunately, to make art the expression of what is permanent, but to protect itself against the ravages of time:

> The art that it desires is conceived less by thinking about
> the finished work than about the mathematical relation
> between its parts. And it [art] is much less the satisfaction
> of a desire than the attempt of a culture always under attack
> to dominate the enemy and its own life, its most pitiless
> adversary (p. 146).

It was not many years later that Malraux modified this criticism of Western art. And certainly, even within the pages of this brief work, the basis for his later appreciation of art as a universal language can be found. The sculpture and architecture of ancient Greece do carry a message for the Oriental intellectual: how else could Ling be so alert to the message of the sculpted Greek head he found in the little museum? Conceivably, Malraux had already discovered the foundations of *The Psychology of Art, The Voices of Silence,* and *The Metamorphosis of the Gods*—that art could effect the perfect marriage between action on the one hand and the quest for a personal participation in eternity on the other. Still, elaboration of these views required much of his literary career: perhaps his fiction was inspired by the recognition that art afforded a solution to his own personal absurdist anxieties. But in *The Temptation of the West,* his interest is not solely in investigating the possibilities of art: he uses the fictional correspondence to point out the failures of Western individualism. And within the pages of this book, art itself is shown to be corrupted by this concept of man.

The letters on art exchanged by A.D. and Ling point out as well as any in the book Malraux's reasons for believing that a reappraisal of individualism is necessary. The romantic artists' hope for immortality through art also seems illusory. And unless the Westerner resorts to some mind-beguiling delusion, he must recognize the bankruptcy of that concept of man on which the greatness of Europe has been built. He cannot avoid recognizing that Europe is now only "a cemetery of heroes."

This remark attributed to Ling is characteristic of the preoccupation with death that characterizes Malraux's fiction. Few of his atheist contemporaries in France or elsewhere in Europe felt so impelled to rescue human values from annihilation by death. Other existentialists have been satisfied to find the meaning of human existence in life itself. For them, social commitment provided direction enough. Sartre, most notably, refused to place life under the dominion of death. Camus, somewhat similarly, held that the individual should maintain the perspective of a person sentenced to death but should refuse to let the remaining moments of his life be contaminated by his sentence. For Malraux, on the other hand, death stands as a reminder of man's alienation in the cosmos. In *The Temptation of the West,* the fictional correspondents describe for one another the European's failure to explain human existence so as to prevent death from draining life of all its significance. By casting his evaluation of Western individualism against a leitmotif of Confucianism, Malraux seems to suggest that Oriental thought offers a valid solution to the absurd and solace from the torment of death. But he then shifts the viewpoint and turns his criticism against the East. Malraux uses shifts of this sort effectively in his first three novels to criticize his characters. In this work, however, it adds a note of irony —incisive but not humorous—and, at the same time, gives another dimension to the title of the book.

The greater portion, by far, of *The Temptation of the West* presents the Oriental's observations on the West. Ling's letters are generally longer, and the responses he receives only confirm his views. The final letters stem, however, from a visit the Frenchman has made to the aging aristocrat, Wang-loh, in Shanghai. A.D. relays to Ling the protracted account of the disintegration of Oriental values given him by the old man. Wang-loh describes the destruction wrought by the young Chinese who have no more respect for traditional values. He is saddened that Chinese youth has succumbed to "the temptation of the West," which is how he sees their desire to change society. Malraux makes only the vaguest of allusions to politics, but it is nonetheless evident that he has in mind the Nationalist and Communist rebellions in China during the 1920s, as well as the technological revolution fostered by European colonialism. But, significantly, he does not represent the political revolts as part of a reform movement: to Malraux, it is a context in which the young Chinese are able to assert their will. He does not describe it in terms of its goals, but in terms of what personal satisfaction it might afford to a young activist.

It cannot be overlooked that, in this book, Malraux presented the Chinese Revolution through the eyes of an uncomprehending and unsympathetic patriarch. But the author wanted his readers to understand Oriental politics from Wang-loh's point of view, and he does not discredit this perspective explicitly. His criticism emerges from an understanding of the concluding exchanges between A.D. and Ling. The last three letters point out that modern China has already rejected its traditional "psychology," which provided the individual a comfortable, albeit insignificant, place in the universe. Like their European counterparts, youthful Chinese activists gave up a religious view of man in favor of one which confers some value upon human will and action. Malraux's message is clear: any concept of man that disregards these essentially human qualities is no more acceptable than one that bases human existence exclusively on them. In spite of Ling's eloquent defense, the Orient offers no better response to the human condition than the Occident. Oriental values may have survived longer, but their fragile survival was dashed by borrowed European political ideals. The knowledge of the Chinese Revolution that a contemporary reader could bring to this 1926 work, even that gleaned from the sketchy newspaper accounts of the time, could only have confirmed Malraux's assessment of Oriental thought.

The Temptation of the West ends on a pessimistic note, seemingly rejecting both the Western view of man and the Oriental alternative. It appears as a nihilistic work, disputing the existence of any human values, except perhaps the formal beauty of art, which alone seem exempt from erosion by history. It would be inaccurate to suppose, however, that Malraux intended his first fiction to be destructive. His aim was rather to describe the plight of the individual who is conscious of the human condition—he might better be called the introspective intellectual, but he is not exclusively European, for he may also be Oriental, Arab, African, or American, so long as he comes to grips with the absurd that casts its pall over modern Europe.

In his description of the absurd, Malraux hoped to lay the groundwork for a new "psychology." He suggests clearly in the fictional exchange of letters that the new concept of man would have to accommodate the Western concepts of will and action and the Eastern aspiration for an integration with the universe, so that death would no longer destroy the meaning of life. It is significant that his characters never despair over their own situation and, quite to the contrary, continue to write with the calmness that testifies to a confidence in the future of mankind. Their letters suggest the author's confidence that the human mind will resolve the European existential problems that have so rapidly spread to the rest of the world.

The Temptation of the West points, then, to the task of a philosopher. In the essay "On European Youth," published in 1927, Malraux annexed the study of ethics to art. While this dense essay can hardly be said to clarify ideas expressed in the previous work, it does restate the absurdist concept of man, identifying it as the source of twentieth-century philosophical problems. Speaking in his own name now, Malraux repeats his view of the absurd as the heritage of a defunct Christianity. He then adds that science also fails to "create a harmony between man and his thought." According to Malraux, it is necessary, first, to redefine the human condition, not just the personality; then to deduce a basis for moral values which restores to mankind a sense of importance.

29

Malraux's Heroes and History

Without so identifying it, he appears to be pointing towards a collectivist view of man in harmony with Confucianist, or even Buddhist, metaphysics or with the Marxist view of society. He is still unable to accept either of them unequivocally, because both concepts deprive the individual of his freedom to judge and act independently. So rather than espouse any view, Malraux invites the youth of Europe to use art to experiment with alternate responses to the absurdist dilemma. Art, he indicates, is a special domain where provisional solutions can be proposed and investigated, and the artist is thus something of a moral experimenter.[15]

Malraux concludes his essay with a question that conveys his own eagerness to assume the artist's moral responsibility: "What destiny lies in store for this violent youth, marvelously strengthened and delivered from the base vanity of calling 'great' a snobbish disdain for a life to which it can no longer attach itself?" (p. 153).[16] Later critics, focusing on the negative aspects of Malraux's thought, have interpreted this conclusion as a prophesy of World War II. Perhaps Malraux was aware that European moral disorder might lead to another war. But that is certainly contrary to the optimism expressed in this essay, an essay that reads curiously like the more publicized Nobel prize speech delivered by Camus in Stockholm in 1957.[17] It is easy to understand why Camus, upon being informed of his nomination for the prestigious award, replied that Malraux was more deserving. Thirty years before Camus, he had defined the responsibility of a generation of writers "rich only in its own negations" and had become one of the first to act upon the precepts of his own manifesto. Although he raised at least one more time the question of whether or not man was spiritually dead,[18] he for one refused to accept *yes* as an answer. Through his fiction he has illustrated that, even without the reassurance of a personal God, life is not meaningless.

The Conquerors (1928) and *The Royal Way* (1930), Malraux's first novels, make no pretense, however, of resolving the tragedy of the absurd. Instead they expand themes of *The Temptation of the West.* In them, Malraux again deals with the futility of giving the personality a reality through historical action. But instead of treating it on the abstract level of ideas, he illustrates it through

The Temptation of the Orient

the adventures of a Swiss revolutionary in Canton, then through those of a Danish political opportunist in Indochina. He chose for the background of these adventures the politics he had come to know during his own trips to southeastern Asia. He took few liberties with history in constructing these stories: his art is in creating characters and projecting them into a historical endeavor condemned in advance to failure. So long as the European must give his personality reality through action, as Malraux illustrates, his life will remain meaningless. His first two protagonists fall victim to the hostility of history, which becomes, in his first novels, an instrument of the absurd and of human tragedy.

3   THE ORIENTAL ADVENTURES

*T*HE optimism that concluded Malraux's 1927 essay, "On European Youth," did not carry over into his first two novels. Neither *The Conquerors* (1928) nor *The Royal Way* (1930) was inspired by the spirit of experimentation announced in the essay. Instead they present fictional illustrations of what Malraux had earlier criticized—the inadequacies of Western individualism. Consequently, neither Pierre Garine of *The Conquerors* nor Perken of *The Royal Way* can be considered exemplars. Perhaps the adjective "accusatory" *(accusatrice)*, used later by Malraux to describe the conduct of T. E. Lawrence in the Middle East, is most appropriate to describe the actions of his fictional European adventurers in the Far East.[1] Their activities, like Lawrence's, spring from a delusion about the individual's place in history, and their example is useful to denounce a mode of life.

Although Malraux has commented on his early novels more than on his later works, little he has written or said helps the reader to understand his conception of Garine and Perken. But his 1939 essay on *Les liaisons dangereuses* provides insights into his own rigorously logical characters.[2] Although Garine and Perken have little in common with the Marquise de Merteuil and Valmont of Laclos's eighteenth-century novel, all four are what Malraux calls "significant characters" *(personnages significatifs)*. Significant characters, Malraux explains, are composed of three elements: "the conception of the goals of man, next the will to attain them, then the application of this will" ("Laclos," p. 32). They are rational beings, he elaborates, who have a clear idea of what life offers them. They determine their goals according to this concept and pursue them with cold calculation—no Freudian unconscious corrupts their intellectual rigor. Products of an undiluted French rationalism, their actions coincide with what their reason proposes. For being able to dominate their feelings, they enjoy a vicious mastery over the more emotional beings about them—at least such is the case with Laclos's protagonists.

Such characters are representatives of an idea; they "signify" the idea they incarnate and thereby test it in a fictional universe. Even though their reasoning may be sound, they fail to win the reader's admiration. The success of the Marquise and of Valmont is won at the expense of those whom they callously manipulate. The tragedy they bring to others exposes them as villains and impugns the idea they signify. So likewise do the accounts of Malraux's fictional adventurers. Through his first two protagonists, accusatory and signifying at the same time, he presents a far more striking criticism of Western individualism than was permitted by the abstract style of *The Temptation of the West* or "On European Youth."

Garine and Perken bring to the Orient attitudes common to Europeans seeking a personal satisfaction in a great historical enterprise. Through the intermediary of admiring observers, Malraux recounts their efforts to dominate history, futile efforts which inevitably lead to their downfall. They are the "fallen conquerors" who, for Malraux's Chinese correspondent of *The Temptation of the West,* symbolize the inadequacy of European individualism.

Although both novels are set in the Orient—*The Conquerors* in revolutionary Canton and *The Royal Way* in French Indochina—Malraux makes no effort to contrast East and West, as he did in the earlier fictional correspondence between Ling and A.D. The Orient of these novels is well along the way toward Westernization. It is a land of political turmoil, and more important to self-seeking European adventurers such as Garine and Perken, it is a land of opportunity. But they are not in search of wealth. They measure their success in terms of political power—a transposition from the bedroom to history of the Malrauvian erotic urge to dominate. Malraux's critics have not overlooked this quality in his characters, who have regularly been reported to search out areas of greatest turbulence to test their mettle, much

The Oriental Adventures

like the heroes of Joseph Conrad.[3] But this assessment must be modified somewhat.

The most rigorous test Malraux's heroes could face would be in a struggle against the established powers of a stable European society. But, in leaving Europe, they seek a society in flux, where the force of their will can have the most discernible effect. They are, in short, political opportunists, and Malraux did not hesitate to so stigmatize them.[4] And, concluding their stories, he deprives them of any reward. His first protagonists are unable to harness the forces of history. Finally, when these forces combine with disease, they succumb to the personal defeat that they sought so much to avoid. At the end of each novel, the protagonist disappears, leaving the narrator alone, as it were, at center stage, disabused of his former admiration. More than just an expository device, Malraux's observers function to fix the reader's attention on the individualistic responses to the absurd, signified by the two European adventurers.

When *The Conquerors* opens, the anonymous narrator is already en route to Canton to join his childhood friend Pierre Garine. It is through him (the narrator) that the reader learns of the historical context of Garine's adventure. Before he leaves the boat, he reads the cabled reports of the workers' uprisings in Canton and Hong Kong.[5] From the reports and their dates (June 1925), the reader is expected to supply much of the background of this Chinese political upheaval.

Supported by a powerful warlord with a flair for political reform, Sun Yat-sen set up a military government in Canton in 1919. He ruled as generalissimo for some eighteen months, until 2 April 1921, when he declared Canton a republic. His hopes to spread his Nationalist revolution from Canton were largely ineffective. But in January 1923, he negotiated an agreement with Adolph Joffe, a friend of Trotsky. Joffe committed the Chinese Communist party to Chinese Nationalism under the leadership of the Kuomintang and agreed to furnish military officers and political organizers. According to terms of the agreement, the Russians were to act simply as advisors and were to make no attempt to subvert the Chinese Nationalist movement. Evidence of Moscow's bad faith soon appeared.

Malraux's Heroes and History

Michael Borodin, who had already earned a reputation as a skilled communist organizer, arrived in Canton in September 1923 with some forty advisors. By the time of Sun's death on 12 March 1925, Borodin and his Chinese and European agents had infiltrated the Nationalist movement, and he was able to turn it into a communist revolution. Although a lieutenant of Sun was elected president of the Cantonese republic on 1 July 1925, Borodin replaced Sun's government appointees with Communist party members. By January 1926, he had completed the purge of the Kuomintang members.[6] The fictional Garine, represented as having no commitment to "scientific socialism," became a victim of this purge.

Garine belonged to the losing side in this historical episode which Malraux preserves rather faithfully.[7] Rather than tamper with history, he uses it as a dramatist uses the public's knowledge of a plot to develop the tragic sense of inevitable failure. Garine's story unfolds in the same tragic atmosphere, but the events belong to a still obscure phase of Chinese history. Few readers could have brought to this novel the same knowledge that the theatre public brings to the performance of Oedipus or any of the familiar tragedies.

Anticipation of Garine's purge is not, however, limited to readers informed about the vagaries of Chinese politics. Better known events—those that form the background for Malraux's 1933 novel *Man's Fate*—would have revealed to readers of 1928 that the Communist party had taken over the Nationalist movement. They would have understood, too, that Borodin, somewhat paradoxically, was also acting out a tragedy similar to Garine's.[8] Malraux supposes that his reader has this information: in an "aside" to the reader, the narrator brings into his account a clear reference to the better known events of 1927 when Chiang Kai-shek overthrew the Communists in the Kuomintang.[9] This reminder conveys enough information for the informed reader to appreciate the context of Garine's drama.

It is only after the narrator disembarks in French Indochina that the reader begins to learn how the fictional Garine fits into this historical framework. In Saigon the narrator meets Gérard, a former teacher in the French *lycée* in Hanoi and now a political

36

activist in the Indochinese Kuomintang—a situation not greatly different from Malraux's during the same period.[10] And like the author, the fictional revolutionary Gérard receives information from party members who were able to keep him informed, in spite of censorship, about political developments in China. He is thus able to fill in the narrator, newly arrived from France, on Garine's participation in the early stages of what history now calls the Chinese Revolution.

Garine, so the narrator is reminded, joined Sun Yat-sen's movement in its earliest days, attracted to it principally by the spirit of adventure. With other Europeans, he came to Canton with the hope of finding a direction for his own life. He brought with him no idealistic zeal and acted exclusively out of personal motives. This self-centered individualism has not prevented him, however, from serving the Revolution effectively. As director of the propaganda service in the newly established Nationalist enclave of Canton, Garine was far more successful than the doctrinaire Borodin. While Borodin's collectivist party line inspired no enthusiasm among the Chinese coolies and peasants, Garine's appeal to self-interest appeared to carry the promise of personal dignity. Through propaganda, he has succeeded in building a disciplined labor force capable of acting as a unit against the British colonials and their Chinese collaborators. His success apparently inspires no jealousy among the Comintern delegates in Canton. So long as he is effective, Borodin tolerates him but certainly does not trust him. Gérard suggests that Garine's authority depends on the Comintern weakness. Once the Communists in the Kuomintang become stronger, he will be purged and his adventure ended.

While Gérard could recount Garine's activities in China, only the narrator is able to give the European prologue to this Chinese adventure. During his boat trip from Indochina to Canton, the narrator reads and comments on a British intelligence report documenting Garine's political activities. As would be expected, the insights an admiring friend brings to the report are far more revealing than what British agents could uncover. From his memory and from letters he has kept, the narrator draws the information to clarify the brief report. This information allows the reader to understand, long before he meets Garine, the motives of this curious revolutionary devoid of any political commitment.

Garine's activism stems from a hunger for power, a hunger that dates from schooldays when he found his own explanation for the failures of Napoleon and the revolutionary terrorist Saint-Just. While he had nothing but scorn for their ideals, he sympathized with their ambitions for power. Even in those early years, the exercise of power had become the ruling passion of his life. He joined the anarchist movement in France before World War I, and until his arrest, he was responsible for arranging illegal abortions for pregnant women who contacted the Anarchists. During the course of his trial, his already pronounced antisocial attitudes were strengthened. He denied in a letter to the narrator that his defense in court was inspired by any sense of justice or desire to protect his reputation. He simply refused to be imprisoned by an absurd society built on worn-out conventions.

Garine's sentence was suspended. After a brief experience in the Foreign Legion and after gambling away his money, he found himself involved with the Bolsheviks in exile in Switzerland. He admired their revolutionary technique but, not sharing their political ideals, did not join the Communist party. When the Russian Revolution began, he was disappointed not to be called to Russia. Perhaps that was just as well: it was the opportunity in social upheaval that attracted him, not the business of administering the revolutionaries' socialistic programs. When a call arrived from a French acquaintance to join him in the propaganda bureau of the Chinese Nationalist government in Canton, Garine accepted without hesitation. China promised the perfect political climate to the adventurer. The goals of the Nationalist revolt were so remote that Garine could expect a long, exhilarating tenure of leadership. He could make of the propaganda bureau a permanent base of power, confident that the consummation of the revolution was too distant to concern him.

While his quest for power has led Garine into politics, he has never had any delusions about improving the state of his fellow man. For him, life is absurd, and because the basic absurdity of human existence cannot be overcome, no social progress is of any consequence. But political authority alone gives direction to his life, and a political organization is but an instrument of personal power to be manipulated for one's own selfish satisfaction. Garine thus finds himself in the equivocal situation of working within a political organization in violation of its principles. This curious collaboration is explained by the views on eroticism that Malraux earlier wrote in *The Temptation of the West* and "On European Youth."

Although prostitutes make a fleeting appearance in the novel,[11] Malraux avoids casting his protagonist as an erotic figure. In his quest for personal satisfactions, Garine manipulates the Chinese workers much as one might manipulate a sex partner. He transposes his sexual urge to political intrigue. Along with Ferral of *Man's Fate,* he illustrates how political conquests can offer a relief from the absurd superior to the more patently sensual pleasures: but they certainly offer no redemption from the absurd. Unlike the psychopaths created by Camus and Sartre early in their careers,[12] Malraux's adventurers are not dazed by the discovery of the absurd. They are spurred on by a basic drive which Malraux insists is sexual in origin. The urge to dominate and the pleasure it brings lose sexual connotations and are translated into a lust for power. Like his counterpart in *Man's Fate,* Garine leaps into politics aware that it affords the thrill of power.

His motives may differ but little from those of even the most loyal Bolsheviks. In a ten-page section that Malraux withheld from a later part of his novel, Garine himself explains the psychological needs that brought an unnamed Latvian officer to China.[13] Had the passage been retained—at the risk of further slowing down the action of the novel or denigrating any political idealism—the resemblance between the disciplined revolutionaries and Garine would have been more pronounced. It might also have aided the reader to appreciate the self-interest that Malraux attributed to his first political activists. Through Gérard, he is nonetheless able to represent his protagonist as a self-seeking adventurer; the narrator simply calls him a gambler. Although the term is somewhat inappropriate, it does convey Garine's apathy towards any ideology—religious, social, or political. His commitment to a political goal goes deeper than the gambler's commitment to the gaming table. So long as he can continue to play and can hope for the thrill of winning, he remains in the game: he stands to gain prolonged "relief and deliverance."

The narrator does not explain what torment Garine seeks to be delivered from. The existential context of *The Conquerors* suggests that it is the Pascalian concept of the torments of man without God. The seventeenth-century Jansenist apologist described the nonbeliever's life in negative terms: he represented it as a meaningless wait for death; all that Pascal's atheist could hope for was some diversion from his morbid fixation. To religious thinkers such as Pascal or Saint Augustine, the atheist's activities have only the negative value of making him forget that his life is useless. And so too for Garine, if not also for Malraux at this stage of his career. The Swiss adventurer-gambler is unwilling to make the compromise with the absurd that Albert Camus proposed in *The Myth of Sisyphus:* Garine cannot find any respite from the human condition short of those moments of forgetfulness that come when he is absorbed by his revolutionary activity.

This protracted introduction constitutes the first of the three parts of the novel. It shows what the character searching for an individualistic response to the absurd signifies—in the sense that Malraux interpreted Laclos's characters as significant characters. Part Two, entitled "Powers," chronicles six days of Garine's activities—five days of frenetic political activity concluded by a last day of confinement in the hospital.

Along with Borodin, Garine is engaged in strengthening the Nationalist position in Canton. His role appears far more demanding, far more absorbing than Borodin's. He has already succeeded in bringing under his control the police and military operations of the infant republic: Malraux credits him with founding the Whampoa Military Academy (actually founded by Chiang Kai-shek), and from his command post at the ministry of propaganda, he directs the defense of Canton. Perhaps more important for the plot, he also directs the economic offensive against the British interests in Hong Kong. He is manoeuvering behind the scenes to effect the passage of a boycott decree against all ships stopping at the British enclave of Hong Kong. To show the intensity of Garine's commitment to his project, Malraux multiplies by seven the number of people Garine must persuade: a fictional seven-man ruling committee replaces the president who, in fact, had the authority to issue the decree.

Because the economic risks to the Cantonese may be as great as the burden on the British in Hong Kong, there is strong opposition to Garine. The leader of the opposition is a Gandhi-like figure, Tcheng-dai. Later it will be seen how Tcheng-dai's moral position stems from a self-interest every bit as reprehensible as Garine's. The two characters make wonderful adversaries for one another, and it is their conflict over the decree that constitutes the plot. It provides a frame for the portrait of the self-interested adventurer. In spite of his claim that he has no love for his fellow man, Malraux's adventurer works tirelessly for them until overcome by chronic dysentery and swamp fever. Confined to a hospital bed with no projects to occupy him, Garine turns his attentions inward. He reflects on his past and particularly on his trial. He gives an explanation for his own individualistic brand of activism and thereby confirms what the narrator has already allowed the reader to understand: that real progress is impossible, that action is purposeless, and that life is vain. All that remains will be his fall from office, a fall already presaged by the announcement of Borodin's usurpation of all civil and military authority in Canton. The communist political "realists" have come to power. Through the focus provided by the narrator, they are seen to reduce Garine's individualism to a vain passion in the concluding section of the novel.

Garine's release from the hospital triggers the conclusion of the plot. He learns upon his return to his office that Tcheng-dai has died. An aide has brought him one of the numerous posters that appeared late in the evening proclaiming Tcheng-dai's death as a suicide in protest against the proposed boycott. In reality, the wily Chinese understood that he was marked for assassination and very likely chose suicide to preserve his reputation. The real circumstances of his death remain undetermined. The posters nonetheless threaten the projected boycott. In spite of his weakness, Garine spends his first night out of the hospital in an effort to counter the suicide announcements. At the end of a night's feverish activity, new posters have been printed, announcing that his political adversary has been executed by the British, and a team is gluing these posters over the initial announcements. By the time Canton awakens, Garine has deprived Tcheng-dai of his posthumous glory and has assured the success of his own project, by now a project that holds little interest for him. But Garine does not stop exploiting Tcheng-dai's death at this point. He delivers a funeral oration which rallies the coolies behind his anti-British campaign.

The following day reveals the fragility of Garine's situation in the Kuomintang. His authority is violated as terrorists in his service are captured and executed. Moments later, he discovers the mutilated body of Klein, his German aide in the propaganda ministry. Ominously, he recalls the futility of Lenin's deathbed opposition to Stalin. Pathetically, now, he resolves not to be so humiliated.

Borodin chooses the preparation for Klein's funeral as the moment to assert his authority. In the name of discipline, he orders Garine to deliver the eulogy. It could hardly have been the traditional eulogy, but, instead, the sort of revolutionary rhetoric that Garine had earlier expounded at Tcheng-dai's graveside. Then, at the height of his political authority, he had no scruples about turning an adversary's death to his own advantage; now the order to deliver a comparable speech seems repugnant. His friendship for Klein undoubtedly contributes something to his feelings, but the resentment Garine displays comes mostly from the frustration of defeat. He has been forced to submit to Communist party discipline and is now painfully aware that power is slipping from his grasp. Chinese communism has progressed far enough for Borodin to replace adventurers with zealots.

From this point on, the narrator assumes a larger role in the story, recovering the importance he had in the introduction. He interprets, step by step, the defeat that Garine could hardly be expected to acknowledge. He begins by explaining the adventurer's incongruous association with the socialist revolutionaries. Although his friend is not a Marxist, he is not opposed to Marxism. Quite the contrary, socialist idealism serves his self-centered goals: it has proven to be an effective device for recruiting from among the workers the shock troops on which his power depended. Not unlike a power-hungry pig on an Orwellian animal farm, he exploits the idealism of the oppressed. Since his ambition is for personal power, he may as well be involved in a fascist revolution (Malraux uses the adjective "Mussolinist") as in a socialist revolution.

Reprehensible though his political cynicism may be, Garine does not appear hypocritical. He understands his motives and acknowledges them. He never ceases to pursue his absurdist individualism to its logical consequences. And, unless the reader is a committed revolutionary like Leon Trotsky,[14] he does not resent Garine's perversion of the revolutionary movement to his own ends. The narrator defends Garine against the criticism of communist ideologues—not, however, on philosophical grounds but for political expediency that Communists might easily appreciate. The defense explains Malraux's title: it is self-centered "conquerors" like Garine who will prevent the right wing of the Kuomintang from taking over the Revolution in China. Malraux expected that the reader, drawing on his own knowledge of Chiang's betrayal, would exonerate Garine.

The purge of Garine is announced to the narrator by Nicolaieff, the Russian Communist assigned to Garine's police force. Disease made the departure inevitable, but the Swiss adventurer would certainly have preferred to die without having to capitulate. For him, the purge is a bitter defeat. He sneers at Borodin's explanation for the purge, which, to the disabused individualist, reveals only the naiveté of the communist zealots. He sees their hope for social progress as an illusion: "Borodin says that what is erected by men like me working alone cannot last. As if what is erected by men like him . . . Oh, how I'd like to see China in five years." And he ends his remark with a criticism of those idealists who hope that their political activity will have a lasting effect: "Permanence. As if it was a question of that" (p. 153). In his scorn is the resignation to the absurd that historical works cannot redeem. And it should not be overlooked that the situation Malraux has chosen for his first novel confirms the pessimism he attributes to his characters.

Garine has not yet been stripped of his authority. On the day before his departure from Canton, he enjoys a final opportunity to assert his power. Two former propaganda agents have been arrested in the act of poisoning a well in Canton. Nicolaieff is unable to get the confession that will reveal the extent of this plot. Arriving at the scene of the interrogation and feigning impatience, Garine resorts to the most cruel abuse to get a confession. He kills one of the Chinese traitors on the spot. His aim is to frighten the other into a confession. The spectacle loosens the tongue of the remaining traitor, but not enough. More effective are a blow which sends him sprawling and the threat of death by slow strangulation: the water supply can be protected. But by now it is clear that no such goal justifies Garine's cruelty. He used this incident to demonstrate the value of the cynical political adventurer to the cause of the revolution. It also afforded him the fleeting satisfaction that can come from the assertion of authority, but this final paroxysm of power does not belie Nicolaieff's assertion that "the time of men like him is drawing to a close" (p. 151).

Garine's time in Canton has ended. In the last scene of the novel, he discusses his return to Europe with the now more critical narrator. The scene presents a pathetic picture of the individualist who refuses to admit his weakness. He draws at any straw in the wind in the hope of restoring some direction to his life. It was expressly to conclude on this pathetic note that Malraux composed this portrait of the conqueror—this title epithet is far more appropriate than that of gambler: Garine needs much more than the gambler's titillation of risk. Not the gaming tables but the advancement of the British Empire appears as the framework in which his personal satisfactions could be found. He announces his hope to go to England. But the narrator—and consequently the reader—are sure that Garine will die before reaching his destination; the wish sounds all too hollow. He repeats nonetheless his hopes for power where individualism is encouraged: "Now I know what Empire means. Tenacious, constant violence. Directing, deciding, enforcing. That's where life is" (p. 161).

When nothing remains before the adventurer but his death, he appears tragic—more deserving of sympathy than of admiration. The tragedy the narrator has witnessed in order to transmit it to the reader is Malraux's illustration of the death of man—the

The Oriental Adventures

death of the Western concept of mankind that Ling interpreted for his French correspondent in *The Temptation of the West.* This is the message to which the adventure of this "significant character" testifies.

In this portrait of the political adventurer, history is the arena where individual ambitions are expressed; it is, moreover, the framework where the virile European tests his worth. But it is an amorphic framework of isolated political events. Unlike Saint Augustine, Hegel, Marx, Tolstoy, or, more recently, Arnold Toynbee, Malraux sees history as having no direction. He reduces it to a collection of random projects undertaken in ignorance of the absurd or to forget the absurd. No undertaking can acquire any permanent value. Not even the hope of an immortality through history can redeem the life of Malraux's protagonist from the absurd. The individualist conscious of the futility of any action can, at best, make history or politics—which is but the day-to-day expression of history—an arena for personal satisfaction. The view is cynical, but the only one open to the lucid absurdist. At the end of his life, debilitation and disease inevitably make a victim of the conqueror. Garine has pursued individualism to its logical consequences only to illustrate its futility and to expose history as the arena of human tragedy. So long as Malraux finds no alternative to individualism or to history as tragedy, his characters can but act out this tragedy.

Not all of Malraux's characters act on the absurdist view of history. One need go no further than *The Conquerors* to find a character whose view is more in harmony with that of contemporary political "realists" who believe in social progress. Tchengdai illustrates the alternative to Garine's absurdist view of history. And Malraux makes the alternative appear every bit as futile. Still, it receives scant development. Malraux investigates at length in *The Royal Way* a comparable hope for a redemption from the absurd through history. There, it propels the Danish adventurer Perken into an adventure that might have been the stuff of a "Terry and the Pirates" episode from the Sunday newspaper. Through this, Malraux's second novel, it is possible to arrive at a fuller appreciation of his view of the tragedy of the individual in history.

Malraux's Heroes and History

When it first appeared in 1930, *The Royal Way* was announced as the first of a three-part series entitled, "The Forces of the Wilderness." Parts Two and Three never appeared, and, thus far, Malraux has revealed nothing of his original plans. He has admitted his disappointment with the novel and quotes a criticism of one of his friends in *Antimemoirs*.[15] According to this admirer, publication of *The Royal Way* could be justified only if it served as a prologue to following works. Consequently, it is tempting to speculate that the tedious story of David de Mayrena recounted in the autobiographical essay [16] was intended as part of the projected triptych. If so, it may have been withhheld from earlier publication because it turned out to be an even weaker story than the 1930 novel. That Malraux chose to incorporate it into his 1967 autobiography would then testify to his confidence in his reputation as an author, for it brings no further light to his past.

It is easy to understand Malraux's disappointment with *The Royal Way.* Several elements can be summoned to justify critics' views that this tale of adventure predates the more polished novel, *The Conquerors.* Most noticeable, but perhaps of less importance for dating the book, is the subject, which is drawn from Malraux's first trip to the Orient in 1923.[17] And it is difficult to overlook how the novel continues with little elaboration the notion of eroticism sketched in *The Temptation of the West* and repeated in "On European Youth." Here again, as will be seen later in more detail, the "erotic game" remains the only response of the Western individualist condemned to find meaning for his life through his actions alone. Malraux does incorporate, however, into this novel a view of art, also drawn from his first work of fiction, which appears as an alternative to historical action. He fails, though, to juxtapose the two so that his intention emerges clearly. Finally, he has trouble respecting the limitations of the observer from whose point of view Perken's adventure is related. In *The Conquerors,* Malraux used the narrator effectively to criticize the absurdist individualism of his protagonist, but in *The Royal Way,* a comparable character threatens the unity of the novel.

In the initial pages, Malraux clearly establishes the point of view of Claude Vannec, a French adventurer modeled to some degree on the author himself. Vannec is not, however, a narrator in the accepted sense of the term. He has been endowed with a personality and has a place of prominence in the story greater than that normally held by a narrator. At best he is an unreliable observer, and, seemingly to underscore this point, Malraux does not permit him to recount the story in the first-person usually reserved for a narrator. He uses instead the third-person, which permits him to violate Vannec's point of view when the needs of the exposition require it—as they do on two important occasions.

Like Malraux in 1923, Vannec goes to Indochina to pirate temple sculpture for resale in Europe. During the trip, he meets Perken, the character based on the legendary Mayrena. Like the original, Perken aspires to establish his own kingdom in the yet-unconquered Indochinese hinterland.[18] His project to establish a personal empire is already far advanced. Although his scheme draws much from the nineteenth-century adventurer Mayrena, he explains that his motivation is different. According to Perken, that French adventurer who ruled his own isolated kingdom for three years as Marie I, King of the Sédangs, lived his biography as an actor played a role. Where the Frenchman was a posturing actor aiming only to impress his admiring contemporaries, the Dane Perken expects to be a creative hero.[19] He intends to build an independent kingdom that will survive as a monument to his existence. Since it would be more substantial than a reputation left to posterity, this "scar on the face of the earth" must be more permanent. Creating this political enclave is his way of protecting his existence from the destruction that death represents for him. Influenced by European admiration for history-book heroes, he sees history as the domain where his metaphysical needs can be satisfied. But different from his nineteenth-century predecessor, Perken acts in response to twentieth-century existential anxieties. He seeks a hedge against death in a grandiose venture under-taken in the face of overwhelming opposition.

Vannec is attracted to him from the moment of their first meet-ing in a Djibouti bordello. During the remainder of the voyage, an attachment develops, nurtured by the adventurer's spiritual resemblance to Vannec's grandfather. In the brief pages covering the trip across the Indian Ocean, Vannec comes to understand

Malraux's Heroes and History

what he admired about his defiant grandfather. Like the hero of *The Royal Way*, he refused to submit to any degradation up to the moment of his undistinguished and even foolishly self-inflicted death. Malraux interrupts the story to give the biography of the grandfather—in reality Malraux's own—a retired sailor with whom the fictional Vannec lived after the death of his mother.

Vannec recalls how his grandfather, tormented by the memories of dead relatives, envied the deaths of Dunkerque sailors, who drowned at sea without having to face the humiliation of age. Finally, in a reckless demonstration of prowess when age has sapped his skill, he accidentally splits his skill with an ax and dies. The recollection, which disrupts the unity of the opening pages, presages the nature of the adventure on which Claude Vannec accompanies Perken. The body of the novel recounts Vannec's discovery of the vanity of the Dane's struggle against death's destruction. Perhaps by the conclusion of the adventure, played out largely along the overgrown Royal Road linking the ancient Khmer temples in Cambodia, Vannec might have also lost his admiration for his grandfather—but that is a question that Malraux does not bring up again.

By the time the novel begins, Perken has already spent the previous fifteen years as a civil servant of the Siamese government. During that time he laid the groundwork for his personal empire. He failed to get machine guns in Europe but accepted an assignment to find the lost adventurer Grabot—presumably for money to buy the machine guns. Then, Vannec's offer to share his booty commits each of the characters to the other's adventures. It permits Vannec to witness the foolhearty heroics of an adventurer determined to wrest his life from the insignificance to which death appears to condemn it.

Although Malraux replaces the image-conscious Mayrena with a Nietzchean hero, he retains the French adventurer-king's scheme in his novel. But he transposes it from the end of the nineteenth century, when French colonial administration was still in its infancy, to the 1920s, when the Foreign Legion and industrialization brought most of Indochina well under colonial domination. Malraux has made a hero out of an historical anachronism. Perken has no chance of success, and his struggle

The Oriental Adventures

becomes a vain gesture in the face of inevitable failure. Through Vannec, Malraux warns the reader that Perken's scheme is suicidal. But Vannec withholds his criticism from his companion. In this respect, Malraux's narrator functions like the chorus of a Greek tragedy: he lets the public in on the impending tragedy. Like Garine's and Tcheng-dai's, Perken's efforts to find some meaning for his life are condemned to futility—not by the gods, but by an equally relentless adversary, history.

Although it is Perken who most interests Malraux, he gives the first half of the novel over to Vannec. To the young French fortune hunter are attributed only the most materialistic of motives, but, at the same time, he is credited with insights into the posterity of art. By way of justifying his expedition before the incredulous director of the Far East French School, Vannec sketches the theory of the "imaginary museum" that Malraux used to introduce his *Psychology of Art* seventeen years later.[20] Here, the concept of an art lying dormant until revived by a comprehending generation is given in a rudimentary form. But it is only with the benefit of hindsight that it is possible to see how *The Royal Way* anticipates Malraux's evolution towards art as a redemption from the absurd. Without making a real effort to understand Vannec's novel theory, the French functionary reluctantly approves the expedition. With Perken's help, Vannec prepares his expedition and sets off along the ancient Royal Road that in the past carried pilgrims from one Buddhist temple to another.

Adept as he appeared in the manipulation of colonial functionaries, Vannec now shows himself to be particularly ill-adapted for an expedition into the unexplored Cambodian jungle. His account of the trek back into this Oriental "heart of darkness" makes the Indochinese jungle appear as hostile as Joseph Conrad's Congo: insects, reptiles, and even plant life appear to menace the expedition, and Malraux's fearful observer even speaks of the road obscured by jungle growth as a river. Other similarities invite further speculation about Conrad's influence on Malraux, but Clara Malraux, who shared the adventure that inspired this picture of the jungle, fails to give any clarification. Writing of her own impressions, she only notes that there is more anticipation than recollection in these similarities.[21] Nonetheless, Malraux's Vannec discovers, as did Conrad's Marlow, that away from the protection of civilization, the primitive world becomes man's greatest enemy. In the face of nature's hostility, mere survival is an act of heroism. Vannec is constantly alert to the dangers lurking in the jungle. His fear stands in stark contrast to the confidence of his companion, for whom danger is a challenge to be accepted. In spite of whatever limits it might have as a vehicle of exposition, Malraux's characterization of Vannec effectively underscores Perken's heroic *sangfroid*.

After an initial disappointment, Vannec, Perken, and their native helpers fall upon the crumbling Khmer temple of Banteai-Srey. At first, Vannec does not even see the wonderfully preserved bas-reliefs or the statues of the dancing girls that have remarkably resisted centuries of erosion. The following scene of the struggle to wrest the statuary from the temple is one of the most vivid of the book. The stone that ceded under the ancient sculptors' chisels resists the adventurers' feverish efforts and wears down their equipment.

Once the statues have been removed, Malraux drops the theme of art and concentrates on Perken's tragedy. Thus, the scene at Banteai-Srey culminates Vannec's part of the story, the lengthy introduction to Perken's. Because of its length, the novel loses focus. But it is likely that Malraux intended the theme of the eternity of art associated with Vannec to stand in this novel or in one of the projected sequels as a counterpoint to Perken's futile attempts to preserve his life from the hostility of time and nature. Only this intention would justify the long introduction and the place given the observer. Malraux may have hoped that the reader would associate the permanence of art with the timorous companion who survives Perken's futile effort to build a personal kingdom. Such a conclusion is prepared by Vannec's adventure. Still nothing in the temple scene points to such a symbolic meaning. It appears simply as a literal representation of one incident of the novel. So this interpretation must remain a speculation. The evidence to support it is far from conclusive and is based on the always dubious supposition that stylistic weaknesses prevented Malraux from giving his theme the relief it deserved. Had his subsequent novels not given further evidence of a stylistic obscurity or pointed towards an esthetic response to the absurd, such a speculation would be idle indeed. Instead, the difficulty of fixing Malraux's meaning reveals the problems that continually confront his readers.

Vannec's dream of making a fortune from the statues and that of Perken to finance the defense of his kingdom are soon dashed. During the night, the native laborers and the guide flee, leaving only the cart on which the precious statues had been loaded. Abandoned in the hostile jungle, unable to transport the statues but unwilling to give them up, the European adventurers set out to find Grabot, a potential rival of Perken who might nonetheless be able to help them. At this point Vannec recedes into the background, and the story becomes Perken's. Driven by his "erotic" impulse to resist death, the Danish adventurer will provide a spectacle of heroism that Vannec first admires, then appears to criticize.

It was at their meeting in the Djibouti bordello that Perken interpreted eroticism as a mainspring of action. Paradoxically, this discussion followed—as the reader learns only later in the novel—a first experience of impotency. He explained to the young Vannec that youth could not appreciate the force of eroticism. They confuse it with love or sensual pleasure. As he talks, Vannec wonders whether or not his still unfamiliar interlocutor is a sadist, for he is quick to discern in Perken's ramblings an urge to dominate. But he determines that Perken does not seek a sadistic domination of a partner. The aging adventurer prefers to forget that the partner even exists: the partner should be seen only as "the other sexual organ" (p. 10), the necessary instrument to a satisfaction that is sensual only in its most rudimentary expression.

Self-consciously, Perken insists that his interpretation is not a perversion. As an example of perversion he cites Grabot. Without identifying the lost French adventurer by name, he describes his perversion as masochism. For Perken, perversion is the willingness to submit, the loss of domination. Grabot's mysterious adventure into the unexplored Khmer region of Siam is explained as an act of compensation: he was so ashamed of his

51

passive sexual submission that he sought to prove his courage, at least to himself, in a dangerous venture. Perken respects this "special relation to eroticism" (p. 64) where he could not respect submission—he even found the refined sadism of some of his "cerebral" bourgeois acquaintances far less contemptible than Grabot's masochism.

Elaboration of Perken's eroticism comes little by little, throughout the novel. Early in the story, however, Vannec is able to observe how his newfound companion resists any degradation with a force "as imperious as a sexual urge." He understands Perken's eroticism as the mechanism of his resistance to death: it is in response to a physical, erotic impulse that Perken attempts to prevent death from reducing his life to nothingness. He acts as though he were conceived to exemplify Ling's observation in *The Temptation of the West:* in the face of the absurd, his actions are but an "erotic game."

Novelists before Malraux have used the same concept. Stendhal and Barrès, to name but the best known, have shown characters responding to a comparable egocentric impulsion. They called it simply energy. Malraux insists, however, that Perken's energy is erotic. Deep in the jungle in search of the lost Grabot, the Danish adventurer explains that his survival in a particularly dangerous escape filled him with a sensual thrill:

> I almost died: you don't realize what exaltation comes from
> the absurdity of life when you're face to face with it, like
> being face to face with a woman un . . . He made a gesture
> of tearing off clothes . . . undressed. Nude, just like that . . .
> (p. 109).

Today, writing of this sort would probably expose Malraux to charges of male chauvinism. His first wife saw it as an expression of his misogyny,[22] which may be no different. Whatever the epithet, his concept of eroticism denies any dignity to the partner or the adversary, making that person only an instrument of psychological or metaphysical satisfactions—but certainly not of physical pleasure. Although he may well have warranted his wife's accusations, he was no less critical of this expression of individualism than she. The protagonist of *The Royal Way* illustrates the tragedy of the European whose life has been reduced to an erotic game. In terms of the Laclos essay, he can be said to "signify" European eroticism.

This Danish adventurer has developed an elaborate concept of the absurd. His sexually rooted individualism appears to be rigorously consistent with it. But, compared to Garine or Laclos's protagonists of *Les Liaisons dangereuses,* he is a weak signifying character. He understands only superficially the politics of the world in which he acts. So, rather than illustrate eroticism as a response to the absurd, he makes it appear too obviously as a paroxysm of the will. Malraux has evidently set him up for a defeat, but a defeat which earns little sympathy from the reader.

Perken is Malraux's only "erotic" protagonist. Afterwards, he investigates other, more egalitarian responses to the absurd but casts eroticism as an aspect of capitalistic decadence in one last political adventurer: he holds up to the reader's scorn the sexual exploits of the industrialist Ferral of *Man's Fate,* published three years later. The introduction he prepared in 1932 for the French translation of D. H. Lawrence's *Lady Chatterly's Lover*[23] allowed the contemporary reader to anticipate the disappearance of this theme from his later fiction. Here he criticized Lawrence's naive hope that eroticism might be the means of escaping from the isolation that constituted the human condition—at least from the human condition as the British novelist saw it. According to Malraux, rather than permitting an escape, the eroticism in *Lady Chatterly's Lover* only reinforces the solitude of the partners. Even though the two novelists have conflicting interpretations of the human condition, Malraux is able to conclude that eroticism is as ineffectual in restoring a sense of social communion as in combatting the absurdist's feeling of cosmic isolation. His essay on the British novelist reaffirms the conclusion of *The Royal Way.*

The last two sections of *The Royal Way,* those which recount Perken's adventure, thus provide Malraux's most complete indictment of eroticism. In them, he shows how Perken's erotic drive permits him to rescue Grabot from the savage Moi tribesman and later drives him in a futile race against the Foreign Legion to regain his kingdom.

Malraux's Heroes and History

The search for Grabot, which follows the defection of the native workers, is brief. Perken and Vannec discover him reduced to slavery in a remote Moi village far from the frontiers of colonial administration. Blinded and turned into an animal, he has been forced by his captors to turn a mill wheel. Horrified by the discovery, Perken recalls that the primitive Indochinese tribes also castrate their slaves. Malraux does not explain whether Grabot's castration has been real or figurative. His sexual energy has nonetheless been destroyed. He becomes a living dead man, everything that Perken scorns. More than that, however, Grabot is a reminder to the Danish adventurer of his own human condition, and as such, he is an inspiration to greater acts of heroism. Perken makes the dangerous situation in the isolated, hostile village a test of his own mettle before the admiring but timorous Vannec.

In one of the scenes Vannec could not witness, Perken negotiates the rescue of Grabot. It is a show of guts with a dose of cold-blooded witchcraft. But in his performance, Perken falls on one of the sharpened bamboo shafts that protect the village. Even though the shaft is not poisoned, it plants an infection deep into the knee joint. Vannec gets the disabled but still determined Perken to the nearest town; there a dissolute English physician diagnoses the infection as incurable and forecasts death after a painful illness of two weeks.

For the first time in his life, Perken sees himself as a victim. He reads in the doctor's eyes a scorn for his own debilitation, and he suppresses an urge to kill, to efface the image of his weakness. He feels he must reassert his domination to recover self-esteem. Weakened in body but not in will, he is angered that his unresponsive body drags him into the degradation against which he is powerless. Still, so long as he retains his reason, he will resist the inner death of submission. He has his Vietnamese driver bring him a prostitute: fornication will prove that he has not yet lost his ability to dominate others.

In this scene of Perken and the prostitute, Malraux violates his observer's point of view for the second time: he has sent Vannec off with his own prostitute, thereby preserving him from the indiscretions of a voyeur. For all its vividness, the scene Malraux paints for the reader is hardly titillating. The gestures of the woman are described so that she is seen to submit to Perken. But the sensual elements fade as Malraux focuses on Perken's face: "Just four inches away from the face with blue eye lids, he looked at it as though it were a mask, almost unconscious of the savage sensation which attached it to this body which he possessed as though he had struck it" (p. 157). He continues to draw satisfaction from that submissive face until the strength of physical pleasure annihilates his consciousness. After the humiliation he experienced at the doctor's office, sexual domination affords a spiritual rejuvenation. It gives him the reassurance he needs to continue his adventure.

Following Vannec's report to colonial authorities, an army is dispatched to punish the dissident tribesmen. Vannec stores his statues away and sets out with Perken for the kingdom in the hinterland. At no time during the trip ahead of the advancing military column and the fleeing warriors does Perken acknowledge the menace of death. His energy resists pain and fever, as does his heroic image of himself. Vannec observes, often with astonishment, how his companion continues to make long range plans for his "people" when his death is so imminent. But the plans are now seen as a vanity by Perken's once-admiring observer, and Perken himself appears as a diminished and pathetic figure of his former self. Like the narrator of *The Conquerors,* Vannec becomes more critical of his companion at the end of the novel. Through him, the reader understands that Perken may have retained some of the dignity that Grabot had lost during his enslavement, but very little.

A tribal chieftain allied with Perken threatens mutiny. Perken understands that he has lost the respect of his allies, but he refuses to accept the image of defeat that he again reads in the eyes of his dissident warriors. He kills two of them in a demonstration of strength. He remains resolved to combat the menace carried by death to reduce human life to insignificance. But he understands that he can no longer preserve the meaning of his existence in a political combat—it is with the opinions of those about him that he must struggle. His enemy is the image of his own degradation that he reads in their eyes. But this struggle is the last-ditch effort to protect his own self-respect. He is reduced to manipulating images rather than acting upon reality. In terms of Perken's eroticism, this can be seen as an effect of impotency.

Finally his combat is reduced to a wish: "My death must force them at least to be free" (p. 177). Exempt from the agony of death, the young observer is surprised by Perken's concern for his "subjects." Vannec fails to understand that the survival of Perken's kingdom will constitute a monument to his existence. His hope to rally the dissident tribesmen against colonial expansion carries the desire that history give his existence some permanence: it is the hero's wish for the historical immortality of a Ceasar or a Napoleon. Perken's last words convey his resignation to a biological death but, more important, his vain hope that it will not totally efface his existence: "there is no death; there is only I, I, who am going to die" (p. 182).

Malraux prepares this last scene by underscoring the separation of the spirit and body. Weakened by fever, Perken fixes his attention on his hand. It moves, seemingly independent of his will. Perken takes comfort in the separation of body and will. He understands it to mean that the death of the body need not drag his whole being with it. Perhaps a reputation can survive beyond the grave. That is the only chance the European individualist, whose absurd life is defined by what he does, has of rescuing his life from death. But Malraux does not let Perken's hope materialize. He has set his character up to be destroyed by history.

Perken ignored the political and economic evolution of Indochina. In the last part of the novel, where two weeks are condensed into but a few pages, political realities intrude. The drama of Perken's illness is played out against a background of colonial expansion. The mistreatment of Grabot has provided a pretext for military intervention in the dissident regions of Indochina. While the column of the Foreign Legion is advancing, railroad construction continues. The sound of gunfire and of railroad ties being laid in the forest punctuate Perken's trip back to his kingdom. As would be expected, the modern colonial army travels faster than the European adventurer. The reader understands that, had not illness felled him, the advances of twentieth-century Europe would soon have put an end to Perken's nineteenth-century ideal. And *The Royal Way* concludes, as did *The Conquerors,* with the observer, alone after the fall of the protagonist, focusing the reader's attention on the vanity of Western individualism.

In one sense, *The Royal Way* repeats *The Conquerors.* It treats for a second time the tragedy of the European adventurer who discovers defeat. But where Garine's ended with his fall from power, Perken's begins with his first experience of impotency. As his story begins, he is already a condemned man, and his attempt to establish a kingdom in Laos is but a futile enterprise to wrest from history some permanence for his existence. He conveys a far less successful denunciation of European individualism than does Garine with his more modest hopes. Nonetheless, both behave according to the pattern of the "significant character." Their actions evolve logically from their interpretation of the individual's place in history—the egocentric European notion that Malraux attributes to them. Their tragedy does not signify that they are weak, rather that the concept of the self that inspires their Oriental adventures is false.

Malraux has condemned his first two protagonists to seek the personal satisfactions of domination. Both Garine and Perken believe that history is the domain where these satisfactions can be found. Both exploit a historical situation in pursuit of personal goals. That one should seek personal power in history and the other immortality does not change their relation to history: Malraux closes this, the only domain where man's actions could take on meaning, to his protagonists. Their successes and failures in pursuit of their goals lose all significance. The author has turned the historical context of his novels into the domain of tragedy. Rather than find history to be the framework of their satisfactions, his protagonists discover it to be the mechanism of their downfall; instead of giving meaning to an individual existence, history functions as an instrument of the absurd, draining human life of any significance. So long as the individual seeks a redemption from his absurd destiny in history, he will remain the tragic victim of the absurd. It was to destroy the delusion about the individual's place in history that Malraux conceived of his two "significant" protagonists. More than any of his following novels, these two initial works denounce, as the critic René Girard observed, "man's stubborn adjustment of environment to his own measure."[24]

Because of the attention given art in *The Royal Way,* it is easy to see how an esthetic response—perhaps reminiscent of Marcel Proust's religion of art—could have been Malraux's alternative to history. The numerous art studies Malraux prepared after he ended his career as a novelist give ample support for it. It is quite unlikely that, as early as 1930, Malraux had already reserved redemption from the absurd for the creative artist. His evolution from the period in which he was describing the tragedy of the individual abandoned by God to that final stage in which art becomes the solution to the absurd is far from direct. Before concluding that art could replace history, his thought took a significant detour towards Marxism.

4 THE HUMAN CONDITION

> Let us imagine a number of men in chains and all
> condemned to death, where some are killed each
> day in the sight of the others, and those who
> remain see their own fate in that of their fellows
> and wait their turn, looking at each other
> sorrowfully and without hope. That is the picture of
> the condition of men.

Pascal, *Pensées*

WITH his third novel set in the Orient, Malraux presents a new type of hero, one not destroyed by history's adversity. Kyo Gisors, the leader of the 1927 Shanghai uprising represented in *Man's Fate,* acts out of a sympathy for the oppressed and exploited Chinese. His commitment to the Communist Revolution in China does not, however, elevate him above the absurd human condition. He is betrayed by history, and his slight accomplishments appear futile; still he is spared the degradation of his self-centered predecessors in *The Conquerors* and *The Royal Way.* Far lower in the revolutionary hierarchy than Garine and far less ambitious than Perken, he retains his dignity and grandeur in the face of death and defeat. In telling the story of the fictional leader of the Shanghai uprisings, Malraux presents an alternative to Western individualism, one based on a more modest view of man's relation to history.

While the hero of *Man's Fate* illustrates a human dignity different from that sought by the protagonists of Malraux's earlier novels, he remains unable to make the conquests that, in themselves, make a single life important. Again, the author has chosen a historical situation that dooms his protagonist in advance. But in this novel, Malraux shows how human worth can be protected from the ravages of history, and, as it did for *The Conquerors,*

Malraux's Heroes and History

recorded history provides the plot. The framework of Kyo's story is the betrayal of Kuomintang socialism by the right wing of the Chinese Nationalist party, the betrayal predicted by the nameless narrator of *The Conquerors.*

Starting from Canton in 1925, Chiang Kai-shek overthrew the Mandarin governments in the southern provinces. By the spring of 1927, he was engaged in a northern campaign against the warlords loyal to the Mandarins in Peking. Then, against the advice of Borodin, he turned his army against the European colonial bastion of Shanghai. In this industrial city, Chou En-lai had already organized the workers. On 21 March, he called a general strike and thereby initiated a model Leninist uprising which soon gave the Communists control of the Chinese quarters of the city. Within twenty-four hours, the insurrectionists seized the police stations, the arsenal, and the military garrison and proclaimed a "citizens' government." This uprising may not have been coordinated with the advance of the Nationalist army, but it was undoubtedly planned to coincide with its arrival. When Chiang did arrive, he found the workers' committees in control. Malraux depicts in *Man's Fate* the last pocket of government resistance, the armored train that Chiang's forces destroy as they enter the city. It is unlikely that even this resistance remained, so effective was the workers' uprising. Their show of power must have frightened the Nationalist leader. Because of his own ambitions, he had little reason to wish the Communists success, and having been the target of a kidnapping plot, he had every reason to distrust them.

Soon after his arrival in Shanghai, Chiang negotiated an agreement with the directors of the foreign interests. In exchange for their financial support, he turned against the Communists in Shanghai. According to some sources, he did not deign to send his regular troops against the communist insurgents in the city. Instead, patrols of hoodlums organized by the army brought the workers and revolutionaries under attack. Chiang may have realized that he could not count on his regulars to betray Chinese revolutionaries—it was but a short time later that his entire first division defected to the Maoist camp. The squads of irregulars seem, however, to have been as effective as veterans in mopping up the insurrectionists. Only a few escaped, among them Chou En-lai, who eluded the sweep and took refuge in Canton. The Nationalist repression soon reached there: again Chou escaped, but now, as Edgar Snow reported, with a price of $80,000 on his head.[1]

Malraux's novel is the fictional representation of what Sinologists have come to call Chiang Kai-shek's "blue terror." It takes the Chinese nationalist movement a step beyond the situation of *The Conquerors,* where we saw the tenuous collaboration between the Chinese Communist party and the Comintern on the one hand and the Kuomintang on the other. The events of *Man's Fate* represent rather accurately the political conditions in Shanghai, which, because of its economic importance and its labor unions so effectively organized by Chinese Communists and their Russian advisors, became the focus of the Communist-Nationalist schism. Unlike the background of *The Conquerors,* the Shanghai political intrigues receive the development necessary to situate the characters clearly in their historical framework. And the novel reveals Malraux's insight into the political conditions in China in 1927. In Part Three, for instance, he uses the differences between the Maoist and Comintern views of the Revolution, on the one hand, and the Stalinist-Trotskyite controversy, on the other, to create the tragic atmosphere of the novel.

In the Maoist interpretation, advanced by Kyo during his brief meeting in Hankow with the Comintern representative, the peasants would necessarily be the main revolutionary force in a poorly industrialized country such as China. Through ignorance of Chinese politics and economics, Vologuine anticipates a Marxist revolt effected by the urban worker. Because China's slow economic development has not yet created a militant proletariat, the policy that he enforces dooms its rebellion to failure.

As though this background were not enough to cloak the events of the novel in the pall of tragedy, Malraux also makes his Shanghai revolutionaries the victims of the Stalinist-Trotskyite struggle. As Goldmann explains in his concise analysis of this intraparty debate, the Stalinists chose to strengthen socialism in Russia before exporting the revolution.[2] In opposition to them, Trotsky sought an immediate world revolution. It is in the latter direction that Kyo and his comrades-in-arms are working. But their efforts are to be thwarted by the Stalinist functionaries of the Comintern. Having taken control of the party in Russia and in China, they dictate the goals of the rebellion. In the Stalinist doctrine that he enforces, Vologuine finds justification for ordering the Shanghai workers to lay down their arms and cooperate with the Nationalist Army as Chiang had demanded. Their obedience leads to their destruction.

Although sympathetic to many of the goals of International Communism, Malraux clearly did not allow his sympathies to lead him into party obedience. Instead, he appears particularly critical of the party, and his depiction of communism in Hankow conveys much of his criticism. Besides the commissar's narrow-minded dogmatism, he reveals that the model socialist state established there survives only through abuse of the coolies' good faith. In his novel, the party faithful in Hankow and Shanghai become the victims not only of Chiang's defection but also of Comintern manipulations. And the Communist party appears as one of those elements of history capable of destroying the individual. Malraux's characters assume their heroic stature less for their party activism than in spite of it—an implication that did not escape Malraux's doctrinaire critics.[3]

Man's Fate could hardly have accommodated a hero whose efforts, even in the infant Chinese Revolution prior to 1929, seemed to augur success. A character such as Chou would be decidedly out of place in this tragic atmosphere. He did not have the stamp of a victim of history, and his progress toward his goal alone conferred a value on each of his undertakings. Malraux could not, of course, have anticipated the outcome of Chou's adventure. Still, it was necessary that Chou be replaced in the novel by a victim of history. The fictional hero of the abortive uprising has so little in common with Chou that he can hardly be said to be modeled on the organizer of the Shanghai uprisings.[4]

Kyo Gisors has little that is Oriental about him. His mother was Japanese, but his father was French. He married a China-born German educated in Europe. The wealth of his family afforded him the comforts of a European colonial. In spite of these barriers, he has come to think of the Chinese as "his people." This commitment is not one that has been thrust upon him; it is one he has freely chosen. His willfulness places him in the lineage of Malraux's European protagonists, but his political ideals clearly distinguish him from the egocentric adventurers of Malraux's two previous novels.

Like his father, who has lost his university chair for his political views, Kyo is a Marxist. And even his concept of Marxism bears the stamp of the European who chooses and acts independently. Because of his insistence that all action be willed rather than determined or conditioned, Kyo is unable to accept Marxist economic determinism. He shares his father's respect for Marxism as a will (*une volonté*) but rejects the fatalism that threatens the European quality that Malraux identifies in this and his next two novels by the adjective "virile."[5]

By rejecting the determinism that underlies the Marxist philosophy, Kyo also casts doubt on the inevitability of communist victory. For him, victory is not preordained by a dialectical evolution of history but must be won by courageous men fighting for social or political justice. Since the enemy is well established, the risk of defeat is great. But it is a risk Kyo accepts, where a more doctrinaire Communist—a Chou En-lai perhaps—would be reassured that final victory is inevitable. Kyo's activism is thus inspired by a personally conceived idealism, not from a Marxist historical necessity. His commitment to the Chinese people stems from a personal desire to aid them in their struggle for human dignity. So, while he retains the will of Malraux's European individualists, he does not seek the same gratification in personal achievement. In place of the individualist's personal goal, he has a collective goal. He no longer struggles against his fellow man but with him in pursuit of a common victory that is too remote for him to enjoy.

In the atmosphere of historical adversity that Malraux has chosen for his novel, victory is impossible. His hero seems aware that his efforts are threatened by defeat. Still, he is not resigned to failure. He searches for a concept of action that, even in failure, does not destroy the meaning of an individual's life. He finds it in a definition of an individual not as the sum of his acts, but in his inherent worth as a human: not in what Kyo later calls his "biography," but in his "being," to which even his abortive acts testify.

How a political defeat can be transformed into a personal victory is the subject of Kyo's story. In recounting it, the author carefully avoids suggesting that Kyo's activism is in itself a distraction from Pascal's grim representation of the human condition (cited as the epigram). Rather, Malraux intends that his hero illustrate political commitment as an alternative to contemplation. In a letter to the noted French critic, Gaëton Picon, he expressed his aims this way: "The essential drama . . . is in the conflict between two ways of thinking: one questioning man and the universe—the other suppressing all questions by a series of activities."[6] The remainder of the novel builds up to the lyrical scene of Kyo's death and that of his Russian comrade-in-arms. It gives a response to Pascal—that defeat and death need not drain the life of the godless man of all its worth. By descending from the immutable realm of metaphysics to the social arena where human actions have some value, his hero finds all the spiritual comfort he needs to sustain him.

The account of Kyo's activities between 21 March and 13 April 1927 furnish the plot of *Man's Fate,* if indeed such a loose series of tableaux can be said to constitute a plot. One critic has described its composition appropriately as a cadenced sequence of events, not unlike a movie *montage.*[7] This structure is due in part to the absence of a narrator who, in the previous novels, strung the various episodes together and, at the same time, functioned as an interpretive mediary between the action and the reader. The latter function has been given over to one of the characters of the novel, Kyo's father, whose penetrating intelligence permits him to speak in Malraux's stead. And at the end of the novel, old Gisors assumes the importance of Malraux's previous narrators, evaluating his son's life in the existentialistic context that the young revolutionary rejected.

Kyo's story does not begin until after the dramatic assassination scene that opens the book. Shortly after midnight, the terrorist Tchen stabs to death a Chinese businessman and takes a bill of lading from his wallet. The document should permit the revolutionaries to get the arms they need for the next day's uprising.

The Human Condition

The leaders of the insurrection are impatiently awaiting Tchen's return in the record shop that has become their meeting place. Once he arrives, they listen to the instructions for the uprising. They have been recorded by Kyo on a phonograph record interspersed among the vocabulary drills of a French lesson. Having heard the record through, Kyo asks why another voice was substituted for his own—he has not recognized his own voice. One of the revolutionaries explains that no one recognizes his voice the first time he hears it on a recording. Kyo is not satisfied by this explanation. In the following pages, he repeatedly recalls the incident. Clarification comes only after two conversations, one with his father, the other with his wife.

After having sought out the curious Clappique and making further arrangements with him to get the arms held on a boat in the Shanghai harbor, Kyo returns home. Arriving there, he leaves the intrigue of the revolution and enters his father's world where "man and the universe are questioned." In the company of old Gisors, "his will was transformed into intelligence, a transformation he did not like" (p. 208). Not that an antagonism sets father against son—quite the contrary. A strong affection unites them, but it does not prevent Kyo from rejecting his father's pessimism. The aging intellectual is intensely aware of the absurdity of the world, and in the face of this absurdity, life seems tragic, and all effort seems futile. To the old man, widowed by the death of his Japanese wife, expelled from his university post for his politics but now barren of any hopes for the future of China, life brings little but the tormenting awareness of the absurd tragedy of the human condition. Only his affection for his son seems to sustain him. Thus he welcomes his son's arrival and the conversation that fills his sleepless nights.

After briefly recounting his activities of the evening, Kyo relates the incident at the record shop. Old Gisors had a similar experience, which he mentions only briefly without his characteristic penetration. By now he wishes only to return to his opium pipe, his refuge from the torments of the absurd. He closes the conversation with the observation that we perceive our own voice with our throat, while others hear it with their ears: our understanding of ourselves comes from within, but others must interpret the superficial qualities that we allow to rise to the surface.

In this casual remark lies the theme Malraux identifies with the hero of *Man's Fate,* a theme developed step by step in the opening pages where Kyo is introduced. The young revolutionary allows the reader to understand the implications of his initial experience in the record shop as he himself methodically sounds its meaning. It leads ultimately to the discovery that the revolutionary camaraderie identified by the redundantly masculine expression "virile fraternity" can rescue an individual life from annihilation by death and defeat. That insight comes only after Malraux investigates, then discredits, love as a possible redemption from the human tragedy.

Love as a refuge from the absurd is studied through the marriage of Kyo and his German wife, a physician at a Shanghai clinic. Upon her return after an especially saddening day with her patients, May reveals to her husband that she has gone to bed with one of her colleagues. Kyo's pride is deeply wounded, but, beyond that, he feels a sort of sympathy for his wife. He believes she has unwittingly allowed herself to become the victim of an erotic game. He attributes to May's colleague the eroticism of a Perken, who sought a personal gratification in the domination of women. Kyo, however, has risen above this individualistic urge. Even though his love remains quite possessive, it permits him to respect his wife as a person with an inherent human dignity. She is not a sexual conquest. But this respect has one curious effect: it changes their marriage from a conjugal to a fraternal union. Their love is based on a shared revolutionary activism. The bonds that join Kyo and May also unite him to the revolutionaries of Shanghai. More important, however, Kyo interprets them as bonds of understanding which permit a penetration below the surface of existence to the very marrow of one's being. This fraternal attraction between people is thus the key to giving life a reality when historical adversity prevents any measurable accomplishment.

This insight comes to Kyo only after he has left the house. He meets Katow out on the street, and together they head to the harbor where the boat laden with arms is anchored. Walking alongside his comrade, he mulls over his love for May and recalls his father's explanation of the recording episode:

> We hear the voices of others with our ears, our own with our throat. Yes. And our lives too we hear with our throats, and the lives of others? . . . "But me, for myself, for my throat, what am I? A kind of absolute, the affirmation of a madman. An intensity greater than all the others. For others I am what I have done." But for May alone, he wasn't what he had done; and for him alone, she was something more than her biography (p. 218).

Like the individualist's eroticism that turns him into an adventurer, the revolutionary's love also has a generalized expression. It is transposed to a political level, but he is no more impelled to conquest in the political domain than in his relations with women. Kyo expects that his wife's understanding can give his life the significance that victory gives the conqueror. Thus love renders victory unnecessary. For the militant destined for defeat, it is an alternative to victory, and in anticipation of defeat, Kyo appears to look to love as a compensation. It is a satisfaction outside of history that historical adversity cannot wrest from him. But for Kyo's love to sustain such a burden is impossible: it soon shows itself to be an inadequate compensation for victory. Just moments before his death, he discovers in virile fraternity a more substantial replacement, but one which still rewards being rather than doing.[8]

In spite of his wavering love and the failure of his revolutionary mission, Kyo never loses his appeal for the reader. His beauty lies in his refusal to sacrifice human dignity to victory. Throughout the novel, he continues to honor his fellow man above success. While this makes him a compelling character, he is a poor revolutionary—and later, in *Man's Hope*, Malraux was to criticize another of his characters produced from the same mold. Kyo nonetheless exemplifies the Kantian "practical imperative" to respect the individual as an end and never use him as a means, the imperative that became the motto of the politically committed existentialists who emerged in Paris after World War II.[9]

67

Malraux's Heroes and History

Part Two of the novel, undoubtedly the section with the most action, recounts the events of the insurrection of 22 and 23 March. It is reported from several perspectives. The first is that of the colonials, or, more specifically, of Ferral, the French industrialist who is one of Malraux's most interesting erotic characters. Then the scene shifts to the revolutionaries: in the most exciting episode of the insurrection. Tchen is shown leading the bloody assault against a police station. In the late afternoon, the scene returns to the headquarters of the colonial police: from there, the results of the uprising are reported to Ferral. Communist victory is imminent, and Ferral decides that the only course open to the foreign interests in Shanghai is to buy off Chiang Kai-shek. He feels confident that the colonials can exploit Chiang and the military strength he has behind him. Finally, the reader sees the conclusion of the insurrection from the perspective of Kyo and Katow, who direct the siege of the last bastion of armed colonial resistance. But already the two revolutionary leaders are speculating that the right wing of the Kuomintang will take over the revolution and disarm the revolutionary army, the Worker's Guard. Overhearing their conversation, Tchen conceives the idea of killing Chiang.

Events of the next week confirm the communist leaders' dire anticipations. But Kyo does not wait to act. He leaves almost immediately after the uprising for the Comintern headquarters in Hankow. There he appeals with no success the party decision that the Shanghai workers yield to the authority of Chiang's Blue Army. The party functionary Vologuine answers Kyo's appeal with his defense of the Stalinist policy for China. The 1933 reader could hardly have avoided recognizing the tragic consequences of this policy for the Chinese Communists: by then the world was well informed of Chiang's 1927 betrayal of the left wing of his Nationalist party. And so as to underscore the plight of the party, Malraux has his fictional Stalinist Vologuine explain that the apparent success of socialism in Hankow is but a fraud. Only the party propaganda succeeds in concealing its failure. If the revolution is to enjoy any success, cooperation with Chiang is essential.

This section, a rupture of the unity and concentration of the novel, serves Malraux well. It creates the tragic atmosphere in

which the remainder of the novel will be played out. At the same
time, it advances the story of Tchen. On the way to Hankow, Kyo
encounters his companion, quite by accident. Tchen explains his
intention to ask for official endorsement of his assassination plan,
endorsement which Vologuine cannot give. He does not, however, detain the determined terrorist. Tchen returns to Shanghai
to carry out the plot to which Malraux gives considerable attention later in the novel.

Upon his return from Hankow, Kyo sets about organizing a
communist resistance to Chiang's right-wing nationalism: the
atmosphere is now heavy with impending tragedy. Kyo's politics
have not yet made him a target of the Nationalists, but his role
in the initial arms theft has. The ubiquitous Clappique appears
at Kyo's house in order to warn him and, at the same time, to ask
for money to manage his own escape from Shanghai. Kyo will not
leave, though. He is determined to stay on to protect his communist comrades from the menacing Blue Army.

By now, however, even the obtuse Comintern functionaries
have become aware of the danger that Chiang's strength represents. No sooner has Clappique left than a messenger arrives with
the order for the Communists to hide whatever arms they still
hold. Kyo must deliver the message to the local party headquarters. But since he is sought by the Nationalist agents, he risks his
life merely venturing out into the streets. In the hope of sharing
her husband's adventure, May asks to accompany him. The discussion provoked by Kyo's initial refusal reveals how tenuous are
his hopes that love can give a person's life a reality.

Kyo is still deeply hurt by his wife's infidelity, and he discovers,
somewhat to his own surprise, a suppressed desire to punish her.
His refusal might be motivated by that desire or, more respect-
ably, by the desire to protect her from danger. May understands
the refusal as a punishment: she reproaches Kyo for having given
her sexual freedom. Unable to answer, he can only reflect: " 'You
shouldn't have believed me.' . . . It was true. He had always recognized [her freedom]. But that she should discuss her rights at this
moment only separated her from him all the more" (p. 327).

The conversation continues. Kyo makes a few gestures of con-
ciliation but does not yet permit her to accompany him. Whether

his intention be protection or punishment, there is a common element of authority that he asserts over his wife. The reader understands what Kyo cannot admit: that his respect for her as an equal has disappeared.

Out on the street, he meets Katow with a warning for Tchen, now on a solitary assassination mission. The inconsequential incident sets the scene for Tchen's death a few pages later. But the encounter does not take Kyo's mind off the quarrel as he continues along the way. Now he reproaches himself for "asserting his pitiable protectiveness" over his wife. Do his thoughts imply that he protected May from death so as to be able to survive in her memory? Given his view of love, such an interpretation is not impossible. But the evidence of the text is too slight to support such an interpretation, and Kyo rises above such petty motives. He runs back to the house, and as he enters, he realizes that "allowing the one you love to join you in death is perhaps the complete expression of love, one that cannot be surpassed" (p. 330). May throws on her coat and joins her husband in the foreboding Shanghai streets where death seems to await them. Together, the two become an easier target for Chiang's police, just as Kyo had earlier observed. Now, however, he puts such thoughts out of his mind. To do honor to his wife, he is willing to jeopardize his mission: little does it matter, though, to one for whom victory is not of prime importance.

Before joining his comrades at the headquarters of the Party Military Committee, Kyo and May must keep a rendezvous with Clappique: Kyo has the money for Clappique's escape. Even though he has more information on anticommunist repression to deliver to the young revolutionary, Clappique lingers at the gambling tables. He fails to meet his friends who, after a fatal delay, set off for the party headquarters. As they approach it, Kyo is beaten unconscious by unseen assailants. He awakens to find himself in the custody of Chiang's security police. It is in prison —in this first temporary cell and later in the converted school where he finally dies—that Kyo's example gives Malraux's response to Pascal's terrifying representation of the existence of the godless.[10] For Malraux, the prison is not the metaphor of a senseless life that is little more than a base animal survival: it is instead a privileged domain where the hero understands the value of his humanity. In prison, among the defeated communist militants, Kyo discovers the rewards of "virile fraternity." For the man of good will condemned to defeat by history's adversity, it replaces love as the justification of his existence.

During his first hours of incarceration, he, like the other prisoners, is subjected to the guards' insults and humiliation. Imprisonment brings him face to face with the humiliation to which Grabot had been subjected in *The Royal Way*. But, while the French adventurer's emotions were reduced to vengeance, Kyo retains his humanity and self-respect. Not even abuse from the guards weakens his concern for the least human of the prisoners.

Despite their confinement in a single cramped cell, all the prisoners except Kyo have been spiritually isolated from one another. They have withdrawn into themselves for protection or self-pity. The inane ramblings of a madman are enough to bring forth their taunts. Others in the cell, ordinary criminals for the most part, resent his raucous ramblings. His insane calls are answered by angry shouts from the prisoners, who hope that a whipping by the guards will silence him. Only Kyo shows any respect for the poor fellow: he stands at the prison bars, braving the guard's abuse in order to negotiate a bribe. For some unexplained reason, prisoners' personal possessions have not been impounded, and with the money Kyo would have given Clappique to escape from Shanghai, he buys the guard's protection for the mad prisoner.

Several hours later, Kyo is summoned for interrogation by König, Chiang's security chief. König, the reader has already learned, retains the adventurer's concept of dignity. Serving as an interpreter for the White Army in the closing days of the Russian Revolution, he had been captured and was cruelly and gratuitously tortured. After that humiliating experience, he could conceive of no other way of regaining his self-respect than in revenge against the Communists. His sense of dignity is thus of an individualistic sort that comes from a personal victory.

The vengeful police chief acts on motives similar to those of Malraux's first two protagonists. Like Garine and Perken, he has no sense of his own worth unless he is asserting his domination over an adversary. In *Man's Hope,* written after the rise of German nazism, Malraux identified as "fascism" any political activity not directed by a sentiment of solidarity. In retrospect, the self-seeking adventurer König, as well as the industrialist Ferral and their counterparts from *The Conquerors* and *The Royal Way,* seem to earn this opprobrium. But in *Man's Fate,* Malraux avoids any political propaganda.

Kyo's confrontation with König represents that of two concepts of dignity. The police chief hopes Kyo will reveal the hiding place of the weapons in exchange for his life. Kyo's betrayal of his comrades would be König's victory, but the alert revolutionary sees through the police chief's cheap tricks. With a threat of torture, König dismisses Kyo, who is taken to the converted school where other communist insurgents are awaiting torture or execution: nothing is resolved by this confrontation, but it does permit Malraux to define dignity and humiliation. It serves as a prelude to the lyrical scene depicting Kyo's death.

On his way back to his final prison, Kyo begins to interpret his experiences in religious terms. He thinks of himself, for instance, as a monk returning to his brothers of the Order of the Revolution, a mendicant order. Before the hero's death and that of Katow, which immediately follows it, Malraux accumulates several more such references. The scene soon acquires the religious dimension appropriate to a response to Pascal, and the principal characters are shown to merit the veneration due holy men.

A short while after Kyo returns to confinement, guards begin calling prisoners for execution. He will not be executed: he can spare himself that indignity by taking the cyanide that all the revolutionary leaders have been given. Before ending his life, Kyo recalls again the phonograph incident. It is associated in his mind with his love for May. But that love is no longer seen as the means of giving his life a reality in a world where accomplishment is continually frustrated by history's adversity. Instead, it appears as nothing more than a deliverance from solitude. It gives way, however, to a greater love, the fraternal affection for those with whom he fought and with whom he would so have liked to live. He thinks that, in the city beyond the walls of this makeshift prison, these martyrs to the Revolution are already being venerated. Lying on the floor, arms in a funeral position across his chest, Kyo realizes that it was not love but virile fraternity that gave his life its direction, and now, in the face of death, it offers the deliverance from solitude that he had earlier expected from marriage: " . . . he was dying, like each of those men lying about him, for having given a meaning to his life. What would a life for which he had not accepted to die have been worth? It is easy to die when you do not die alone" (p. 406).

What Kyo had expected to find in marriage, he discovers in the bonds of a revolutionary camaraderie cemented by a common struggle. The affection of his comrades—even those who are dying—is stronger than his wife's. Not even his awareness that, one by one, they are being led off to what must be an excruciating death weakens this newfound faith. Death now appears as an important element of the revolutionaries' bond. For Kyo, it is "a death saturated by this fraternal lament, an assembly of the vanquished in which multitudes would recognize their martyrs, bloody legends from which are made the golden legends of the saints. How, already facing death, could he fail to hear that murmur of human sacrifice which cried out to him that the virile hearts of men are as great a refuge for the dead as the mind" (p. 406). Then the cyanide extinguishes Kyo's thoughts.

During the last moments of his life, Kyo undergoes—with a sense of satisfaction, not torment—what Pascal had described as the existence of the godless. With no hope of salvation, imprisoned and aware that his friends are being called out to their death, Malraux's hero experiences the exaltation that Pascal believed was the reward reserved for the Christian faithful. By means of the religious elements worked into his text (only a few could be cited here), Malraux illustrates how revolutionary zeal could stand in the stead of religion.

Like many expressions of zeal, Kyo's involves only will and effort, but stops short of real achievement. Malraux insists that achievement is secondary to the assertion of the will: he offers his hero a redemption without success. It is the opposite of the redemption of ultimate victory offered by Marxist materialists, who require that the individual be dissolved in a collective, dialectical praxis. And, contrary to Marxist doctrine, Kyo illustrates how effort spent in battle, though not in victory, brings a reward. Victory is too remote. It exists only as a matter of faith, and like a religious faith, it creates the conditions of martyrdom—with all the gratification Kyo draws from it.

He is, however, not the only revolutionary martyr of the novel. The example of Katow is perhaps even more worthy of Malraux's "golden legend" of revolutionary saints. The reader meets Katow at the same time he meets Kyo, when it is explained that he had participated in the abortive 1905 revolt in Odessa and had subsequently taken refuge in Switzerland. Hereafter, his biography is obscure: all that is seen of it is a period he spent as a prisoner working in the Siberian lead mines. His confinement all but destroyed his revolutionary fervor. Only a woman's affection was able to rescue him from solitude and introversion. After her death he participated in the 1917 revolutions. As in the case of Kyo, love based on respect, not on sexual domination, linked Katow to the revolution. Now his respect for his fellowman finds its most exalted expression in his final sacrifice.

Like his dead comrade next to him, Katow carried concealed in his belt buckle enough cyanide to kill two men. To take it would spare him the pain of being burned alive in the boiler of a steam locomotive.[11] But, with a supreme fraternal gesture he gives half his poison to each of the two collaborators lying on the side opposite Kyo. This is his effort to be "stronger than solitude, stronger than fear" (p. 408). The scene is played out in a semi-darkness in which the horror of the impending death is communicated by the strident whistle of the steam engine. Terrified and weakened by their injuries, the condemned Communists allow the cyanide to fall from their hands. The men risk losing this precious gift, the gift of a humane death: so great is the gift that Malraux describes it as being "greater than life itself." Success in the search for the capsules is punctuated by the hushed exclamation: "Oh, resurrection!"

The interjection seems at first incongruous in the situation where godless men find the weapon of self-destruction. But it recalls the religious motif introduced by Kyo. The two revolutionary martyrs bear witness to a new religion which offers the redemption that Christianity held for Pascal some three hundred years earlier. A militancy founded on a respect for dignity stands as the faith that restores to the European the justification his life lost with the death of God. Because of their faith, Kyo and Katow are spared the tragic fate of their individualistic predecessors, Garine and Perken. In their defeat, the two revolutionaries find the heroic stature which the egocentric adventurers failed to attain. Their example provides an answer to the question raised early in the novel by old Gisors, "What to do with a soul if there is neither God or Christ?" (p. 226)—and, to Gisors's conditions, one might add another: "and if history condemns all endeavor to failure."

Had the novel ended with the death scene, it might have conveyed the endorsement of the revolutionary ideals of the two heroes. But the last word on Kyo's death is reserved for those who survive him, May and his father. For the bereaved wife, Kyo's death is all a martyrdom should be: an inspiration to continue the fight.

Having recovered the body from outside the school, she combs the hair in preparation for a funeral. She imagines that the body is still warm. The impression is symbolic: for May, Kyo's life had not been terminated. She will continue his revolution, but more out of a desire for vengeance than political zeal. It is her way of responding to his love. Because of it, as Kyo had once believed, his life seems to acquire a significance not confined to the importance of his acts. But in the face of her father-in-law's reaction, May's resolve appears hollow, and it is Gisors's judgment that prevails in the conclusion of the novel. Like the narrator or the observer in each of Malraux's two previous novels, he focuses the reader's attention on the limits of the hero's response to the absurd—limits that he perceives once he overcomes his sorrow. The intellectualism that Kyo sought to avoid during his life returns after his death to devaluate his actions.

While opium is old Gisors's refuge from life, Kyo was his attachment to it. With his son's death, the world loses the scant meaning it had for him. He feels as though time has lost all meaning and he has entered a realm where such notions as progress and social change do not exist. All that he retains is a fear of death. When May reminds him that the victory of workers is yet to be won, he can only deprecate their cause. For the old man, death remains the only reality of life—a reality that political commitment cannot dispel:

> "It is possible to cheat life a long time, but in the end it always makes us what we were intended to be . . . Men should be able to learn that there is no reality, that there are worlds of contemplation—with or without opium— where all is vain . . ."
>
> "Where one contemplates what?"
>
> "Maybe nothing besides that vanity . . . That's a great deal" (p. 429).

This concluding scene is Malraux's reminder that militancy fails to satisfy the metaphysical longings of man. More precisely, it prevents him from arriving at an understanding of life which is not destroyed by death. As Malraux later suggested in *The Walnut Trees of Altenburg*, political commitment constitutes one of those "destinies" which prevent man from finding a way to integrate his life with the eternal. That this is also Malraux's criticism at this stage of his career can be inferred from his previous fiction as well as from the structure of *Man's Fate*. Had he not wanted to cast his own doubts on Kyo's example, he would certainly not have ended his novel on a negative note. The reader is left to conclude with Gisors that what belongs to history fails to offer a redemption from the absurd. The old man states his conclusion in terms that register his absurdist perspective: " 'Everyone suffers,' he thought, 'and everyone suffers because he thinks. Fundamentally, the mind conceives man only in the eternal, and the consciousness of life can be nothing but anguish' " (p. 430). Through Gisors, the absurd returns to the fore. And, while Malraux could hardly propose the opium addict as a model to follow, he does use him to reveal limits of revolutionary militancy as a way of coping with the problems of human existence. Kyo does not overcome the tragic absurdity of human existence. He only succeeds in devaluating it. But he attains thereby the stature of a true Malrauvian hero.

The Human Condition

While there can be little doubt about Kyo's being the principal character of *Man's Fate,* the importance of his comrade Tchen cannot be overlooked. He is the central figure of the four most animated scenes of the novel, and, in the condensation prepared for use in French classrooms, fully two-thirds of the text are devoted to his adventures.[12] Although the editing of that textbook exaggerates Tchen's importance, it nonetheless testifies to the fascination he holds for the reader. He represents better than any other Malrauvian character the drama of the Christian who has lost his faith, the condition that Malraux had posed initially in *The Temptation of the West,* as the source of the absurd. Since he is the only Chinese character to receive a complete development in the novel, it is perhaps surprising that Malraux should attribute to Tchen torments that for Malraux characterize the European. The explanation lies in Tchen's Protestant education that made him spiritually more European than Oriental.[13]

From the American Lutheran missionary to whom his education was entrusted, Tchen acquired a European religious sensitivity. He learned the comforts of the Christian's relation to God and came to see his own grandeur in terms of divine grace. To his misfortune, perhaps, grace was interpreted to him by Reverend Smithson, for whom it represented a boundless charity. Early in his youth, however, Tchen was taken out of the mission school. It was somewhat later that he met Gisors at the University of Peking. There, the aging professor taught him "other forms of grandeur," and Tchen lost his religious faith. Unable to live without an ideology he could transform into acts, he sought the miscreant's grace in revolutionary terrorism.

Tchen's story begins with the first episode of the novel, which initiates him to the thrill of assassination. That thrill is the subject of the scene. Malraux allows the reader to see only the assassin's emotions. So absorbed is Tchen by his act that he feels no pain from the stab wound he inflicts upon himself. That there is a human victim involved all but passes unnoticed. And Tchen almost forgets the motive for his act: just before departing he remembers to take his victim's wallet with the bill of lading needed by the revolutionaries awaiting his return at the record

77

shop.[14] There he turns over the document (which proves to be of little value), receives his instructions for the next day's uprising, and makes arrangements to see Kyo's father.

It is less to confess his act than to understand the emotions accompanying it that Tchen seeks out his former mentor. So confused is the assassin that he is unable even to describe his feelings. Perspicacious old Gisors understands what his pupil could only feel. By allowing Tchen to interpret his feelings as a form of eroticism, Gisors helps him to appreciate them: the young revolutionary's eroticism appears as another product of his European education.

For Malraux's erotics—Perken, Ferral, and Tchen (they disappear from his fiction with *Man's Fate*)—eroticism is associated with domination. In response to Gisors's question about his feelings after having first gone to bed with a prostitute, Tchen admitted feeling a certain pride in not being the submissive partner. During the discussion, he discovers the "erotic" urge to dominate death. Since death is inevitable, the only domination is in being the cause of death rather than falling victim to it.

As his conversation with Gisors continues, Tchen realizes that his new cause is not just a substitute for sex, but a higher form of domination. He thinks scornfully of those who have not killed as virgins *(puceaux)*: his experience has distinguished him from others.[15] Rather than uniting him with other revolutionaries, his initial act of terror has isolated him from them. He is no longer interested in the goals of the Revolution because, as Gisors allows the reader to see, he "wants to give death the meaning others give life" (p. 224). While at first Tchen appears to regret his isolation, he soon comes to prefer it. He asks Gisors how he could "possess" the exalting experience of assassination the way a sex partner is possessed in marriage. Gisors advises that it is possible only if he succeeds in transmitting his obsession to others.

Gisors does not explain his curious advice. That may be because it is intended principally as a preparation for the remainder of Tchen's story. Tchen himself appears to discard it with a remark that reveals at the same time his pride and sense of solitude, "Who would be so worthy?" (p. 224). A hope for transmitting his death fixation nonetheless completes his terrifying drama, a drama whose next act is played out at the siege of a police station the next day.

Although he is the hero of a violent battle, his participation in it only reinforces his isolation. Even in anticipation of the fight, he understands that no common goal unites him with the men fighting at his side. He rediscovers only the thrill of violence, a thrill so strong that he can forget the pain of the previous night's wound reopened in the battle. In an especially revealing episode, Tchen is depicted supporting the weight of three insurrectionists lying on the sloping roof of the police station in order to drop hand grenades into the windows below. Exposed to death as much from the grenades as from the police fire, he thinks that "in spite of the imminence of death, of the fraternal weight that tugged him apart, he was not one of theirs." The grenades miss their target; Tchen then slides down the roof to throw his own grenade while hanging from the gutter. A miss would mean his death, but he throws anyway, successfully, so he survives to undertake an even more desperate attempt against the life of Chiang Kai-shek that he announces to Kyo and Katow the evening after the insurrection.

Intoxicated by the hope of killing Chiang, he seeks Comintern approval in Hankow. There he encounters Kyo Gisors. During their conversation, Tchen reveals his fascination with death, or more precisely, his desire to be stronger than death. Enjoying the family's gift of perspicacity, Kyo understands Tchen's morbid fascination to be a vestige of his religious training:

> Thirst for the absolute, thirst for immortality, thus a fear of death: Tchen could have been a coward; but he felt, like all mystics, that his absolute could only be seized in the moment. From whence undoubtedly came his disdain for everything that did not lead up to the moment which would join him to himself in a dizzying embrace (p. 290).

Through the interpretations of Gisors, then Kyo, Tchen is shown to have replaced the Christian God with death. Having lost his faith, he has found another absolute through his revolutionary activity which permits a comparable exaltation. He stays with the Revolution not out of a commitment to revolutionary goals but because it offers a framework for satisfying his spiritual needs. And, for Tchen as for other religious mystics, risking one's life only intensifies the thrill. Neither concern for his own life nor the official opposition of the Comintern weakens Tchen's determination to kill Chiang: it is a thrill he must have. To Kyo's question about why he insists on killing Chiang rather than allowing someone else to execute the plot he replies: "Because I do not like the women I love to be screwed by others" (p. 290). With this response, Tchen places his terrorism next to Perken's eroticism, likewise a residue of a lost religion, but one that involves no metaphysical aspirations.

Preparation for the bomb assassination of Chiang gives a direction to Tchen's life. Failure of a first attempt leaves him all the more determined. He combines the assassination with his suicide. Rather than kill themselves, Tchen's two accomplices withdraw from the plot. He is not discouraged. Again, as in each instance when he is involved in an act of violence, he is entirely self-possessed. He attains that state of insensitivity to anything outside his own immediate goal—here, to the pain of another self-inflicted wound. He takes leave of his accomplices, asking them to bear witness to his own special martyrdom.

Later in the evening, as he awaits Chiang's car, Tchen finds a higher meaning to his solitary terrorism. He reflects on the police repression and the fascist opposition to workers that it is supposed to elicit. But, he supposes, the fascist repression could not be any greater than the blue terror purges already undertaken. So, by killing Chiang, Tchen reasons, he would be teaching the workers the only response open to oppressed men for whom the future holds no hope. Tchen thinks of himself as a model in a life of futility that evitably ends with death. His act would give the Chinese workers an understanding of their oppression; it would give birth to an army of terrorist martyrs. Although he does not connect his somewhat lyrical meditation with the advice that old Gisors had given early in the novel, he sees himself as transmitting to others his fatal passion. In his last moments, he imagines he is transforming terrorism into a religion, the only faith that

The Human Condition

can replace the Christianity he has lost. Then as the headlights of the military car emerge from the fog and darkness, he lunges at the vehicle with an ecstatic joy.

By one of the historical ironies common in Malraux's fiction, Tchen is cheated of his martyrdom. He does not die in the explosion, but only when his reaction to a policeman's kick fires off the revolver he has thrust into his mouth. Later, the reader learns that Chiang escaped: he was in the preceding vehicle, the one Tchen allowed to pass. Unaware of that, Tchen died, seemingly satisfied that his life had fulfilled its mystic purpose. Unlike Kyo and Katow, he enjoys the particular grace of dying ignorant of his failure. He alone from among the characters of this and previous Malraux novels need not acknowledge failure in the inexorable domain of history. It is, significantly, the grace granted the least lucid of Malraux's victims of history's adversity.

Although Tchen shared few goals with the other Shanghai revolutionaries, he did share with Kyo a pessimism about man's place in history. Kyo's view of his place in the revolution contained not really a defeatism but rather an accommodation of defeat. It is implicit in his hope that individual worth rests on something other than victory. Tchen's more nihilistic view was that even the revolution was hopeless. Consequently, he sought no victory in the historical struggle in which he was engaged. At this stage in Malraux's evolution, history is no more capable of furnishing an absolute than of permitting progress. So Tchen's drama appears as futile as that of any of Malraux's heroes. But more than futile, it was destructive of all human values—dignity, fraternity, equality. In the concluding parts of the novel, his efforts receive the condemnation they warrant.

Just before dying, Katow explains that Tchen failed to kill the Nationalist generalissimo. Then, in the concluding scene, May acknowledges him only in negative terms. She has just received a letter from one of his former accomplices, now in Moscow; she notes especially that Pei makes no mention of Tchen. Already the memory of the fanatical terrorist is disappearing. Not even old Gisors, who shared Tchen's torments of the absurd, remembers him in the closing pages.

Malraux's Heroes and History

By yet another of Malraux's ironies, the character presented as one of the least deserving of the novel comes through the rebellion unscathed. Clappique escaped from Shanghai to reappear three decades later in one of the two long fictional accounts of the *Antimemoirs.* There he again shows the same mythomania for which he was criticized by old Gisors. But it is in *Man's Fate* that his shortcomings are exposed: the characterization of Clappique underscores the totalitarian nature of Malraux's thought.[16] This portrayal serves as an index to his scorn for those whose actions serve only to mask the reality of the human condition. Disdain for them is registered as early as Clappique's first scene where, during his five-page conversation with the night-club prostitutes, his prattle arrests the political intrigue of the novel.

After the phonograph episode, Kyo had gone to the Black Cat Club to arrange the second step in the arms theft. Clappique would later negotiate the delivery, but before being able to speak with him, Kyo waited patiently out of sight, listening to his conversation. Through the aid of the young revolutionary, the reader observes the performance of the *mythomane* as he acts out his role of cosmopolitan playboy. Kyo offers no comments on the spectacle, but after finishing his business with Clappique, he returns home and describes the episode for this father.

Old Gisors identifies Clappique's mania as one response to the human condition, but a cowardly response. Gisors's analysis of the *mythomane* suggests more than it explains, but it points out Clappique's refusal to come to grips with the absurdity that underlies human existence. Rather than finding in the absurd an imperative to create human values, so Gisors implies, the *mythomane* acts as though it has deprived all life of value. He adopts a nihilistic attitude: "nothing exists: everything is a dream" (p. 209). This attitude does offer a certain compensation, however. It spares Clappique the anguish that accompanies the absurd. The little suffering that he cannot avoid is but superficial, not of the sort that drove Kyo to seek a metaphysical justification for his life in political activism. Clappique is, rather, a character caught up in history. His actions, as Gisors notes, constitute a denial of life. They testify to a belief that life need have no more justification than the pleasure afforded by any of the roles the mytho-mane momentarily portrays.

Clappique's remaining appearances in the novel reinforce Gisors's interpretation. Calling on Kyo to report that the arms can be unloaded from the boat, he is unable to appreciate the seriousness of his mission. He sees himself playing out the part of Fantomas, the hero of the popular thrillers. But he is not without his endearing side—he does warn Kyo of Chiang's crackdown against the Communists. Yet, when he has further information that might save many of the revolutionaries, he is paralyzed at the gaming tables, unable to bring himself to deliver the message. Finally, when he escapes from Shanghai, he is startled to discover how easily others are taken in by his disguise.[17] This last role is his biggest success, and one of Malraux's most vivid scenes. It stands with some of his portrayals of Tchen as the most visual of the novel. More important, though, it underscores the differences between Clappique, who finds nothing worth struggling for, and those who enter a historical struggle with the most serious of intentions.

Clappique, it is necessary to note, is but one of Malraux's rogues, but he is the best developed. Because he is associated with the revolutionaries, Malraux could afford to draw him in detail without losing the perspective of his novel. Still Ferral, on the enemy side, also received much of the author's attention. His sketch of this erotic character in *Man's Fate* registers the evolution of his thought. Measured against the example of Kyo, Ferral's erotic response to the absurd appears even more futile than did Perken's in *The Royal Way*. He joins König and Vologuine whose manias have likewise become the object of Malraux's scorn —König for his vengeance, Vologuine for his party loyalty. When Gisors's criticism of Clappique is turned against these three characters, each can be seen to withdraw before the reality of their existence. They all fail to meet Malraux's criteria of heroism. But since such characters are found on either side in the Revolution, Malraux's scorn is not a matter of politics. He limits his admiration to those characters of *Man's Fate* who are engaged in the fraternal struggle for dignity—a struggle which is metaphysical before being political.

Malraux's Heroes and History

The two heroic martyrs of *Man's Fate* and the individualistic, self-seeking adventurers of *The Conquerors* and *The Royal Way* shared the hope of giving their lives a meaning through participation in history. All four applied their will and intelligence to wrest from history a redemption from the torments of the absurd. But the differences between the characters are nonetheless great. They can be explained best by the different views on the individual's place in history which the author attributed to them.

As the analysis of Malraux's first two novels revealed, the characters who sought a personal victory were the most tragic, for Malraux's concept of history offers no victories. Although second in time by its date of publication, *The Royal Way* offers an earlier view of history, one inherited from a confident, optimistic nineteenth-century Europe. The protagonist Perken, for whom victory meant a personal immortality, appeared most pathetic. Garine, skeptical about progress and immortality, sought the thrill of power; but when the course of politics deprived him of power, history appeared as an instrument of the absurd rather than an escape from it. With Kyo, and secondarily with Katow, Malraux offers a different concept of man's role in history. Through them, he illustrates how a redemption was possible once the personal domination that victory represents ceased to be the goal.

The two Shanghai revolutionaries, with a latent comprehension of history's adversity, identified their interests with those of their fellowman. An abstract faith in social progress—but not the inevitable social or economical evolution often preached by Marxists—provided a direction to their lives. But it was not their contribution to progress that yielded the satisfactions they sought. Rather it was in a sense of fraternity over which history has no sway. A hope for progress brought them to history, but their personal conquests lay outside it. That Kyo and Katow understood how such victories were possible gives their examples a moral force that Garine's and Perken's lack. Even if the individual cannot overcome the tragedy of history and of the absurdity to which it testifies, at least he can "devaluate" it.[18] This is the lesson of Kyo and of his Russian comrade.

The Human Condition

To these heroes of *Man's Fate,* the Revolution did not offer the redemption from the absurd that it offers to a more doctrinaire Communist. Dedicated Marxist revolutionaries might very easily find in the dialectical interpretation of history the sort of absolute that Tchen was looking for. But at this stage in his career, Malraux does not permit his European heroes to see Marxism as a substitute for Christianity—unless one so interprets the political faith of the Belgian expatriate who operated the Shanghai record shop. Once free of the threat of reprisal against his ailing wife and child, Hemmelrich thrust himself into the struggle with the zeal of a new convert. At the collapse of the Shanghai uprising, he fled to Russia. The mindless tasks that he is reported to perform in a factory there seem to fill him with a sort of grace. Although his appearances in the novel are so brief that they fail to explain what the Revolution holds for him, it evidently offers him more than virile fraternity. It is through Kassner, the hero of his next novel, that Malraux first illustrates how communism can become a religion capable of saving man from his tragic destiny.

5 TRANSITION FROM DESPAIR TO HOPE

$\mathcal{T}$HE success of *Man's Fate* catapulted Malraux into political as well as literary prominence. His participation in left wing European causes provided the background for his next novel, but it is no more—nor less—autobiographical than *The Royal Way.* He was one of the founders of the World League Against Anti-Semitism and of the Committee to Aid Victims of the Nazis; he headed the group working for the liberation of the Bulgarian Communist imprisoned for participating in a Reichstag bomb plot. In 1934, he appeared as one of the principal speakers at the Soviet Writers' Congress in Moscow and, the next year, helped organize the International Congress for the Defense of Culture held in Paris. Although sympathetic to communism, his talks at these two meetings left no doubt about his rejection of the official Kremlin esthetic of socialist realism. In its place, he defended the artist's privilege of free investigation. He reinforced this stand in 1935 with the preface to *Days of Wrath,* his first novel to be set in Europe.

Malraux's declaration of nonconformity is far less important, however, than the collectivist view of man conveyed by the brief preface. Following what seems to be a *pro forma* disclaimer of political intent, he repeats his criticism of the nineteenth-century individualism that was already the subject of *The Temptation of the West.* [1] This time, however, his criticism acquires a political tenor lent to the preface by a new view of history. Malraux restores it as a domain where an individual's actions are not condemned in advance to failure. He proposes, as an appropriate twentieth-century exemplar, the hero who is able to "identify his actions with the social order struggling to be born." Such a character becomes the hero of *Days of Wrath,* and his story is told in such

Malraux's Heroes and History

a way that he never appears as the tragic victim of metaphysical absurdity or malevolent history.

This 1935 novel must have disappointed the admirers won by the prize-winning novel, *Man's Fate.* It fails to capture the tragic poetry which is the beauty of the earlier fictional representation of the 1927 Shanghai uprisings. During the two years that separate the two works, Malraux reassessed brotherhood and man's role in the historical process, arriving at a view more in harmony with communist notions of history. *Days of Wrath* illustrates how the virile fraternity of *Man's Fate* ceases to be the consolation for the futility to which history condemns human enterprise and becomes the key to social progress. More important, however, than this political evolution, but nonetheless closely associated with it, is the change in the view of man in the universe to which the novel also attests. Through a fraternally inspired activism in a domain where progress is possible, the hero achieves a metaphysical union with the absolute. Communist activism replaces Christianity in Malraux's thought as an attachment to the creative forces of the universe without, as he represents it, destroying the individual personality. Ironically, political views that the author renounced shortly after the outbreak of World War II detract from the novel announcing his new orientation. Still, this brief work, which Malraux withheld from the 1970 collective edition of his fiction, should not be overlooked, for it marks a major turning point in his literary career.

As it was for Kyo and Katow, the bond of brotherhood proves to be a humanizing force for Kassner during the imprisonment, which constitutes two-thirds of the text. To a large extent, *Days of Wrath* repeats the adventure of the two Shanghai revolutionaries. But Kassner is to be freed, and after his release, his sense of virile fraternity becomes the foundation for his communion with the political activists of Prague, then with all mankind.

Although Malraux found in Europe the same sort of political turmoil that provided the background for his first three Oriental novels, he failed to give the Nazi-Communist antagonism in Germany the amplitude of the previous tragedies. In scope, it more resembles a single chapter of *Man's Fate.* Its conclusion is abrupt, and the development of the ideas leading up to it is curiously truncated. In addition, all secondary plots have been sacrificed. Malraux focuses on a single character, the German revolutionary Kassner, from whose point of view the adventure is recounted.

Here, too, *Days of Wrath* marks a departure from the Oriental novels. Since the story is told from the viewpoint of the protagonist, its meaning is not filtered through the sensitivities of an aloof, critical intelligence—the narrators of *The Conquerors* or *The Royal Way*, or Kyo's perspicacious father, old Gisors. Their observations serve to criticize what may appear to be the discursive logic of the novel. As reported by their witnesses, Garine's and Perken's efforts appear as futile gestures in the face of the absurd, and Kyo's sacrifice remains an isolated tragedy. But when Malraux seeks to represent a heroic venture sympathetically, he cuts down the esthetic distance and permits a more direct identification between the reader and the hero. It is as though he seeks to reduce the area for criticism while he introduces an immediacy into the story of Kassner's nine-day confinement in and subsequent release from the ordinary prison that Malraux calls a Nazi "concentration camp."

Kassner's story begins as he awaits interrogation by Nazi storm troopers. His biography is briefly sketched through a series of flashbacks. The reader learns that, by the early 1930s, he has already enjoyed an active career as a communist militant. He has just been arrested in a raid upon the apartment of a party member. Anticipating the raid, he had gone to the apartment to destroy a list of names that would have compromised members of his clandestine cell. His action meant certain arrest, but the reader is not yet sure whether his personal sacrifice was inspired by concern for his comrades or by automatic obedience to the party, or even whether the two motives are distinct.

The Nazis have an intelligence file on Kassner which seems curiously incomplete: it does not provide the information necessary to identify him positively. And the Communist militant refuses to admit anything. He is confined to the dank solitude of a cell. There he gradually becomes aware of gimmicks being employed by the storm troopers to destroy his will and to loosen his tongue. He recovers surprisingly well from a beating at the hands of the sadistic prison guards but discovers that a greater danger is the insanity brought on by isolation from the world of human beings. Despite his resolve not to lose control of his mind, the first stages of his captivity betray his weakness.

He thinks of his wife, safe in Prague and away from the Nazi menace; but since he cannot share her life, he thinks illogically that she must be dead. He invents childish little tests to prove that she is still alive but fails to convince himself. A first link with his fellow man appears to be broken. He soon finds another social attachment in music. More than a consolation, it carries with it a kind of spiritual communion: "Music takes the head of man in its hands to raise it slowly towards virile fraternity" (p. 57). Music in general becomes in his mind the communist "Internationale" and calls forth a series of more remote recollections from the time of Kassner's participation in the Russian civil wars that followed the 1917 Revolution. The imagined anthem releases the past like a Proustian *madeleine.* Since Kassner's past is one of militancy in the cause of international brotherhood, it triggers recollections of revolutionary activity, but as a memory-releasing mechanism, music receives no special endorsement from Malraux. There is no reason for interpreting the "Internationale," in anticipation of *The Psychology of Art* and *The Voices of Silence,* as an art form that functions as an "antidestiny."[2] Malraux represents the hymn as an attachment to the party, and through this attachment, his hero retains his humanity. Memories of mass singing of the revolutionary hymn dispel Kassner's feelings of isolation, but the charm is short-lived. Once the strains stop, he reverts to the subhuman condition of a prisoner, and, shortly afterwards, he is tormented by his recollections of the plain-chant of the orthodox church and the music of Bach and Beethoven: the repetitious, haunting strains seem to be but another threat to his sanity.

His attention is soon captured by tapping from an adjacent cell. A sense of fraternity is transmitted through the cell walls, but for Kassner, real communication requires that the irregularly spaced taps be decoded. His first efforts are interrupted by the visit of the guard, who throws him an end of rope to unravel; since it is the only thing in the cell, it becomes a constant invitation to fall into the degradation of an idiot's pastime. But the tapping resumes, and the code is deciphered. Kassner decides that only the essential need be transmitted, that he need only reassure his comrade and protect him against the temptation of his own rope. Although the code is understood, words seem useless to express such basic ideals; the essential is communicated with the most banal words, and even with fragments of words. Deciphering the code merely occupies Kassner's mind and preserves one element of human dignity, the intelligence, from atrophy.

The prison episodes constitute what can best be considered Malraux's illustration of the functioning of "virile fraternity" on the private level. Here it can be seen as the force that preserves the prisoner's own humanity. It is significant that Malraux's fraternity involves a willful expression: one's humanity is not a birthright inherent in human nature, but a noble prize wrested from the dehumanizing forces in the world. In this novel, as in all of his novels, jails, guards, and police chiefs represent what is dehumanizing and humiliating: prisons and their wardens are instruments that serve to isolate the individual and reduce him to an animal state. The notion of the prison as a place where humanity is tested recalls Pascal's representation of man without God. Rejecting Pascal, Malraux illustrates in *Days of Wrath,* as he does in *Man's Fate,* how dignity can be retained in prison. But besides appearing as a place where the individual wages a solitary fight for his humanity, Malraux's prison is associated with the spirit of domination characteristic of the individualistic society. If the individual is to reap the benefits of his hard-won humanity, he must escape from the metaphorical prison of an individualistic, competitive world. This escape, or transcendence, is the subject of the concluding chapters of *Days of Wrath,* which mark Malraux's departure from the world of tragedy.

Kassner is a Malrauvian exemplar capable of casting aside values that isolate man socially and metaphysically. Because he is needed to illustrate the compensations of communist militancy, the author allows him to be rescued from his cell. He is able to discover after his release what previous Malrauvian exemplars were deprived of by their deaths: how the fraternal bonds, which in the first stage protect an individual's humanity, can constitute a metaphysical redemption from tragedy. This discovery involves a whole new outlook upon the world and requires an entire reconstitution of values for the former prisoner accustomed to protecting his humanity in an individualistic society. Kassner's release comes as he is practicing a speech that he might give to a Communist party meeting: it is the last of the inventions he uses to cheat isolation and solitude. He has been spared further prison degradation, less by his own efforts, however, than by the sacrifice of another party member who, under the name of Kassner, has surrendered to Hitler's police.

Shortly before beginning this novel, Malraux set out on an air expedition with the aviator Corniglion-Molinier in the hopes of discovering from the air the lost capital of the Queen of Sheba. Reports of the expedition were initially published in the Paris daily, *L'Intransigeant,* in May 1934. Soon afterwards, the account of the flight through the hurricane over Tunisia was repeated as Kassner's return flight to Prague.[3] More than a literary transposition of an aviation adventure, it is the transition to the most provocative part of the novel. In *Days of Wrath,* it forms a dramatic connection between Kassner's imprisonment and what Malraux calls a "return to the earth" in his autobiographical work. He uses this device twice again, both times in his last novel, *The Walnut Trees of Altenburg,* first published in 1943. In that work, as in this, it leads to a higher understanding of the individual's place in the world.

During his confinement in prison, the world died for Kassner in the same way that his wife had presumably died: the prisoner's existence had been reduced to recollections somewhat distorted by his memory and his concentration on the psychological struggle against his jailors. Now the world begins to take on a new meaning for Kassner: as he resumes his marriage, the world appears as the domain of the interaction between society and the individual. The flight to Prague becomes a symbolic rebirth to the world, the grace which Kyo and Katow were deprived of.

The freed prisoner risks a dangerous flight because of his impatience to leave Germany and return to Anna. He and his nameless pilot chance the return trip against three-to-one odds. Only luck can explain their arrival in Prague. Considering such a stroke of luck along with the good fortune of Kassner's release from a Nazi prison, the reader realizes that man's fate is no longer adverse. For the first time in Malraux's fiction, the accidents of history favor the hero. But Kassner's good fortune brings him to an alien world in which nothing he sees carries the warmth of familiarity. Only his surprisingly chaste affection for his wife is able to restore the meaning of the world. His singular experience provides Malraux with an opportunity to demonstrate, in a manner that recalls Jules Romains's unanimism or Emile Durkheim's collective consciousness, how a sense of group solidarity is created.

Once Kassner had become reconciled to Anna's presumed death, his mind had turned to her for only one brief moment during the remainder of his prison confinement—and he thought of no other woman. Unlike the inmates of Arthur Koestler's *Darkness at Noon* or Jean Genet's prison accounts, Kassner is surprisingly free from sexual desire. Malraux avoids the theme of eroticism, which evidently remains associated in his mind with a domination of one partner by the other. His men of good will view their women as equals engaged on equal terms in a struggle for human dignity. The respect that united Kyo and May of *Man's Fate* in a "fraternal" marriage also joins Kassner and his wife. Anna Kassner is not, however, so defeminized as May Gisors, but her marriage is hardly more believable: in both unions, affection gives way to an ethical attachment to mankind. Malraux does not succeed in infusing much more emotion into this representation of husband-wife relations than can be found in a *Little Red Book* of party directives or, worse, the Orwellian caricature in *1984* of marriage as a party duty. He is far more successful in representing male-female antagonisms. His failure to breathe any life into his exemplary marriages lends some credibility to the accusation of misogyny that Clara Malraux wrote into her memoirs.[4] Perhaps they clarify why her former husband chose the redundantly masculine expression of "virile fraternity" as the basis of human values!

Upon his release from prison and again when the small plane escaped the danger of the storm, Kassner had the impression that Anna's life had been saved. Malraux uses the wife again as Kassner's link with life. Before the freed prisoner can experience any sense of living, he must be stimulated by some sort of affection that only his wife can give. So he heads for their apartment, unresponsive to the life on the streets or in the shops. To his disappointment, Anna is not at the apartment when he arrives. Had he bought the party newspaper before going to the apartment he would have known why. From the paper he learns of the "Meeting for Imprisoned Antifascists." Because of Anna, the newspaper acquires a significance. The process of integration to life has begun. Kassner's experiences at the meeting continue this process based on the emotions and not on the rigorous logic of Malraux's "significant characters." Like Kyo before him, Kassner's actions derive from the heart and not from the mind.

Kassner joins 20,000 other antifascists at the overflowing Lucerna Hall, but he has gone in search of his wife, not out of interest in the program. An elderly woman is speaking when he arrives. He registers more an aloof comprehension of her embarrassment than real sympathy. He supposes, however, that he and his wife are sharing the same experience of listening to the old woman's voice. The conclusion of the halting talk gives him a chance to search for Anna among the crowd. He mistakes one cat-eyed girl for his wife. It will be impossible to find her, Kassner realizes, because he is projecting his recollection of Anna's face on all the young women in the hall. Rather than causing any despair, this realization comforts him. He understands that he is with Anna just because she is somewhere in the same crowd. He ceases his search and fixes his affection on the whole assembly. Freed from the impulsion to continue his search, he listens momentarily to the talk of a party intellectual next on the program. It reminds Kassner of his own imaginary discourse to the shadows of his cell: a unity between him and the speaker is created. Then the faces of the crowd appear to take on an animation and " . . . before that multitude, [to which Kassner had] not yet been linked by the communion of will, he found the passions and truths which are only given to men assembled together . . . And all that bewildered, grave and fierce communion with which he was beginning to identify himself became fused with his invisible wife" (pp. 163–64).

The speaker continues his talks on the degradations to which prisoners in Nazi concentration camps are subjected. The subject awakens no recollections in Kassner's mind: he is again intent on finding Anna. He understands, though, that Anna has come to the meeting to give her concern for him a more general expression. Her affection, Kassner thinks, has a solid foundation in the emotions and is, thereby, far more sincere and enduring than one which is reasoned out; only such emotional responses can resist an enemy's cruelty. He concludes the chapter with the observation: "No spoken work penetrated so deeply as cruelty, but virile fraternity met it [cruelty] even in the most remote reaches of the soul, in the forbidden places of the heart where torture and death are lurking" (p. 165).

In this chapter, Malraux's style becomes especially dense, if not obscure. He is juggling three or four ideas at once, all of which are evidently fused in his thought. On the most immediate level is his plea for a faith in the force of emotions. The plea is tied in with his hope of making virile fraternity into the foundation of social unity. And beyond this, he attaches these emotional responses to a redemption from the absurd based on a political activism. Besides the multiplicity of ideas, Malraux is also wrestling with difficulties presented by the characterization of Kassner. Since the story has been reduced to two characters, "the hero and his sense of life" ("Preface," p. 8), Malraux has no other spokesman. Kassner receives the double burden of transmitting a complex message and, at the same time, making a case for the emotions. To respect the latter, Malraux sacrifices interpretation. He deprives Kassner of that intellectualism that characterizes Malraux's earlier heroes, and permits him only to praise the emotions that unify the participants at the antifascist rally. Here, as elsewhere in his works, Malraux's narration suffers from too great a condensation. André Gide, who collaborated with Malraux in his political enterprises during the time of the composition of *Days of Wrath*, might well have turned around a criticism which he had leveled at Proust and applied it here: where the author of *In the Remembrance of Things Past* received criticism for building a novel and leaving the scaffolding standing, Malraux seems to deserve it for having removed so much of the scaffolding that the narrative hardly stands as a completed novel.

Malraux's Heroes and History

The last chapter takes Kassner, in an equally condensed manner, to a state of religious exaltation while it recounts his reunion with his wife and son in their Prague apartment. The scene begins as a monologue. Anna speaks and Kassner listens, first to the bedtime story being read to their nameless son, then to his wife's restrained welcome. He is curiously unresponsive to Anna's coy expression of regret that she cannot be the "joy" of his life. Kassner cannot devote himself to a single person; his commitment must be on a higher level. He mirrors the impulsion to participate in a vast historical movement that Malraux attributed to the expatriate Belgian shopkeeper Hemmelrich in *Man's Fate.* Kassner is not restrained, however, by his family responsibilities, and his wife and child need not be killed for him to realize his ambitions. Anna's concerns rise to meet her husband's: she ceases to see herself in the individual role of wife and mother and becomes aware of being part of a group united in motherhood. As her husband, scant moments before, found identification with a group through his affection for his wife, so Anna finds a comparable identification with other Prague mothers through her son.

Kassner's attention is called away from his wife by the neighbors' clatter in the hallway. His gaze then shifts out the window to the city. It is a moment of epiphany for him as the city takes on the meaning that it lacked earlier in the day, after his arrival at the airport. He sees a child emerge from a building across the street and thinks, "One of those illuminations which make men believe that a God has just been born bathed that house from which a child came out only to disappear in the shadows, and it seemed to Kassner that, although mired down by all the blood he had just slogged through, the meaning of the world was emerging and its most secret destiny was going to be accomplished" (p. 183). The revelation is presented so briefly that it fails to attain the lyricism of a Joycean epiphany, but its meaning is clarified somewhat by the concluding paragraphs.

The moment is bathed in a divine light, as Kassner experiences a new sense of the eternal. Unlike religious eternity understood in terms of the resurrected souls of the dead, Kassner's eternity will be historical. It is composed of the unending succession of human lives and is, as he indicates, "the eternity of the living and

Transition from Despair to Hope

not the eternity of the dead" (p. 184). Kassner's illumination is one of mystical attachment to the human race in its entire historical continuity. He sees human life as part of a vast evolution that, according to the political context of the novel, must be the dialectical evolution described first by Hegel and given an economic interpretation by Marx. It involves a continual progress, presumably toward some classless, fraternal society that Malraux wisely avoids describing in the novel. Still, the story of Kassner rests on an assumption of progress quite contrary to the view of tragic history presented in the Oriental novels. This concept of historical change permits the individual to redeem his life from the absurd, which, in the earlier novels, rose up to destroy human values. This new view of history gives individual endeavor a significance which justifies human existence. It is this existential response to the absurd that Malraux finds in Marxism, not the economic materialism of more doctrinaire Marxists.[5]

Because history can now be taken as a continuous process, an individual has the function of fostering progress. By espousing the dialectical movement that directs history, the activist gives his life a permanent value that comes from what he lends to this all-encompassing historical evolution. Malraux's new concept of history restores to the individual the place in the universe that he lost with the death of God. Taken as an eternal succession, history becomes something of an absolute—the only one man can know in a universe from which God appears to have withdrawn. Participation in the Communist Revolution affords a salvation, without, of course, the promise of Christian immortality. Kassner is not so transported by this mystical experience as to exaggerate the nature of his new-found redemption: he realizes that "in all his acts, he would express what remained in him of the spirit of his comrades and, the day he would be killed in Germany, this instant would be killed with him" (p. 184).

Although communism assumes the proportions of a surrogate religion in his 1935 novel, Malraux is hardly a zealot of the new religion, as his opposition to the esthetics of socialist realism has already shown. In addition, the hero of *Man's Fate* and the character who often appears to be the author's spokesman in the novel both had already rejected the economic determinism of Marxism

97

as a "fatalism." *Days of Wrath* contains no such direct attack on Marxist economic theory—which may explain why it was the only one of Malraux's novels to circulate freely in Stalinist Russia. Nonetheless, the author represents brotherhood as a social bond, stronger than any materalistic force and equally capable of satisfying the metaphysical needs that attracted Malraux and many other French intellectuals to Marxism. When virile fraternity is mentioned a second time in connection with the party rally, it is to explain Kassner's being raised from an individual consciousness to a higher state of group consciousness.[6] On the last pages, through the intermediary of his wife, he realizes the full implications of this consciousness, that of identification with all human society throughout all time. To give expression to that vast consciousness, Kassner needs a greater field than that of his intimate apartment. He must go out on to the Prague streets, streets that only hours before held no meaning for him despite their teeming life. Ironically, then, Kassner no sooner finds his wife than he loses her; or, more accurately, no sooner does he find her than he transcends the need for a wife.

Into a few hours, Malraux has condensed Kassner's spiritual itinerary from personal consciousness to metaphysical redemption. A mystical aura places the conclusion of his experience in a religious framework not unlike that which illuminated the last moments of Kyo and Katow, the exemplars of Malraux's tragic period. The religious elements of Kassner's adventure are not, however, restricted to the conclusion. The account of his entire nine-day ordeal is punctuated with examples of martyrdom, temptation, prayers, self-denials, and persecutions at the hands of Nazi devils. Some thirty years after composing this work, Malraux raised, somewhat rhetorically, the question of whether or not "a civilization can be anything more than a civilization of doubt or one in which the present alone counts, and if it could establish its values very long on anything besides a religion."[7] *Days of Wrath* had already pointed to the necessity of a religion, but a secular religion founded on a depersonalized God. Malraux has based his new faith on the Marxist, dialectical concept of man as a cultural being, united with an unending succession of men who have gone before and who will follow. Through it, redemption is offered to the elect of the Communist party who enjoy the special grace of virile fraternity. This restriction confers on the book its political bias. Although Malraux may be faulted for representing communism as the only instrument of salvation, he has investigated an outlet from the torments of the absurd. Leaving the hostile Orient for a seemingly friendly European setting, he ceases to show his protagonist as a victim and accords him reason to hope for the recovery of dignity and a place in the universe, but gives no place to the improvement of his material lot.

During the moments of his greatest despair in prison, Kassner conceived the scheme of growing a fingernail long enough to cut open the vein of his wrist and kill himself. In the constant darkness of his cell, only the realization of this desperate project gave meaning to time. Kassner repeated the discovery made by Kyo moments before his death that only where there is hope to bring a project to fruition does time have a meaning. Illustrating hope as a function of its opposite, despair, does, on the surface, appear incongruous. Kassner's plan, however, is to preserve for himself some dignity by ending his life before he is reduced to a subhuman state. It is all one can hope for in a tragically absurd universe.

When Kassner is released from prison, the novel and Malraux's fiction in general take on a decidedly optimistic tone. Upon the rebirth symbolized by the airplane flight to Prague, the Malrauvian hero emerges into a different universe. He stops acting as though his efforts were condemned by historical adversity to be nothing more than futile gestures. A new sense of history permits him a reprieve from the torment of an absurd, metaphysical alienation.

This view also inspires several of the revolutionaries that Malraux depicts in *Man's Hope,* a novel which offers a more ample and critical development of the themes of *Days of Wrath.* Like this 1935 novel, the vast fictional representation of the Spanish Civil War grew out of his experiences at the side of Republicans. In the novels composed during his brief association with them, he restores history as the domain where human activity acquires meaning. As he became active in European politics, he ceased to condemn human endeavor to the futility which he had assigned to it in the Oriental novels. In the absence of any confirmation from Malraux himself, it is idle to speculate on whether it was his return to Europe or his sympathy for communism that explains his changing view of history. It is possible to conclude, nonetheless, that the first novel he set in Europe annexes his metaphysical quest to the European impulse to give meaning to life by influencing history.

6 THE HUMAN
CONDITION REVISITED

$\mathcal{B}$EFORE dawn on 17 July 1936, Franco set
in motion from his garrison in Morocco a *putsch* which was supposed to leave him master of Spain within a few short days. He
had counted on the factionalism within the Republican government to prevent any effective opposition to his military insurrection. But he failed to assess the zeal of organized labor or to
anticipate the defection of numerous police units to the Loyalists.
By 20 July, the uprising was forestalled and a long period of civil
war began; by 21 July, André Malraux had arrived in Madrid,
presumably to prepare a report for the Comité de Vigilance des
Intellectuels Antifascistes.[1] The report was soon forgotten as he
set about, almost upon his arrival, to organize an air squadron in
support of the Loyalist government—the International Squadron
depicted in *Man's Hope.* On 20 August, the Squadron undertook
its first successful mission, bombing Franco's army advancing on
the road near Medellin—an incident recounted in the novel. Malraux held the post comparable to that of the fictional Squadron
Commander Magnin until the entire unit fell victim to the war's
attrition in February 1937. Although the novel renders history
rather faithfully, Magnin's activities are of little help in clarifying
the author's role in the war.

Malraux was no longer serving in Spain when the battle of
Guadalajara, the last episode of his novel, took place in March
1937. One of his last military responsibilities was to arrange the
rescue of the flight crew of a bomber which had crashed in the
Teruel mountains shortly after Christmas, 1936. This episode,
which later would become Malraux's first film venture, was sand-
wiched between the preparations for the battle of Guadalajara
and the victory of the Republican forces over the better equipped

Malraux's Heroes and History

Italian regulars sent into Spain by Mussolini. Malraux transposed the crash of the "Canard Déchaîné" from 27 December 1936 to 13 February 1937. He turned this mishap into a tableau of peasant and military solidarity coinciding with the first major Republican victory. The book was rushed into print and appeared in December 1937—in view of its length, a remarkably short time after the scenes it depicted. Its initial popularity can, to a large degree, be explained by the public curiosity about the war, and the book undoubtedly served well the author's unconcealed intention to create sympathy for the Spanish Loyalist cause.[2]

Malraux was well situated to write an eyewitness account of the Spanish Civil War. In addition to his participation in the early military phases, he remained on as something of a propagandist for the Republican struggle. He was one of the principal organizers of the Writers' Congress held in Madrid in the summer of 1937. And, from accounts in memoirs which have since been published, he was present at several conferences on the war in Paris and at the Neutrality Commission in Geneva. But writing a work of history was not his intention: he used his experiences to create a work of fiction in a style of journalistic immediacy. He explains his technique early in the novel through a conversation between the Spanish sculptor Lopez and the American journalist Shade.[3] Lopez advances the view that a style will be born when people who must speak are thrown together with people equally avid to learn. The Spanish Civil War appeared to the artist to be the necessary meeting ground, and out of it, he expected a fresco style to develop. Malraux may have had in mind the murals of the Mexican revolutionary artists, Siqueiros, Orozco, and Rivera[4]: his disjointed narrative appears as the literary counterpart of their graphic frescos. The unity of the novel comes not through the development of character or events but through the development of the theme of the individual's role in history—or, more specifically, those cataclysms of history we call war.

To follow the novel, the reader must bring his own knowledge of the Spanish Civil War to his reading: Malraux provides none of the background. He further complicates his novel by shifting its focus from character to character and battle to battle in order to compose his vast panorama of men at war. Successive scenes bear little relation to one another even though they follow a chronological order running from the military uprising of 17 July 1936 to the Republican victory at Guadalajara on 18 March 1937. Malraux is less interested in placing the events in a military context than in tracing the relation of the individual to the events. But in order to understand the view of history that Malraux develops, some consideration must be given to the background of the war. It is necessary to keep in mind that, when the Spanish under Franco revolted against the Republic, the defense of the government was left to a handful of loyal officers and police units, a militia of zealous anarchist syndicalists and a maverick group of foreign volunteers. During the course of the novel, Malraux shows that only the rigorously disciplined Communists could turn this heterogeneous mass into an effective army. The Communists, led by the political commissars placed in each Republican military unit, required what every army requires: an exclusive dedication to victory. Through his novel, Malraux illustrates that such dedication involves, first, that the individual sacrifice his personal idealism and, concomitantly, that the adversary be regarded as a dehumanized opponent to be vanquished. To make this point, all incidents of *Man's Hope* are presented from the point of view of the Loyalists, the enemy being identified simply as "Fascists," with no consideration of the range of political opinion from Carlist and Legitimist to Phalangist that constituted the Nationalist opposition. This orientation gives the work a decidedly communistic flavor, making it appear to the eyes of some critics far more propagandistic than it really is.[5] Rather than being read as an apology for communism, *Man's Hope* can be more profitably studied as an illustration of the conditions under which history can provide a redemption from the absurd.

It cannot be overlooked, however, that Malraux treats communism with disarming sympathy. He presents it as a coherent explanation for history in which can be found a redemption from the absurd. But, so far as his own sympathy for the political goals of communism are concerned, his association with the communist militants comes principally from a shared antifascism. For whatever collaboration he offered the Communist party in Spain, France, or Germany, he refused to join the party and regularly

Malraux's Heroes and History

repudiated official party esthetics. And his political independence did not escape the Comintern hierarchy. They refused to allow *Man's Hope* to circulate in Russia after having approved Malraux's previous novel, *Days of Wrath.*

It is worth noting in passing that the views Malraux illustrates parallel those Ernest Hemingway attributes to the hero of his Spanish Civil War novel, *For Whom the Bell Tolls,* but differ from George Orwell's. The British journalist came upon the scene some weeks after Malraux had relinquished his command to the communist cadres. Perhaps for having been a victim of the communist purges in Spain, Orwell acquired a more pessimistic view of the Stalinization of the Spanish Civil War. His *Homage to Catalonia* carries an anticommunist invective quite opposed to what may be considered Malraux's theme. But unlike Orwell, the French novelist does not limit his considerations to politics.

Malraux's fictional account of the Spanish Civil War continues the optimism of party solidarity first depicted two years earlier in *Days of Wrath.* In that politically inspired novel, he was principally interested in exploring the foundations of a single militant's commitment to communism and in illustrating the metaphysical comforts it offered. For *Man's Hope,* he has chosen a much broader canvas and has peopled his vast tableau with Spaniards, Frenchmen, Germans, Russians, and Italians attracted to the Spanish Republican cause by any manner of idealism. Malraux's collection of characters evolves through repeated questioning and redefinition of their commitment to the Republican struggle, which the author prefers to call a revolution. During the course of the first months of the war, the idealism of some is condemned; others discover a new personal relation to history that, within the context of the novel, gives their actions a permanent value. Through their identification with the Marxist view of history, the communist militant Manuel and the most autobiographical of the characters, the French squadron commander Magnin, achieve a sense of integration with the universe that more closely resembles a religious experience than a political one. But, because their importance is developed only in the second half of the novel, they are most profitably studied in the light of Malraux's criticism of

The Human Condition Revisited

his "idealists," those from whom he withholds the satisfactions of metaphysical comfort. The tragic adventures of the Catalonian anarchist Puig, the quixotic French volunteer Mercery, and the Spanish captain Hernandez exemplify, in the first sections of *Man's Hope*, the futility of the personal heroism of the sort Malraux earlier praised in *Man's Fate*. In a European setting where history ceases to be hostile, the actions of the Kyos and the Katows, more dedicated to the expression of good will than to victory, receive the author's condemnation.

Puig's appearance is limited to the account of the Republican capture of the military installations in Barcelona during the initial uprisings. This zealous Anarchist is the first in the novel to incarnate the naive hope that the cause of the workers and peasants can be won by inspired acts of individual heroism. Ignorant of the mechanisms of progress and historical change, he sees the socialist revolution simply as a series of exemplary revolts; political activity need not be made part of a vast, coordinated movement. Malraux identifies this heroic impulse as the "Lyric Illusion," the theme and title of the first portion of the novel. Puig's brief role in the revolution points out the error of this romantic view of politics.

During the early moments of the workers' assault on the barracks, Puig watches his comrades fall before the fire of the small but disciplined unit holding the military installation. He feels a curious admiration for the fallen workers, an admiration that betrays a martyr's death wish. It impels him to charge a gun emplacement in a near suicidal rush with his car. While the first effort is successful, the same manoeuvre a few moments later in a truck commandeered for the purpose ends his life.

Puig's heroism is inspired by something other than a genuine concern for the welfare of the impoverished workers and peasants, but the explanation of it must await clarification by other, more developed characters who share his seemingly suicidal motives. Still, history tells us what Malraux only suggests: at the cost of the lives of many idealists such as Puig, the Anarchists defeated the insurgent army forces under the command of General Goded and paradoxically passed from being criminals to being defenders of the established Republican government.[6] The battle illustrates, nonetheless, that the cost of such victories is out of the reach of the undisciplined workers.

While the solidarity that seemed to inspire Puig and his fellow Anarchists may have been enough to carry the day at Barcelona, it would inevitably fail to bring victory in the protracted war that the military uprising was to become. The commander of the Civil Guard who had brought his men over to the side of the Anarchists was able to observe to Puig moments before his final suicidal dash, "Your men know how to fight but they don't know how to wage a war" (p. 458). While Malraux's play of words is lost in translation,[7] the force of the trained police officer's criticism is not lost on Puig: catching sight of the bloodstained stretchers being brought to the barricades for more wounded, he is forced to acquiesce.

During the early stages of the novel Malraux accumulates episodes such as the assault on the Barcelona barracks to expose the tragic naiveté of the Anarchists' optimism. One Marxist critic has described the novel as a dramatization of the ideological dispute between the Anarchists and the Stalinists, who, in the name of victory, sought to impose a communist discipline on the entire Republican force.[8] Although he presents an accurate summarization of the diffuse work, Lucien Goldmann overlooks the diversity of spirit that exists among the noncommunist Republicans drawn by Malraux. The novelist has made an effort to present a nuanced indictment of misplaced zeal. His criticism is not always conveyed in the serious tones of the Puig episode: the misadventures of the French idealist Mercery injects some humor into Malraux's otherwise dour fiction.

Had Malraux chosen to give his caricature of the zealous French volunteer greater relief, Mercery might have become a symbolic character. Appearing briefly, however, in but four disconnected episodes, he appears to be but one of several characters who serve Malraux's thesis. Mercery's appearances in the novel occur, nonetheless, at significant moments. He is introduced in the headquarters of the International Air Squadron shortly before the air attack on Franco's columns near Medellin was to earn for the Squadron the distinction of the first victory over the Fascists. Why Mercery has chosen aviation is not explained, but Malraux shows with a comic twist how his character has been attracted to the cause of the Spanish Loyalists. His wife had been in Madrid attending a philatelists' convention at the time of the military *putsch.* She had written back to her husband in the industrialized Paris suburb of Noisy-le-Sec that no man should be able to tolerate such injustices. Acting on a mixture of his wife's suggestion and his own libertarian convictions, Mercery put his military experience "at the disposition of Spain": he had been a noncommissioned officer in the First World War and since then had been a fire captain. Magnin's whimsical reaction indicates that Malraux intended his readers to feel something of the mockery for this fire captain that the French reserve for firemen in general. Still, Magnin supposes that, beneath Mercery's idealistic extravagance, there may be a reserve of good will and that his experience may very well qualify him as a captain in what is still a ragtag army. The Squadron commander's attitude toward his compatriot reveals more about his own views of the war than about Mercery's personality. Mercery's first appearance highlights the attitude that lay behind the Air Squadron's first successful mission: it points out Magnin's personal "lyrical illusion." For all its success, the Medellin mission does not prevent Franco's advancing army from joining Mola's forces in the north. By the conclusion of the first section of the novel, the Fascists have occupied the entire western half of Spain. The Spanish Republicans and their foreign volunteers are forced to admit that they must bring something more than good will into battle if they, the forces of justice, are to prevail over the forces of evil in the apocalyptic struggle.

This view will be reinforced in the longer account of the fall of Toledo to Franco's army, recounted in the following section entitled "Prelude to Apocalypse." It treats, for the most part, the drama of Captain Hernandez, a career officer who, by remaining loyal to the Republican government, became involved first in the siege of the Alcazar of Toledo and then in the defense of the city against the Spanish regulars. That a Mercery should serve with Hernandez as captain is already an indication that the Toledo militia will fail in both its objectives.

The reader first learns of Mercery's new role when Hernandez avers that only the worst of his officers are able to get along with the militia of the Iberian Anarchist Federation. This socialist

107

labor organization was responsible for the Pyrrhic victory over the insurgent army forces at the Barcelona barracks; several of the characters from that episode reappear in Toledo where they are commanded by Mercery. According to Hernandez, the Anarchists do not take the French officer's leadership seriously, but at least they appear to like him. He parades his ridiculous zeal in exhortations to his troops quoted from his wife's letters, in his officious conduct before the communist major inspecting the Toledo siege, and in his explanations of the obvious. During the truce arranged in a vain effort to effect the release of hostages held by the defenders of the Alcazar, Mercery contributes his homilies to the discussion between the Communists and the Loyalist militiamen. Taking the side of a Barcelona veteran now under his command, he defends the nobility of the Anarchist's ideals and those of Hernandez against the Communist insistence that these "beautiful standards" be sacrificed in order to assure a military victory over the Nationalists:

> "Please allow me, comrades," said Mercery, his hand on the table and his heart in his hand. "One of two things must happen. If we are victorious, those opposing us will come before History with the Burden of Hostages, and we with the freedom of Madame Moscardo [the wife of the commander of the Alcazar]. Whatever happens, Hernandez, you give a great and noble example. In the name of the Peace and Justice Movement, to which I have the honor of belonging, I take off my cap to you" (p. 605).

The communist major Garcia wonders whether such theatrics necessarily accompany idealism. He recognizes that the war is a grand ego-trip for Mercery but grants that he does give evidence of a sincere opposition to fascism. Before he has gotten into combat, it is already evident that Mercery's contributions are to be of limited value, if they are not altogether wasteful.

The undisciplined militia is unable to hold Toledo against the assault of the "Moors" of Franco's Moroccan division, and Mercery and his unit retreat to Madrid with the main body of Loyalist defenders. There Franco's forces lay a siege, but not until after

The Human Condition Revisited

the defenses have been set by the better organized communist cadres. Franco's assault is able nonetheless to breach the defenses temporarily. During the heat of the fighting, the German commanding one sector of the defenses receives the muddled report about a soap factory being retaken and two tons of soap being recovered: Mercery has misread his map and "recaptured" a factory that had never been lost. Less indulgent than the Spaniard Garcia, Colonel Heinrich has Mercery relieved of his command. Shortly after this incident, but hardly because of it, the Republican defenders push Franco's troops back across the Manzanares River. From this position, the Nationalists launch an indiscriminate artillery and air bombardment of Madrid, which Malraux captures in detail to discredit the Fascists.

While the Republican failures cannot be attributed to Mercery, they can be attributed to the mentality that permits a Mercery to hold his command. Once a policy of victory is determined, the quixotic idealists must be cast aside or placed in positions where they are able to make a serious contribution. Mercery's career in Spain serves as a barometer of Republican military policy. His demotion marks the moment when the Republican forces cease to be an army of "operetta" soldiers. He does not drop out of the story, but makes one final appearance after having been assigned to the task he can perform well—fighting the fires started by the Nationalists' shelling. As the siege intensifies, he will lose his life in a final, glorious gesture.

When one of his firemen is gunned down by an unseen machine gunner, Mercery takes up the hose and climbs the ladder. Surrounded by flames, he confidently sets about extinguishing the fire. Putting out one blaze, he momentarily enjoys the vision of himself as the protector of innocent children—to his last moments he remains an incorrigible romantic. Then, through a gap in the flames, he catches a glimpse of a fighter plane speeding towards him. Answering an impulsion to act, he sprays the cockpit of the plane as the pilot makes his pass, machine guns ablaze. He is struck by a bullet; his vain act ends his life. He becomes another of the idealistic victims of the first revolution to be waged with twentieth-century political concepts and—the author did not overlook this—twentieth-century technology. Mercery suc-

Malraux's Heroes and History

cumbs because he has allowed his romantic, individualistic idealism to delude him about the contribution he is able to make to a modern political movement. His idealism proves to be as suicidal as Puig's lyrical illusion. The comedy of the well-intentioned character turns into a tragedy as his crusade runs athwart of modern warfare.

The theme of misplaced idealism is developed at greater length in the drama of Captain Hernandez. Through this tragic character, Malraux appears to announce a theme which will be even further developed by French existentialist dramatists and novelists. He anticipates the suicides of such would-be idealists as Camus's Kirilov, Sartre's Hugo Barine, and Antigone and Joan of Arc, the two characters from Anouilh's theatre that existentialism appears to have spawned. More important, however, Hernandez' sacrifice recalls the deaths of Kyo and Katow in *Man's Fate.* The Spanish officer dies serving his fellow man, but Malraux presents the circumstances of his death so that he appears far less worthy of the reader's admiration than did his predecessors in the 1927 Shanghai uprising. Behind the criticism of Hernandez lies a different appreciation for the Marxist dialectic. As the next chapter will show, Malraux's exemplars no longer denigrate it as a "fatalism," the charge leveled against it by Kyo and his father in *Man's Fate.* Through Hernandez, whose life is extinguished early in *Man's Hope,* Malraux repudiates the view that an individual's basic humanitarianism can compensate for his failures, the view presented with such sympathy in his 1933 prize-winning novel. By the time he composed his 1937 novel, Malraux appears much more inclined to believe that, where victory *is* possible, any compromise with defeat, such as that which Hernandez repeats after Kyo, is reprehensible.

The reader first met Captain Hernandez as he was showing Major Garcia about the Toledo installations. It was then that he described Mercery as one of the worst of his officers. And in further responses to Garcia's impatient inquiries about the Alcazar siege, Hernandez reveals his resignation to an eventual Republican defeat. The leadership of the militia units is fragmented, each labor union retaining the command of its own troops and refusing to respect any other authority. For Hernandez, a career

The Human Condition Revisited

army officer trained at the military academy of the now-besieged Alcazar, the situation should be intolerable. He accepts it, however, renouncing thereby any hope for a military victory in preference for a personal concept of justice and honor. It is these principles that explain his loyalty to the Republican cause, but at the same time, they prevent him from seeing the Nationalist defenders of the Alcazar as the enemy. He accepts the request from the Alcazar commander to transmit a letter to a Madrid clinic where the fascist general's wife lies ill[9]; he has already defended against charges of corruption a friend who had determined to disrupt the Republican government's land distribution plan. For Garcia, the Moscow-trained revolutionary committed to a military and political victory, Hernandez' acts of generosity are characteristic of the 1917 adolescence of the socialist revolution. The Spanish captain acts on values that, according to Garcia, are not only outmoded, but even dangerous to the Republican cause.

This Spanish intellectual, identified first as one of Spain's foremost ethnologists and characterized later as taking advantage of every opportunity to speak, has more function than role in the novel. Like old Gisors in *Man's Fate,* he is something of a spokesman for the author. But his communism is far too doctrinaire to be identified with Malraux's own politics. Garcia can best be considered a stand-in, giving the author's criticism of the humanistic idealists attracted to the war and explaining the evolution of the war. He enjoys the additional privilege of pronouncing on such heady questions as "what is the best thing a man can do with his life" (p. 764).[10] And it is also Garcia who introduces into the novel the religious elements that, as in *Days of Wrath,* become important in the dramas of Manuel and Magnin. By identifying the war as an apocalypse, he suggests that the struggle between the loyal Republican forces and the ignoble Fascists is the Armageddon announced by Saint John the Divine. Like the second-century Christian visionary who borrowed so much from Manicheanism, Garcia sees the Spanish Civil War as a battle between the forces of Good and Evil, an opposition that allows no middle ground. Only by respecting this opposition can the Republic expect victory in the "adulthood" of revolution. It is in

111

terms of these quasi-religious criteria that he judges Hernandez's participation in the war.

Yet another religious note innocuously sets the scene for Garcia's condemnation of Hernandez. In the barroom banter which parodies libertarian anticlericalism, one Anarchist attacks his interlocutor as a priest of communism and chides him for his all too zealous popery. The religious motif is dropped, but Garcia picks up the train of criticism addressed against the Anarchists in order to condemn Hernandez for his misplaced idealism. In agreeing to transmit the letter written by the Alcazar commander, Garcia explains to his Communist listeners, Hernandez was trying to earn the respect of the besieged enemy. The reader must interpret that, implicit in Hernandez's act, is a fundamental respect for the adversary, a respect that prevents him from considering the enemy soldiers as opponents to overcome in an apocalyptic struggle. His respect of the defenders, his recognition of the "noble" motives of the Anarchists explains his apparent indecisiveness in battle. It prevents him from turning his military advantage over the besieged Nationalists into a victory. For Garcia, Hernandez represents all that is wrong with the Loyalist army. The Spanish captain has been attracted to the Revolution only because it offers him the opportunity to give expression to his personal moral code. Then, returning to the religious motif, Garcia observes:

> The captain is a very noble man who sees the Revolution as a way to realize his ethical desires. For him, the drama which we are living is a personal Apocalypse. What is most dangerous in these semi-Christians is their appetite for sacrifice: they are ready to commit the worst mistakes so long as they pay with their lives (p. 609).

For the communist intellectual, the Revolution must be a collective effort: any satisfaction to be derived from the war could come only from victory. No single person could claim victory as a personal achievement. Hernandez and those like him, whom Garcia criticizes as "semi-Christians," are sophisticated enough to understand that the individualist's dream of conquest is impossible. They seek instead the exaltation of dying to bear witness to justice and brotherhood. While they share these laudable ideals with the Communists, they possess none of the comrades' political realism. The reader is left to see how much they resemble the early Christian martyrs who died before they saw Christianity established, feeling nonetheless a personal satisfaction from their efforts. But, in the end, the martyrs' examples were less effective in the evangelization of Europe than Church militancy.

Garcia's criticism of Hernandez is developed further in a private conversation between the two Spanish officers. Hernandez begins it by defending himself. He expresses his hope that the revolution will be effected by the example of the most human of men, even if their example must come from beyond the grave. Garcia, the political realist, counters that being right does not come from moral rectitude, but from victory, which alone permits the revolutionaries to impose a direction on history. The difference between the realistic notion of the Communists and the idealism of Hernandez lies in the concept of the self. The Communists, whose strongest appeal is to the disenfranchised and destitute, judge their worth in terms of accomplishment; the idealists seek the personal gratification of giving expression to their concept of justice, but without imposing it on others. Garcia succinctly explains this distinction in terms that anticipate Jean-Paul Sartre's *Being and Nothingness:*

> The Communists want *to do* [Malraux's italics] something.
> You and the Anarchists, for different reasons, you want *to be*
> something. That's the drama of any revolution like this one.
> The myths that we live by are contradictory: pacifism
> against necessity of defense, organization against
> Christianity, efficiency against justice, and so on. We must
> organize them, transform our Apocalypse into an army or
> be done in. That's all (p. 613).

Garcia's distinction between *being* and *doing* carries a fresh answer to the question of whether or not the individual is what

113

he does, a question Malraux first raised in his Oriental novels. The adventurer Perken of *The Royal Way* defined his own worth only in terms of his accomplishments, and he met death in a vain effort to *do* something with his life. Kyo rejected *doing* as a definition of human values, believing that the individual was more "than his biography." In the hostile universe where the Malrauvian hero could give only inadequate expression to his ideals, the individual had to be more than the sum of his acts. Definition of the self on the basis of inherent qualities that lead to failure is appropriate, though, only where the adversity of history prevents any significant accomplishment—such was the world of the revolutionaries of *Man's Fate*. With his return to European fictional subjects, Malraux appears to have discovered how a collectivist view of history, one based on cooperation in a common cause, can have an influence on the course of events. He came to see the possibility of progress in organized, concerted activity. History ceased to appear hostile to him, and again he is able to judge human worth in terms of *doing*, in terms of accomplishment and progress.

In the less tragic Occident, then, good intentions that lead to no results are to be damned. They are inappropriate to the maturity of the revolution. Hernandez reflects the nineteenth-century mentality that inspired the Russian Revolution and the early Chinese revolts, Garcia suggests. Paradoxically, it appears from the logic of the novel, such attitudes only place the goals of a modern revolution farther away. Without really intending to reform his fellow officer, Garcia concludes the conversation on a critical note: "Moral perfection and nobility of spirit are individual problems far removed from any direct connection with the Revolution. The only bridge between the two is, for you, alas, the idea behind your sacrifice" (p. 614). These remarks set the scene for the death of the Spanish idealist, the scene that confirms Malraux's evolution toward a Marxist view of history.

As the loyalist forces withdraw before the advance of Franco's Moroccan Division, now reinforced by Italian troops and equipment, Hernandez stays behind in Toledo to cover the retreat. He is one of the few defenders of the city who has had experience with the automatic weapons, but his decision to protect the rear

The Human Condition Revisited

of the retreating Republican army seems to be prompted as much by his urge to self-sacrifice as by military necessity. In spite of the arguments of Garcia, Hernandez remains convinced that only by sacrifice will progress be won. Moments before his last battle, he confides to a soldier that his recent experiences have provided one valuable lesson: "I have learned one thing, something very simple: we expect everything from freedom and right away, but the deaths of many men are necessary to advance mankind one centimeter" (p. 626).

To his last moments, he views social change as being out of reach. He continues to believe, like Kyo just before his death in the makeshift Shanghai prison, that the only satisfactions to be realized are those of the martyr to an impossible though just cause. But, because Malraux's view of man in history has evolved, Hernandez fails to earn the reader's admiration. When a successful alternative is at hand, the martyr's death appears as a tragic waste.

Hernandez's suicidal hope for a martyr's death does nonetheless inspire his heroic stand in Toledo, where he does succeed in delaying the advance of the fascist troops. Coming up from the south, Franco's army arrives at the city before the Loyalist militia can take the old citadel. The Spanish regulars send the disorganized siege army into hasty retreat. Hernandez almost single-handedly protects the Loyalist rear. He momentarily checks the Nationalist pursuit and, with a sort of ecstasy, orders the last of his codefenders to withdraw. In the solitude of his gunnery position atop the Toledo bullring, Hernandez finds the satisfaction that gives meaning to his life. It is the same satisfaction that Kyo felt moments before he died. But rather than being cut down by enemy fire as he expects, Hernandez is captured, and later executed by a firing squad. He must await execution in the Toledo prison, surviving his own will to live. The pages consecrated to his last moments begin as a meditation on death, only to conclude as an understanding of the place of the individual in history.

Having spent his moral energy and having realized his destiny, Hernandez has no further reason to live. When an opportunity to escape arises, he rejects it and dispassionately accepts death.

115

Malraux's Heroes and History

The spectacle of the execution of other captured Republican soldiers provokes no emotion in Hernandez until he begins to wonder if his acts of nobility are not responsible for the capture of the doomed soldiers. Now he is unable to enjoy that fraternal pleasure that Kyo felt at the conclusion of *Man's Fate*. At this point, the author intervenes to inform the reader that Hernandez is finally learning what history is. Malraux completes the paragraph with the vision, drawn from the imagination of Hernandez, of an infinite succession of wives in mourning. Without the light shed by *Days of Wrath* or later repetitions in *Man's Hope*, the meaning of this truncated image would remain obscure. These references permit the patient reader to see that the image communicates Hernandez's discovery of eternity as a succession of living people, not of dead heroes—the discovery that Kassner made in the final chapter of the previous novel and that Manuel and Magnin are about to make. The Spanish captain only obliquely acknowledges his error: he recognizes just before his death that nobility requires victory. And the clenched fists raised in the Loyalist salute by the three soldiers executed immediately before him express a defiance which Hernandez and, presumably, the reader find far more heroic than passive submission to the enemy.

In his interpretation of the libertarians' sacrifice, Garcia underscores their resignation to failure. It is a reminder of the tragic atmosphere of Malraux's first three Oriental novels, where an intractable history condemned human enterprise to futility. The characters were not permitted to glimpse success. Kyo and Katow alone in these novels died without their lives being destroyed by history's adversity. But they gained their modest satisfaction only by resigning themselves to defeat. In a concept of the self not defined by accomplishment, Malraux found his first redemption from tragedy. With only this humanistic principle by which to judge the actions of Puig, Mercery, and Hernandez, the reader might honor these victims of the Spanish Civil War. But in *Man's Hope*, Malraux develops it in a collectivist concept of history. The political activist can be seen to find a real value for his actions only after he renounces the self and accepts a commitment to the

116

whole of mankind. But that will be apparent only in the following chapter on the exemplars of the true revolutionary spirit. Through them, Malraux illustrates how a collectivist commitment gives a person's action value but, more important, how man can recover his place in the universe through his political activism. Only the false revolutionary seeking to preserve his own personality fails to find these comforts. Such is the meaning of Garcia's—and Malraux's—last remarks about Hernandez.

Some weeks after the death of Hernandez, during the defense of Madrid, Garcia offers his final criticism of the throwback from *The Conquerors* and *Man's Fate*. It comes in a conversation with the Italian art historian, Scali. Garcia explains that, for the thinking man, the Revolution and life in general are tragic because they lead to the irrevocable death of the individual. But, he continues, "if it is to overcome his tragedy that he gets involved in the Revolution, he is thinking backwards—that's all." Malraux's spokesman notes that Hernandez felt the same moral reservations as the reluctant Scali and died because of them. And, he adds, "There are not fifty ways of waging a war: there is only one; that is to win. Neither the revolution nor war consists in self-satisfactions" (p. 766). The true revolutionary, according to Malraux's 1937 spokesman, works for the success of the revolution, not for a solution to an individually conceived tragedy.[11]

Judged by the criteria proposed by Garcia in *Man's Hope*, Kyo and Katow would fail to attain the stature of true revolutionaries. They, too, belong to the adolescence of the Revolution, less for their own shortcomings than for their creator's subsequent rejection of the tragedy of history. They were deprived of success but were presented as exemplars at a time in Malraux's evolution when personal example alone signaled a hope for the betterment of the workers. No higher revolutionary standards stood as a measure of success or failure—at least in the Oriental setting of the novel. Projected against a more typically Western concept of progress, that which underlay Kassner's optimism in *Days of Wrath* and is further developed in *Man's Hope*, the tragic humanism of Kyo and his Russian comrade appears scarcely more worthy of the reader's admiration than that of Puig, Mercery, or Hernandez. Kyo and Katow remain tragic heroes of "virile fraternity," while the historical figure who organized the Shanghai uprisings but then escaped to become the Premier of the Chinese People's Republic better illustrates the mature revolutionary attitude. Kyo shared Hernandez's pessimism, while Chou En-lai shared Garcia's hope. It is one of the ironies of history that Malraux should have chosen a successful revolution to illustrate tragedy and an abortive defense of a socialist republic to illustrate hope. The irony illustrates how little of history and how much of the author's own judgments upon history influenced his political novels.

While the change in Malraux's view of history was first announced in *Days of Wrath,* the scope of this brief novel prevented him from doing much more than identifying history as a metaphysical or religious force capable of redeeming the individual's sense of isolation in the universe. The breadth of the vast revolutionary mosaic in *Man's Hope* permits him to contrast personal and collectivist ideals and to show what the individual has to give up to achieve a redemption from the absurd. The evolution from the adolescence of idealism to the maturity of political commitment is illustrated by characters who outgrow the suicidal "lyrical illusion." Manuel and Magnin discover, in renouncing their idealism, the satisfaction of communion with the only absolute in Malraux's godless universe. Compared to these mature revolutionaries, the idealistic victims of the Spanish Civil War lose all their tragic virtues as the novel acquires an eschatological dimension.

7   THE HISTORICAL
         LEAP OF FAITH

$\mathcal{S}$TANDING in stark contrast to the humanistic Hernandez is Manuel, the dedicated Communist who
appears to accept unquestioningly the party's leadership in the
Spanish Civil War. His attitude is not significantly different from
Garcia's, except that Malraux has made the elder and more
analytical Garcia the communist apologist and the younger man
the activist leader; where Garcia debates and explains, Manuel
acts out his commitment and, during the course of the novel,
discovers his own military vocation. If one character were to be
singled out as the hero of this amorphic work, it would have to
be Manuel. He is the first character to emerge from the confusion
of the early reports of the generals' *putsch,* and his lyrical meditation on his own contribution to the destiny of mankind concludes
the novel. In the eight months that the novel covers, the former
movie sound engineer rises to the rank of lieutenant-colonel. He
commands a brigade at Guadalajara in the battle that, according
to the Republicans' hopes, marked the turning point in their war
against fascism.

When the war breaks out, Manuel shows none of the dedication
to a Republican victory that he acquires during the course of the
novel. Under the tutelage of the colonel who commanded the
Anarchists at Barcelona, he evolves from the jovial optimism of
the intellectual whose only contact with war has come through
French and Spanish training manuals and the works of von
Clausewitz[1] to the seriousness of a hardened military leader. His
evolution is rapid, perhaps too rapid, and by the end of the novel,
he comes to exemplify Garcia's ideal of selfless commitment to
victory. Because of his identification with this thesis, he arouses
little of the reader's interest, and Malraux's efforts to humanize

him by emphasizing his nervous mannerisms fall short of making him a dramatic character. Even the battle scenes in which he appears carry little drama: they are learning experiences or tests where the lesson is that courage lies in sound military organization. Manuel's first lesson constitutes the first episode of the novel.

As the novel opens, Manuel is at the North Railroad Station with a communist comrade monitoring the progress of the military uprising in towns along the rail lines. Hearing news of the generals' first successes, Ramos determines that it is time to act. Together they set out in Manuel's car to deliver dynamite to revolutionaries ready to destroy the bridges along the way of the advancing army. At first, Manuel is concerned about what may happen to his car, but he is soon caught up in the fever of revolutionary camaraderie. The car no longer interests him—a good thing, for it is destroyed during the run. It is at this point that his commitment to the revolution is born. Although he has been a member of the Communist party in Spain for some while, his bourgeois background has evidently prevented him from identifying with the workers' cause. Henceforth, the military success of their cause will be his only interest, as his concern for the workers themselves passes into the background.

The strength of his commitment to victory receives its first test just two weeks later. Early in August 1936, he is serving under Ramos on an armored train sent out to attack Nationalist gun emplacements in the mountains. In his first action, he appears more a buddy to the men he commands than their leader. At the cost of the lives of several of his untrained militiamen, Manuel's unit does succeed, however, in taking its objective, and a short while later, Ramos's forces capture the town formerly held by the Nationalists. But their new position is hardly secure: a carload of Civil Guards undoubtedly loyal to the Army easily infiltrates the lines. The guards are captured, summarily tried, and executed. To show his scorn, a peasant youth dips his finger in their blood and spells out on the wall behind them, "death to fascism." Manuel witnesses this scene with no pity for the slain guards or commiseration for the peasants. He thinks only, "It is necessary to make the New Spain in opposition to both [the Nationalists and the peasants]. And one will not be any easier opponent than the other" (p. 505).

Some moments later, Manuel tries to tell Ramos how the war has already changed him. With typical Malrauvian obliqueness, he explains that he has lost the "virginity of command," the moral purity that he brought into the war which, unlike Hernandez, he is willing to sacrifice in order to enjoy the fruits of victory—but then, he does not share Hernandez's pessimism. From this point to the end of the novel, Manuel's military apprenticeship is to be continued under the indulgent tutelage of Ximenez. The colonel who previously commanded the Anarchists' victory at Barcelona immediately recognizes Manuel's capacity for command in his natural inclination to lead. During the defense of Toledo, Ximenez molds this quality, and even in defeat, Manuel emerges as an officer capable of organizing an army. He comes to see his men as instruments to victory and understands that the military leader must forego the admiration of those serving under him. This lesson is learned only after he foolishly risks his life to win the loyalty of a Falangist linecrosser named Alba.

Along the front near Toledo, several Fascists defected to the Loyalist side. All were assigned to Manuel's company. He calls out the leader of the group in an effort to win his allegiance. Instead of discussing matters in a typically military fashion, the pair sets off across the fields in the direction of the enemy lines. On one calculated pretext, then another, Manuel gives all his weapons to Alba. Malraux does not explain how his hero manages to survive the scene, nor whether he wins Alba's loyalty. The reader sees only that Manuel attempts to create a fraternal rapport between himself and his men. But, if he is to lead an army, he must understand that fraternity is a detriment to the success that can only come through military organization and efficiency. This is perhaps the most difficult lesson for Manuel. Once he has learned it, he completes the apprenticeship he is just beginning during these defensive operations near Toledo.

Ximenez has the responsibility of wiping up several pockets of fascist resistance in the farmland around the old Spanish capital. He uses the situation to form his undisciplined soldiers into an organized unit. At the end of the first engagement, he lectures

121

them on the meaning of courage. It is not the individualistic concept of personal bravery that brings victory, he explains, but the "courage of organization." In anticipation of Manuel's military and spiritual evolution and of Hernandez's tragedy, he relates this collective notion of courage to the soldier's role in history: "Do not forget that the one who contemplates us, I mean History which judges us now and which will judge us in the future, needs the courage that wins and not the courage that brings consolation" (pp. 571–72). The lesson of the lecture is not lost on Manuel. Moments later, in a private conversation with his admiring pupil, Ximenez returns to the same subject.

Adopting his characteristic paternal tone, Ximenez explains that history *does* crown success, but it does not offer the individual the immortality sought by a Napoleon or, in Malraux's own fiction, by the protagonist of *The Royal Way*. It offers only the lesser satisfaction of participating in the forces that give history its direction. He adds, though, that leaders, military or otherwise, have a special nobility, a special relation with history. Because they make history happen, they stand to reap the greatest satisfactions. The young communist officer understands from this conversation that he must sacrifice to victory any desire he might have to win the adulation of his men. He has already learned what Hernandez did not understand until his death: that the revolutionaries "need results more than examples" (p. 576).

Manuel's apprenticeship at Toledo appears as the counterpoint of Hernandez's drama. Since Hernandez disappears from the novel after the Toledo debacle, it is the example of Manuel that the reader retains. At the end of the battle of Toledo, the disciplined communist revolutionary can be seen to be well along the spiritual itinerary that leads him to an identification with the entire history of mankind. By the end of the novel, he recovers a metaphysical comfort that more than compensates for the sacrifice of his personal values. But before finding this gratification, he must prove his ability in turning the retreat from Toledo into a defense of the road leading to Madrid.

Manuel's first real success at command comes at the railroad station at Aranjuez, between Toledo and Madrid. There, he turns the frightened band of irregulars withdrawing from Toledo into

The Historical Leap of Faith

an effective defensive unit. The episode is based on a crowd scene, heretofore infrequent in Malraux's fiction. In his first novels, Malraux concentrated on the individual in history, and his scenes generally represented private dramas. With *Days of Wrath*, however, he investigated in somewhat abstract terms a collective relation to history and the individual's relation to the collectivity. Now, in *Man's Hope*, he illustrates it. Great battle scenes abound in this Spanish Civil War novel, and through them, Malraux develops his concept of a collectivist view of history as a redemption from the absurd.

Manuel's next military engagement, part of a vast military operation set on the Plain of Guadarrama northwest of Madrid, carries his military apprenticeship a step closer to that redemption. Recently promoted to lieutenant-colonel, he is now responsible for defending Madrid from an attack across the Guadarrama Mountains. In the interval since the battle of Toledo, the Republican forces have received equipment and training, but still not the training that could weld them into an efficient army. During a scene in which certain elements recall the patriotic bravura of Victor Hugo, one of Manuel's officers reports that he has thwarted the defection of several Republican volunteers: the soldiers, who had intended to surrender to the advancing Nationalist armored units, have been arrested by the Republicans. They cannot be put on trial for their attempted desertion, however, until the furor of the battle subsides. Later in the day, Manuel convenes the council of party commissars responsible for army discipline and indoctrination. He accepts their decree to execute the defectors. The young lieutenant-colonel encounters the condemned soldiers as he leaves the council meeting. He resists their solicitations for leniency, disdaining any response to their cowardly supplications. Recollections of braver soldiers come to his mind, so no pity softens his resolve to carry out the decree. Gazing into the face of one of the prisoners, he realizes that "never before had he felt as much as then how necessary it was to choose between victory and pity" (p. 759). The scene concludes with no further commentary by the author: the silence registers, however, Manuel's awareness of the solitude imposed by leadership.

123

Malraux's Heroes and History

The next day Manuel recounts his experience to Ximinez. In retrospect, that day which witnesses his feverish commitment to battle in the morning and his resistance to pity in the evening appears to Manuel as the most important of his life, but less for the military victory that it brought than for the personal victory over a self-interested humanism. He has resisted the temptation to trade clemency for popularity; he has thereby transcended the facile idealism that earlier prevented Hernandez from finding a salvation in history.

The last step in Manuel's military apprenticeship is this suppression of his personal emotions and his individuality—some readers may choose to call it a collectivization; others even more critically, a dehumanization. Even for Manuel, it is a climb he had made with some regret. He explains to Ximenez, "There is not one of those rungs that I climbed towards greater efficiency, towards being a better officer, that did not separate me more from the men. Everyday I am a little less human" (p. 774). Ximenez, the Catholic officer who remained loyal to the Republic out of a sense of brotherhood, found in Christianity a way to reconcile the demands of leadership with the search for a personal identity, and at the same time, he found the metaphysical comforts of religion. Neither Malraux nor his hero share Ximenez's religious convictions, but this Catholic Republican clarifies what might be considered Malraux's secular faith. Like some angel of revelation he leads his pupil to a hilltop from which the continuing battle can be observed from the perspective of the divinities: Manuel shares with the communist Kassner and, as will be seen later, with Magnin the privilege of such apocalyptic visions of man in history. From this eminence, he observes individual lives being consumed by the fires of war. Like a twentieth-century Saint John the Divine, the communist leader discovers the vanity of the individual's attachment to his own life.

Ximenez continues his instruction as the flames turn to black smoke and the city below disappears from view. By now, however, Manuel has already progressed beyond the point where the older officer's help can be useful. Ximenez seeks to assure him that he will be able to sentence men to death without compunction. But that reassurance comes only after Manuel has discov-

The Historical Leap of Faith

ered with some surprise that he feels no sympathy for the condemned deserters. The young revolutionary leader has reached this important stage in his career with such ease that any appreciation of its importance can only come through talking about it. Perhaps this is a flaw in the way Malraux drew his character. Nothing in Manuel's evolution to leadership conveys much drama. Only a grandiose setting punctuates the crucial moments of his career, and his rewards seem to be earned with very little effort.

The scene ends when Manuel is summoned to the telephone to be congratulated for the measures taken against the defectors. Because of his action, other Anarchist militiamen have volunteered to serve in a special brigade, one which Manuel has just been selected to command. Heinrich, the German general responsible for the defense of Madrid, meets Manuel to drive him to his new post. During the ride back to Madrid, the conversation reinforces the lesson of the apocalyptic vision. Using a vocabulary more appropriate to the Catholic Ximenez, Heinrich notes brifely that leadership in the Revolution involves the loss of one's soul. Curious about the remark, Manuel asks what losing one's soul could mean to an atheistic Marxist. Heinrich's response is evasive: the reader must furnish his own interpretation, drawn as much from Garcia's criticism of Hernandez's pseudo-Christianity as from Malraux's previous works.

Nothing in the German officer's answer permits the reader to identify the soul as the source of what Garcia spoke of as an individual's "being." It does suggest, nonetheless, that for those who accept the European concept of the soul, it is the source of one's individuality. Its loss then means the loss of one's particularity. The transition from individualistic to collectivist moral values is marked figuratively by the loss of the soul. More by way of reassurance than warning, the experienced general observes to the new brigade commander that it is but one of the losses that accompanies victory: a military leader does not enjoy the privilege of looking on the victory as a personal accomplishment, nor can he indulge in the luxury of pride or pity. But, since Manuel has already made this discovery, Heinrich's inculcations merely underscore the transformation. For the reader, they have the effect of summarizing a step of Manuel's evolution that, because it took place with so little drama, may very well have passed by with little notice. But it is not the final stage of the evolution. His last battle carries his final lesson. Although the loss of his soul may deprive him of any personal accomplishment, his role in the battle against the better equipped Italian army at Guadalajara provides him a greater pleasure than any individualist could enjoy. It is there that he discovers the spiritual comforts that history withheld from Hernandez.

Before the Battle of Guadalajara begins, Manuel's career begins to concide with that of Enrique Lister, the Kremlin-trained officer who proved himself to be one of the most successful field commanders of the Republican army.[2] Like Lister, Manuel commands the special "mixed" brigade during the winter siege of Madrid in December 1936. It is this brigade that, still mirroring Lister, Manuel leads into battle at Guadalajara in March 1937. Historical accounts of Lister's pursuit of the Italian forces in hasty retreat through Brihuega, twenty miles northeast of Guadalajara, clarify many of the chapter's oblique allusions to the battle: they show Lister's disciplined troops capturing the straggling Italian troops and taking abandoned matériel during the fifteen-kilometer pursuit of the enemy along the road leading away from Madrid.[3] The fictional Manuel relives this experience, which soon ceases to be simply a military venture.

At his command post, he receives reports of his troops' advance. Content with the outcome of the battle, he seeks out Ximenez possibly to divide up the captured Italian equipment. But before finding his old mentor, his attention is caught by the work of the Revolutionary Art Committee, already busy in a ravaged church. He wanders in, seats himself at the organ, and plays a Palestrina *Kyrie*. Unexpectedly, the music brings a feeling of discomfort. He explains it briefly for Ximenez, who has been drawn to his side by the sound of the organ. While playing, Manuel realized that he had no feeling for the religious significance of the *Kyrie*. Instead, the piece recalled the past which had lost its meaning. He understood that the war had purged him of his attachment to the past and that he had begun a new life where the Church and its music held no part.

The Historical Leap of Faith

Malraux uses music to trigger the concluding episode of the novel—this time, the secular music of Beethoven. Manuel returns to his own quarters and plays some recordings that he finds at hand. The music suspends his desire to act and again carries him into the past, but only to his experiences in the war. They inspire the lyrical passage by which Malraux concludes his novel—the passage that registers the meaning of Manuel's rebirth in war. Manuel "feels life around him teeming with premonitions as if, behind those clouds that the cannons did not disturb, a blind destiny was silently awaiting him" (p. 858). He then senses within himself for the first time the rhythms of the eternity of the earth and of the human race. Although he never appears to be tormented by metaphysical problems, Manuel does enjoy the religious exaltation that comes from a sense of identity with the universe:

> Manuel was hearing for the first time the voice of
> something more awesome than the blood of individual men,
> more disturbing than their presence on the Earth—the
> voice of the infinite possibility of their destiny; and he felt
> within him that presence, permanent and profound like the
> beating of his heart, mingled with the footsteps of the
> Italian prisoners and the sounds of the rainwater flowing in
> the streets (p. 858).

In the last paragraphs of *Man's Hope,* Manuel repeats the lyrical experience that concluded *Days of Wrath.* Like his German predecessor, he finds a religious dimension to his political commitment. His military apprenticeship now over and his first significant victory behind him, he discovers that his efforts have not been isolated political acts undertaken in the quest of a limited social goal. Instead, they attach him to what Kassner earlier identified as "the eternity of man."

One must be careful not to exaggerate the meaning of Manuel's discovery. His communism fails to provide the spiritual identity with the universe that, according to Malraux, the European has sought since he lost his faith in Christianity. Manuel's political activism does, however, accommodate his will without

Malraux's Heroes and History

inflicting upon him the sense of alienation that tormented the earlier individualists. While he cannot find in his willful activism an integration with the universe, he can find an integration with the history of mankind. Manuel's experience reflects a compromise with the European's religious aspiration. The hope for an identification with all of creation is replaced by the more modest hope for an identification with human destiny.

For Manuel's efforts to provide this attachment to the eternity of mankind, history must cease being the random collection of political events proposed by eighteenth-and nineteenth-century empirical philosophers and illustrated by Malraux in his early novels. Had history no direction, any action would be effaced by time and appear as futile as those of Garine and Perken. But Manuel discovers that history has conferred a permanent value on his acts. Such a discovery is possible only if history is considered to have a direction.

Starting with Hegel, secular philosophers began to analyze the course that history takes. Philosophers of history have seen since then that each moment of the present must grow directly out of the past and lead directly into the future. The dialectics of Marx, Sartre, or, in a far less absolute manner, Arnold Toynbee, describe such a dialectical cohesion.[4] But, in contrast to Hegel, they cannot accept the notion of a preordained evolution. Like Kyo and old Gisors of *Man's Fate*, they reject the historical fatalism that deprives human action of its value. They too view history as a product of man's will. Its direction is that which is imparted by an ever-growing public concern for social justice. Mankind's common goal makes history into a coherent system. Within it each life can acquire the permanent value of being an instrument shaping the continuing struggle for justice.

While there are several more or less dialectical views of history —some idealistic, others materialistic or economic—it is unlikely that Malraux attributed any view other than a Marxist one to his Communist engaged in the Spanish Civil War. These revolutionaries, who judge their actions in terms of its vast dialectic, discover an attachment to an eternity of mankind—not to the divine eternal, or even to the cosmological eternity defined by astronomers, but to the historical eternity limited to the human

128

era. It is only on this human scale that human acts regain their significance. Still, history affords Malraux's revolutionaries a sense of communion with the eternal that his Oriental correspondent in *The Temptation of the West* recognized as the principal function of a religion. And it cannot be overlooked how this historicism offers the European what Oriental religions do not: it accommodates the Western concept of will and action that Malraux so prizes. More than that, it limits the comforts of eternity to those who understand history and translate their insight into action. Because it develops this theme primarily, *Man's Hope* deserves to be considered a philosophical rather than a political novel.[5]

Through his selfless commitment to the party, Manuel finds a redemption from the absurd. With Malraux's European novels, history provides a sort of religious justification for an individual life, but only if the individual ceases to look to it for personal glorification. Like Christianity, which it temporarily replaces for Malraux, the dialectical view of history allows life to acquire a meaning which death cannot extinguish. Malraux is thus able to draw communism in *Days of Wrath* and *Man's Hope* as a surrogate religion but, curiously, not as a political credo. Although some of his revolutionaries express their concern for the lot of the peasants, his heroes function on the more abstract, metaphysical level where religious thinkers weigh their lives.

Although the communist heroes of *Days of Wrath* and *Man's Hope* arrive at the same understanding of the individual's place in the historical eternity of mankind, their insights are produced by vastly different experiences. Kassner's follows his rebirth, but Manuel's comes through Ximenez. He has undergone a period of discipleship that is climaxed by his final vision. When the religious analogy is extended, the devout Catholic officer can be seen as something of an Old Testament prophet. His Catholicism, which occupies an important place in the last episodes of the novel, is the old faith built on the immortality of the soul. It is exceeded by the new religion that he can reveal but not participate in. He has permitted Manuel to understand how political commitment leads to the only salvation man can expect, the salvation of history. While Manuel has sacrificed his personal identity to a political cause, he has given a Marxist meaning to the Apostles' admonition against the quest of immortality for its own sake.[6]

Malraux prepares the reader for this religious interpretation early in his novel by identifying the Spanish Civil War as an apocalyse. The religious motif arises again in Garcia's criticism of Hernandez and in the Anarchists' chiding of the Communists in Toledo. And numerous other references to various aspects of Catholicism follow.[7] The theme is brought to its conclusion on the battlefield near Brihuega. There Manuel experiences a religious ecstasy that contrasts with the emptiness that Hernandez felt before his execution by the Nationalist firing squad in Toledo. It is left to the young communist militant to illustrate the insight of the condemned captain: "There is nobility only in victory" (p. 652). By accepting the discipline of the party and its commitment to victory, he earns for himself a place in the historical paradise of communist activists. During this concluding meditation, Manuel may well realize what Garcia defined as the best thing a man could do with his life. He has "transformed the broadest possible experience into conscious thought."[8] In spite of the inflation of Garcia's pronouncement, the intellectual aspect of Manuel's experience fades in importance behind its religious lyricism. Through the character of Manuel, Malraux has given his political subject a metaphysical force.

In *Man's Hope,* the main characters accept the military command imposed by the Communist party commissars. So far as the war is concerned, the direction of history appears to be determined by the Comintern. Malraux's endorsement here of communist authority should no more be interpreted, however, as an acceptance of party orthodoxy than it is in *Days of Wrath.* Where he is most critical of doctrinaire communism, he presents several characters who oppose its intellectual totalitarianism; where he is most sympathetic, he develops aspects of Marxism that are, at best, of secondary importance in communist doctrine. Besides its metaphysical historicism, he emphasizes the fraternity of the revolutionary struggle—this time without the redundantly masculine adjective "virile" repeated so frequently in *Man's Fate* and *Days of Wrath.* Even Manuel, who appears to lose his sense of

The Historical Leap of Faith

brotherhood, feels a solidarity with those who are working with him for victory.[9] No personal attachments are involved, but rather a feeling of membership in a group defined by common goals. Manuel's evolution to military leadership and his discovery of his historical role do not deprive him of his sense of solidarity, but Malraux evidently chose to investigate the fraternal aspects of the Revolution through another character. Rather than confer all the virtues on a single character, he illustrates revolutionary fraternity through the French aviation commander who is modeled to a large degree on himself. Magnin's example shows, contrary to Ximenez's observations, that fraternity is not impossible in an efficient army, so long as it remains an abstract attachment to a group and does not become an attachment to individuals.

Malraux's fascination with aviation as a literary theme is undoubtedly as strong as that of his contemporary, Antoine de Saint-Exupéry. The drama of his 1934 air exploration of the Queen of Sheba's ancient capital had been transposed as Kassner's return flight to Prague in *Days of Wrath*. Again in *Man's Hope*, the flying experiences of Magnin are based on his own. But Malraux's accounts of air warfare pale in comparison to the descriptions of Saint-Exupéry or the English-language novels of Nordhoff and Hall. The thrill and danger of flying in combat recede behind the administrative problems of command: assigning crews, disciplining them, and keeping up with logistical problems.

Magnin, who, like Malraux, organized an air group that supported the International Brigade, first appears in the novel when volunteer pilots are being tested. They have come from all over Europe and bring all manner of skills and motives with them. The squadron commander shows remarkable patience with these aspiring heroes, a testimony to his respect for his fellowman. During the course of the war, his desire for a military victory will greatly attenuate his respect for individual human dignity. At one moment, he accedes to the communist political commissar's insistence that three German volunteers be summarily discharged. Later, as the tempo of the war accelerates, he dismisses a French mercenary for an act of cowardice. By this time, victory has become more important than respect for his men. He will not be guilty of the misguided humanitarianism which destroyed Hernandez's ability to command his troops. His evolution parallels Manuel's, but, unlike the young Spaniard, he is not a Communist. He accepts the communist supervision of the war, but without entirely accepting communism. Like Robert Jordan, the hero of Hemingway's *For Whom the Bell Tolls,* Magnin appears to have put his moral judgment in suspension until the Republicans have won the war. He is used by the author to focus the evolution of the war from an "apocalypse of fraternity" to a modern, technological war where organization, discipline, and firepower contribute more to victory than good intentions do. During the rescue of the crew of the "Canard Déchaîné," he discovers, nonetheless, that brotherhood is not incompatible with military success. This episode, the longest uninterrupted passage of the novel, was to furnish the substance of Malraux's first film undertaking. In spite of his own inexperience and that of his amateur actors, he was able to use his camera as effectively as he did his pen to capture the theme of brotherhood. But, by the time he was making the movie, a Republican victory was impossible, and as in *Man's Fate,* fraternity became the consolation of defeat.

The drama that leads up to a vast tableau of human fraternity projected against the Spanish landscape begins with a peasant's report of a hidden fascist airfield. Magnin readies three planes for a predawn bombing mission, and peasants bring their trucks to illuminate the Republican air strip for the four A.M. takeoff. The peasant informant, unable to read a map, must accompany the flight. Seeing his town for the first time from the air, he cannot locate the camouflaged installation in the dim light. Only as dawn breaks does he distinguish it. The mission succeeds in destroying sixteen planes on the ground, but Magnin's bombers are intercepted by Franco's Heinkel fighters on their return. The engines of the "Canard Déchaîné" are severely damaged by the machinegun fire, and the pilot tries to set the plane down in the mountains above the village of Valdelinares. The crash landing leaves the Arab gunner dead and the six remaining French, Belgian, and Italian crewmen injured.

Once Magnin's own plane has returned safely to its base, he sets about organizing the rescue of the fallen crew. The men are at a four-hour climb above the town where the road ends and he must leave the ambulance. He leads the doctor and a group of townspeople carrying stretchers up to the crash site. During the lengthy climb, the ache in his muscles is felt as a first proof that leadership has not deprived him of a sense of fraternity. He appears to need evidence of a personal sacrifice made for others to reassure him at this point. Arriving at the damaged plane, he discovers that peasants from the nearby hamlet have preceded them. One old woman, whose son is serving in the Republican army, has killed the last chicken in town, and to show her solidarity, she is offering soup to the wounded flyers. Her gesture might have been more appreciated had she not insisted that the flyer with the injured jaw take her soup: even the peasants in this isolated hamlet are caught up in the "lyrical illusion" of the revolution.

The descent down the mountain is recounted from the point of view of Magnin, bringing up the rear. Like Manuel on the hill with Ximenez, his vantage point affords him a vast perspective of human activity, but against the tranquil background of the Sierra de Teruel[10] instead of battle. It is a viewpoint that Malraux does not respect in his film version of the episode. While the shift in camera angle generally worked to the film's advantage, the lens was not able to give the desolate mountains the animation they received from Magnin's imagination. At one point during the descent, the squadron commander views his wounded men through the branches of an apple tree. The limbs seem to be grasping the foreign airmen in a fraternal embrace: the entire Spanish countryside appears to be in accord with its inhabitants in their expression of fraternal good will. But, by being more than just an expression of humans, the brotherhood of the Spanish peasants takes on for Magnin the eternal dimensions of the rugged landscape. Like the ageless terrain in the background, human affection is understood as one of the unchanging conditions of life. It is associated, most appropriately, with the peasants who, in themselves, illustrate the unchanging qualities of man living off the earth.[11] For the Frenchman Magnin, this affection unites mankind across time and across national frontiers.

Malraux's Heroes and History

Through his representation of Hernandez's misplaced loyalty and Manuel's resistance to pity, Malraux has already discredited personal expressions of affection. Presumably he might have also discredited love: women seldom appear in this novel and then never as lovers. Love and camaraderie are sentiments more appropriate to Kyo, Katow, and Hernandez than to an activist committed to victory. Malraux's character Magnin registers a sympathy for the depersonalized, human collectivity. Far from being an obstacle to victory, his sympathy inspires military success. It is the sort of abstract affection that permits a military commander to order his men into a dangerous battle in the name of a postponed dignity. In his next military venture, he permits the reader to see how this abstract brotherhood that comes less from human contact than from isolation becomes an individual's link with history.

Not long after the rescue is completed, Magnin is called upon to provide air support at Guadalajara. Flying over the battle lines, he again has a chance to view the heroic efforts of an impoverished people united in a common cause. But he soon loses sight of the military objectives. From his bomber high above the battlefield, the engagement appears to him as one of peasants struggling for dignity. His interpretation bears traces of the rescue in the Sierra de Teruel: for the other characters, the army is composed of industrial workers; but for Magnin, it is a peasant army. And, more than reflecting his experience in the mountains, his interpretation translates the war into terms appropriate for a history that reaches further into the past than the industrial revolution of the nineteenth century. The deprived not only come from an industrial society, but go back into the remote past when private ownership first created inequality. But Magnin's sentiments are not those of commiseration. They are provoked less by past outrages to the peasants and workers than by a hope for their future. His admiration goes out to the faceless mass struggling to give birth to a new society, the undifferentiated human mass that has dissolved individual identities. His sympathy for their cause creates a fraternal bond linking him with those who are preparing the future. But as this experience and the rescue illustrate, the emotion requires the lofty perspective of the leader

134

The Historical Leap of Faith

able to rise above the battle and reflect upon his place in history. Magnin's abstract fraternity is the privilege of commanders removed from battle.

Because it registers so little human warmth, the sentiment Malraux attributes to Magnin scarcely resembles brotherhood. Still the word identifies his emotional attachment to the army of anonymous Spanish peasants and workers. But, in the case of the French aviation commander, the emotion has a broader effect. It is the attachment to the mass of humanity that, when set in motion, gives history its direction. A fraternal commitment to a common goal ties the activist to the human continuum that survives after individuals perish. It affords him the sense of participation in eternity. More than the consolation that it was for Kyo in *Man's Fate,* fraternity becomes a mechanism by which human existence is redeemed from the absurd—but only so long as it carries the commitment to victory explained by Garcia and illustrated by Manuel's adventure. Magnin's brotherhood and Manuel's leadership thus appear to complement one another. Malraux shows each of his Republican officers to possess the qualities he has investigated in the other: Manuel feels the emotional tug of brotherhood, just as Magnin feels the leader's commitment to victory. The author has created, however, separate dramas based on distinct motives. And rather than fuse them in his conclusion, he emphasizes their distinctiveness. It is on this note that he ends the story of the character that so resembles him. Talking with the young communist officer and Garcia on the road to Brihuega after the battle, Magnin realizes that he is more affected by the emotional aspects of the victory than by the political. The peasants and their contribution assumed for him an importance that his more analytical comrades could not conceive.

Like *Days of Wrath,* Malraux's Spanish Civil War novel promises a hope that characters of *Man's Fate* did not have. Upon their deaths, Kyo and Katow enjoyed only the comforts of fraternity and of the satisfaction that they had striven, albeit in vain, for the improvement of the human condition: so long as man's destiny was seen as death in a hostile universe where he has been abandoned by the gods, the only response to the absurd was an expression of brotherhood. Starting with *Days of Wrath,* Mal-

135

Malraux's Heroes and History

raux's characters begin to live in a different universe. Heroes from the early cycle cannot be judged by the same criteria as those of the later. Values from the earlier, tragic universe are obstacles to victory in a world where victory is possible. What distinguishes *Man's Hope* from any of Malraux's Oriental novels is not so much the nationality or race of the characters or their concept of honor, but the view of the world upon which their ethics are founded. To return to an earlier religious analogy, Malraux's first two European novels stand to his early tragedies as the New Testament stands to the Old. For all of their dignity, the elect of Malraux's Old Testament fail to merit the salvation promised the hero in his New Testament.

With his first novel set in Europe, Malraux announces a redemption through history. In *Days of Wrath,* Kassner discovers communication with the eternity of living, but the truncated conclusion of that brief novel does not permit the reader to appreciate how commitment to the Marxist dialectic redeems the human tragedy. An understanding of Kassner's insight benefits from the experiences of Manuel and Magnin and from the interpretations offered by the ubiquitous Garcia. Through these characters it is possible to see how history, while providing the battleground where the hero is tested, also provides a basis for hope, hope for the material improvement of the human lot but, more important, hope for a historical redemption from the absurd.

In *Man's Hope,* Malraux's heroes rediscover the religious comforts of an identification with the universe. It was in a feeling of unity with the cosmos that the Chinese correspondent Ling in *The Temptation of the West* found the superiority of Orient over Occident. Now the dilemma of Western man seems to be resolved. The Chinese intellectual, however, saw Oriental serenity in a static universe; Malraux sees man's reality as a vast historical progression marked by the tumultous moments of rapid change that wars are. The redemption of Malraux's hero requires an espousal of the movement of history, particularly at the moment of violent change. Reconciliation with the universe becomes thereby a commitment to the historical metamorphosis, but a commitment scarcely permitting the serenity that Ling represents as the supreme Oriental value. It does afford, however, the

The Historical Leap of Faith

satisfaction that comes from a reconciliation of the individual and his universe, even if the universe is viewed differently.

Before concluding any consideration of *Man's Hope*, a word must be added about the exclusivity of the Malrauvian paradise. For Malraux, salvation from tragedy and reconciliation with the eternal are privileges reserved for leaders. In contradiction to the popular appeals of communism, Malraux does not put metaphysical hope within the reach of the common people. Instead, the peasants and workers are the means to the leader's metaphysical satisfactions. Only those so placed as to appreciate their role in the grand historical dialectic enjoy the hope Malraux offers. As Orwell was to suggest in his *Animal Farm*, they have the advantage of shaping history, so they can continue to enjoy this special privilege.

It should not be overlooked, however, that Malraux has included in his revolutionary fresco characters who anticipate Orwell's anti-Stalinism. Miguel de Unamuno, the art dealer Alvear, and the Italian art historian Scali express unequivocally their skepticism about an intellectual abdication to communism. The reader may well wonder whether their views are not closer to Malraux's than are those of Garcia, Manuel, and Magnin. As it did for old Gisors, reason remains for these intellectuals an obstacle to political commitment. Although the comments attributed to Unamuno and the aging art dealer are but secondary, they nourish the more developed story of Scali. This airman serving under Magnin never succeeds in making the leap of faith which would give his participation in the war a religious dimension. Political action does not afford him the "totalitarian" response to the absurd that the intellectual needs. He seeks something more fundamental to the human condition—attachment to the eternal which does not require the suspension of judgment. At the same time, it should be compatible with his concept of art. Although his drama remains unresolved at the end of the novel, it has attracted the attention of numerous critics—and rightly so. Scali's participation in the futile Republican cause and the possibility of identifying him with the esthetic themes of *The Psychology of Art*, already being published as fragments, make him appear in retrospect as the typical Malrauvian hero. It is the continuation of his quest for a secular faith founded on something more substantial than the historical dialectic that provides the substance of Malraux's World War II novel, *The Walnut Trees of Altenburg.*

Composed only after the Spanish Republic and then the French Republic had come to an end, this last work carries a repudiation of the unified view of history that, in the Spanish Civil War novel, constituted "man's hope." Malraux retains from that novel, however, the hope that a cultural unity can redeem the tragedy of an absurd human destiny. He makes his last fictional work the investigation of his newly conceived "antidestiny," one more accessible to the artist than to the political leader—unless, of course, the political leader were an artist exercising the function of Minister of Culture.

8   HISTORY REASSESSED

*W*ITH the completion of *Man's Hope,* Malraux had provided a solution to the existential problems he had raised at the beginning of his career in *The Temptation of the West* and in his provocative essay "On European Youth." His fiction thus became a complete cycle, and had he been interested only in solving the esthetic problem of creating an internally consistent, Proustian work of art, he might very well have considered his literary vocation to be fulfilled. Malraux, however, accords existential questions as high a priority as esthetics. And when, in 1939, European politics brought him to alter his concept of man as an instrument of historical evolution, he made his changing views the subject of a final novel. In *The Walnut Trees of Altenburg,* he returns to the basic problem of the individual in the search for a salvation, rejecting in his investigation the solution that emerged out of his experiences in the Spanish Civil War.

In January 1939, shortly before the fall of the Spanish Republic, Malraux was forced to flee his movie location in Catalonia. His film version of *Man's Hope* was still far from finished. He continued work in southwestern France throughout the spring and completed the film early in the summer of 1939. Government authorities withheld permission for public exhibition, so Malraux held a private screening to which he is reported to have invited several well-known French communist figures. This gesture of communist sympathy may have well been his last: just days later, the Berlin-Moscow Axis was announced. Soon afterwards, Russia seized Eastern Poland and the Baltic states and, in the fall of 1939, launched an attack on Finland. Russia's collusion with nazism and its unjustifiable military aggression appears to have provoked in Malraux the same distrust and resentment that nu-

139

merous other European intellectuals felt. Shortly, he would align himself clearly behind the noncommunist opposition to the Nazis.

When the French call to mobilization went out, Malraux volunteered for service in an armored division. He had already observed and reported the effectiveness of tanks in Spain and, in spite of his age, evidently chose to make his contribution where he thought it would be most effective. His choice coincides with opinions that de Gaulle had expressed in his study on modern warfare published in 1934.[1] The coincidence does nothing more than mark what may best be considered an initial point of agreement; still it appears fortuitously prophetic.

For the nervous writer who, eighteen years earlier, had been considered unfit for military duty, service in the tanks seemed unlikely. Simone de Beauvoir even reports in her memoirs that Malraux had been rejected. His autobiography indicates, however, that he served as tank commander until captured by the Germans. Through the intervention of an uncle, Malraux was released from the German detention camp to the custody of a farmer in the department of Yonne, not far from the ancient cathedral town of Sens. Clara Malraux sketches in the last volume of her autobiography how the half-brother of her husband, then "already nearly her ex-husband," aided his escape to the Mediterranean village of Roquebrune late in 1940.[2] Malraux has since confided in his *Antimemoirs* that a letter written from there to offer his services to de Gaulle's Forces Françaises Libres went without a response, perhaps, he conjectures, because of his earlier association with Communists. De Gaulle had good reason to distrust the intentions of a former "Red fellow traveler": the French Communist party was in close collaboration with the Nazi occupation forces and remained so until the German invasion of Russia on 22 June 1941.[3] The explanation for de Gaulle's silence lay elsewhere, however: the courier never succeeded in getting Malraux's letter out of France.[4]

Malraux put his enforced leisure to use. He undertook a biographical study of the British adventurer T. E. Lawrence and a long three-part novel to have been entitled "The Struggle with the Angel" and continued work on his long study *The Psychology*

History Reassessed

of Art. While writing at Roquebrune, according to his most recent French biographer, he rejected requests from Sartre and from the peripatetic leftist, Emmanuel d'Astier de la Vigerie, to help form underground resistance groups. Later, his novel finished, Malraux left the intrigue of the Riviera for the calm of the Dordogne Valley. There agents of the Buckmaster network reportedly made irregular contact with him, perhaps encouraged by Malraux's brother Roland, already deeply committed to the Resistance. But it was not until early 1944 that André Malraux became Colonel Berger of the Forces Françaises de l'Intérieur.[5]

Malraux has revealed little of his Resistance experiences.[6] It is still impossible to determine, for instance, whether or not he chose a Gaullist faction in preference to a communist group, or whether he started his underground activity before the Nazi invasion of Russia brought the French Communist party into the Resistance. Nonetheless, he declared himself clearly for de Gaulle, and he served in the Resistance under the hybrid name, French or German according to the pronunciation, that he had used for the family of the only extant portion of the projected trilogy, a family drawn after the Malraux of Dunkerque but transposed to Alsace to satisfy the needs of his novel.

Of the Lawrence study, only one brief chapter has ever been completed.[7] It reads more like a book review than a biography. But evidence of Malraux's research into the life of Lawrence of Arabia has very evidently contributed to his conception of the central character of *The Walnut Trees of Altenburg.* This story of Vincent Berger, framed by his son's World War II experiences, constitutes the only surviving portion of "The Struggle with the Angel." In a prefatory note to the 1948 reedition of the novel, Malraux explains that the other portions of the three-part work were destroyed by the Gestapo. He continues that "it is rare that a writer succeeds in rewriting a novel." Then, in seeming contradiction, he adds that "when it appears in its definitive form, *The Walnut Trees of Altenburg* will be fundamentally modified." Any further modification was to await the refinements produced by Malraux's lengthy association with de Gaulle.

Upon the liberation of France in 1944, General de Gaulle appointed Malraux to the post of Minister of Propaganda in the provisional government. When the French electorate rejected the Gaullist constitution in January 1946, Malraux left the government with de Gaulle. Although he remained a spokesman for the Gaullist Reassemblement du Peuple Francais, he was nonetheless able to devote much time to his art studies. The 1951 edition of *The Voices of Silence* carries, along with the credits for his previous novels, the indication that an edition of "The Struggle with the Angel" was still being prepared. The Fourth Republic died after a turbulent thirteen-year existence, and the Fifth Republic was seven years old when finally a modified version of *The Walnut Trees of Altenburg* appeared.

While Minister of Culture in de Gaulle's government, Malraux published his *Antimemoirs,* the autobiographical work which draws heavily on his experiences in government. Edited portions of his last novel make up the first chapters of the autobiography. Malraux has condensed the sometimes tedious colloquium debates that constitute the novel's central portion. He has also eliminated the narrator's introduction and the apocalyptic visions of man destroying himself by gas in the First World War: World War II provided apocalypses that surpassed in horror anything Malraux conceived in 1941. About midway in the autobiography, the concluding chapter from the novel is repeated to contrast Oriental and Western views of man in the universe. The reader has the impression that the 1941 novel has been updated and expanded by the author into a meditation on the meaning of his own life.

It is tempting to believe that this is the revised version of the novel Malraux had promised in 1948. Equally tempting, and perhaps equally unfounded, would be the hope to find in the pages of the *Antimemoirs* any vestiges of the lost "Struggle with the Angel." The 1967 autobiography is nonetheless useful to the student and scholar of Malraux's fiction: it conveys a reaffirmation of his 1941 views of man in the universe and stands, with the art studies, to confirm that *The Walnut Trees of Altenburg* marks the final stage of Malraux's spiritual evolution.

Perhaps the most significant development to which this final novel attests is Malraux's repudiation of communism as a redemption from the absurd. Carefully situating the body of his story in a period shortly before the Russian Revolution brought

History Reassessed

international communism into existence, he again avoids the practical politics and economics of Marxism: these are of scant importance to a writer whose concerns are metaphysical. Instead, he considers the historical dialectic of Marxism, which, in his two previous novels, afforded the individual a quasi-religious link with eternity. He represents it as but a stage in the European's struggle with the absurd, a stage transcended when he attains a superior understanding of man's place in the universe. But Malraux's ambitions far exceed the possibilities of a novel of the size of *The Walnut Trees of Altenburg*. To complete his story in the relatively small dimensions of the work, Malraux is forced to dramatize as debates ideas better treated in an essay or an autobiography. For that reason, the *Antimemoirs* is a more satisfying work. The novel remains, however, rich in ideas while it is confounding in density. Its wealth and concision, the qualities a reader usually hopes to find in a piece of literature, obscure the meaning of the novel that the author thought important enough to annex to his autobiography.

The story of Vincent Berger is recounted by his son. Imprisoned in Chartres with other French soldiers after the fall of France in June 1940, the young Berger studies the cathedral which dominates the town. Its Gothic decor seems to mirror something in the expressions and mannerisms of the French prisoners of war. For him, this resemblance testifies to an ineffaceable, human unity—the unity which is the principal message of the novel. The young soldier recalls it as a discovery made by his father before him. It would likely have been the theme of the memoirs left incomplete at the father's death in World War I on the eastern front along the Vistula. The young Berger, a writer by profession, will reconstruct the memoirs from his recollections of the notes his father had entitled "Encounters with Man"; in the prison compound where life has no apparent meaning, exercise of his art is the only way for a writer to retain his dignity. In the concluding section of the novel, he continues his father's adventure, discovering in art the metaphysical force that his predecessors had reserved for political commitment. Through his own experience, art comes to provide a salvation. Young Berger, Malraux's first artist-hero, ceases to think of art

143

as a social act, seemingly rejecting the function of communication that was ascribed to it in the early chapters of *Man's Hope.* In the conclusion of *The Walnut Trees of Altenburg,* it becomes, as it did for the narrator of Marcel Proust's *Remembrance of Things Past,* a religion capable of lending a permanence to the artist's fragile existence, but for reasons altogether different from those Proust proposed.

But before young Berger comes to understand the religious force of art, he must first trace vicariously his father's evolution through individualism and Marxism in search of a solution to the tragedy of human destiny. The narrator recounts how his father repeated the adventures of previous Malrauvian heroes, beginning with Perken of *The Royal Way* who aspired to a historical immortality. Like Perken, Vincent Berger set out to leave a political monument to his own existence. But more than a resurrection of a previous character, Vincent Berger is first of all a transposition of the historical figure T. E. Lawrence. In Vincent Berger, Lawrence's activities are projected against the background of the Young Turk movement in the years preceding World War I.

Immediately after completing his studies in Oriental languages, Vincent was assigned to the newly reorganized university at Constantinople. His courses on Nietzsche so influenced the Turkish students that he soon acquired the reputation of leader of the young intellectuals. When student opposition to the Ottoman government came to the attention of the German Ambassador in Constantinople, he asked Vincent to organize a propaganda service to advance the interests of the Germans trying to salvage a political advantage out of the decaying Ottoman Empire. The embassy became something of a military mission, and Vincent supplied arms to the young Turkish militants. He promoted the mercurial rise to power of Enver Pascha, the historical figure who in Malraux's novel corresponds to Lawrence's Feisal. Like the association between the British adventurer and the Arab chief, Vincent's friendship with Enver was cemented by a war. When Italy invaded the Ottoman provinces of Tripoli and Cyrenaica in 1911, Turkey sent its forces under Enver's command to support the North African Arabs. But it was the fictional

History Reassessed

German advisor's military cunning, again reminiscent of Lawrence's, that, in Malraux's fictional version, kept a superior Italian army at bay for a year. Enver, however, was recognized as a hero by his people. With that success, Vincent ceased being an advisor to become Enver's "grey eminence" and the architect of Enver's nationalistic Turan Movement.

Historians confirm Malraux's explanation of Turanism as a plan to unite Turks from Anatolia on the west, across Iran and Afghanistan to the Chinese border, and north to include all of Turkestan.[8] The hope to establish a vast Pan-Turkish Empire now appears as foolhardy as Perken's scheme to establish his own kingdom in the Indochinese back country. And like Perken's dream, Enver's hopes ultimately ran afoul of the realities of twentieth-century politics: the rise of Ataturk, World War I, and communist expansion into Turkestan. After his overthrow by Mustapha Kemal Ataturk, Enver was used by the Russians and would finally be killed by them in 1922 defending his Pan-Turkish illusion in Russian Turkestan. Malraux has resurrected this forgotten fantasy of history to associate his German adventurer with it. Vincent Berger is presented as using Enver, much as the Russians would use him some ten years later, to advance his own motives. He evidently hopes to take over Turanism, thereby leaving his scar on the earth as Perken earlier had attempted to do. But Vincent Berger is spared Perken's fate. While in Kabul to muster support for the movement, he narrowly escapes assassination. Like the slap in the face that T. E. Lawrence received in the Damascus military hospital,[9] the incident impresses the German adventurer with the futility of trying to win a place of glory in history.

The narrator has presented little more than a chronology of his father's experiences in Turkey and Libya. The adventurer's response is neither his nor Malraux's major interest; he is principally concerned with that which transcends individualism. Vincent's adventure becomes, then, Part One of the European spiritual odyssey, an introductory element leading to the discovery of a new Malrauvian salvation. Malraux is able to make certain economies with his narrative, economies that, in large measure, deprive Vincent Berger's Oriental adventure of its existential foundation. He is presented as acting automatically: unlike the adventurers of the early Oriental novels, he does not reason out his motives. Nonetheless, references to Vincent Berger's egocentric desire to leave a lasting scar on the earth show that the hero of Malraux's last fictional work was at first acting upon the same imperatives that drove Perken. Both sought a confirmation of their own existence through their domination of others and sought to give their existence some immortality by leaving an indelible impression on history. And like his predecessor, Berger fails to win an enduring personal glory. Their failures are not those of personal inadequacy but failures which come from misunderstanding human limitations, as Malraux interprets them. A permanent scar cannot be left on the face of the earth. Pursuit of the ill-conceived Turan adventure would only provide further confirmation of the futility of individual human endeavor, the opposite of what the adventurer aspires to.

Although Vincent Berger's Turkish drama does not have the tragic ending of *The Conquerors* or *The Royal Way,* it is played out in the same atmosphere of futility. Until he learned that political history was beyond his domination, Vincent Berger was but repeating the tragedy of Malraux's first protagonists. Then, just a few weeks before the outbreak of World War I, he abandons his romantic dream and returns to Alsace by way of Marseille. He hopes that a few weeks' rest will cure the dysentery ravaging his health and will provide a new direction to his life. But in spite of his disappointment in the Middle East, he refuses to resign himself to an Oriental view of man's place in the cosmos: he retains his Western view of individual dignity and his confidence in the individual's ability to dominate his destiny rather than submit to it. The Malrauvian hero must find an alternative to politics if he hopes to redeem the absurdity of his life. Before arriving at a tenable view of the individual's place in history, Vincent Berger successively encounters and rejects the Proustian hope for a personal immortality through art and the hope for a redemption through a collectivist view of history. Neither of these solutions that so tempted European intellectuals can satisfy Vincent Berger's need for a substitute religion capable of redeeming his existence from the absurd. The inadequacy of art and of the historical dialectic is developed during the intellectual discussions that make up the central part of the novel, the part that begins with Vincent's return to Europe.

The landing at the French port of Marseille is a rebirth for the Alsatian. Like the hero of *Days of Wrath,* he will have the opportunity of finding a new meaning to life. Vincent Berger's experiences repeat Kassner's, to a certain extent, but they require a much lengthier elaboration. He will start from a more primitive state, not enjoying the bonds of fraternity that permitted Kassner to discover his place in the eternity of the living.

Returning to the West from the timeless Middle East, he is surprised, but not disappointed, that the modern warships, new dance steps, and clothing fashions awaken in him no sense of familiarity. He has returned to a world where progress has meaning and where the change in styles marks the time that inevitably effaces individual accomplishment. Vincent Berger feels entirely foreign to the life he observes in the European port. His response to newspaper accounts of an assassination trial reveals his sense of estrangement. He sympathizes with the accused, who discovered in his act of violence the fragility of social conventions like justice. Malraux's narrator must intervene to contrast Vincent's sense of alienation with that felt by a first-time assassin.

Earlier in the novel, Vincent Berger was described by his son as a sort of "shaman."[10] Malraux's intention was not, however, to present him as a mystic but rather as a character subliminally conscious of the world about him and able to respond instinctively long before he understands why he acts. Such a characterization permits the author to focus the reader's attention on the emotions associated with a new idea before elaborating the idea. For this episode to have any meaning, however, the fictional narrator must offer the additional comment that his father's feelings go much deeper than the assassin's. While killing forces the murderer to reassess his personal code of values, Vincent's experiences in North Africa and Turkey have put him in a position to weigh Western values against Eastern. Neither culture offers an acceptable solution to man's tragedy, and Vincent is left with the feeling that all bases of human values have crumbled.

Malraux's Heroes and History

Instead of restoring a direction to his life, his return leaves him with a sense of emptiness. He is aware only of the need for a higher understanding of mankind. He does not experience the metaphysical malaise that reduced the protagonist of Sartre's *Nausea* to a state of hallucinatory impotence; nor is he driven to the violence of Camus's Caligula. Malraux's heroes never appear to be buffeted in a moral void. Consciously or unconsciously, they are sustained by the confidence that human existence is not absurd, that man need not be an unwitting victim of an unfathomable destiny. So it is with an undirected hope that Vincent Berger returns to the family residence in Reichbach. And, having no specific direction in his life, he appears as a passive witness to the events taking place around him. Vincent's passivity notwithstanding, his experiences assume the dimensions of a spiritual drama played out against the background of death and violence: first, the suicide of his own father five days after his return to Alsace; then, the mass asphyxiation of Russian soldiers on Germany's eastern front in World War I, represented as the horrifying experience which forces Vincent out of his passivity and impels him to action.

The announcement of Dietrich Berger's suicide is the first incident of Vincent's reconstructed memoirs. It served as an introduction to his Turkish adventures, presented in the novel as a flashback. Vincent's reputation as the grey eminence behind the rise of Enver Pascha had earned him an invitation to participate in the colloquium of German and French intellectuals sponsored by Vincent's uncle, Walter. Like its French counterparts at Pontigny or Créteil,[11] Walter's debates are held in a restored abbey, the Altenburg Abbey not far from Reichbach. Walter the historian and Vincent the returning adventurer thus have an opportunity to speculate on the meaning of Dietrich's suicide before the intellectuals begin their discussion.

Before he died, pious and eccentric old Dietrich had prepared a note requesting that he *not* be buried by the Church. He had second thoughts, however, and scratched out the negative, making his last request in opposition to the Catholic sanctions against Church burial for suicides. The reason for the contradictory requests, or for the suicide, has been intentionally obscured by the author so that his characters can raise the question of the meaning of a human life. During their conversation at Dietrich's bedside, the son Vincent and the brother Walter announce the themes to be developed during the later debates on "The Permanence and Metamorphosis of Man." Their conversation shows that the two have little in common, and perhaps it might not even have taken place had the circumstances of Dietrich Berger's suicide not been so puzzling.

Apparently resigned to the impossibility of fathoming the meaning of his brother's suicide, Walter generalizes that, "for the essential, man is what he conceals ... A miserable pile of secrets."[12] He understands man in the Western, humanistic framework of the personality, an individual with a full set of motivations, mostly concealed or subconscious. Vincent, on the other hand, has already moved towards a view of man similar to the one proposed about the same time by Jean-Paul Sartre in *Being and Nothingness.* He responds vehemently that "man is what he does" (p. 90), rejecting thereby his uncle's implication that the meaning of a man's life lies in some hidden psychological motivation. He understands old Dietrich's suicide as a continuation of his revolt against Church traditions and local prejudices. In more Sartrian terms, this was the "situation" in which his will had to be expressed if his life were to acquire any meaning. Vincent sees his father's final violent act as part of the struggle to wrest his life from the insignificance to which conformity might have condemned it.

Here Malraux violates his own characterization of the profoundly religious Dietrich Berger. For the Christian, belief in the immortality of the soul and in the possibility of communion with God guarantees the significance of human life: no revolt is necessary. Malraux's intention is clarified, however, by his error. He assigns to the act of protest or revolt a metaphysical significance, but one which the narrator does not explain for the reader. Instead, he will show Vincent's confidence that redemption from tragic futility can be found outside of Christianity.

Vincent's hope is communicated by a meditation which carries his attention back to his father's suicide. With some regret, he thinks how Dietrich Berger's destiny might have been different and recalls how he became aware of the change in his own destiny in Marseille. Briefly he relives those moments when he first realized that the old directions of his life had been lost. But he does not linger over the gratuitousness of life. He immediately feels a metaphysical pull. The starry nocturnal sky reminds him of the eternity of the universe in which the individual is able to give his life some meaning.

Unexplainedly, as though he had overheard his nephew's thoughts, Walter interrupts the silent meditation on eternity to confess that he, too, had once experienced the same metaphysical reassurance. Then he recounts a railroad trip he made across Switzerland with a mad and delirious Friedrich Nietzsche. His narrative is punctuated by the rain falling out of doors: the reader wonders why the stars, which for Vincent pointed to the still unexpressed meaning of human life in a godless universe, were not obscured by the clouds that brought the rain. However inconsistent his imagery might be, however, Malraux has succeeded in casting the scene in the ominous darkness of tragedy which pervaded all of his early tragic novels. Only when a way out of tragedy is announced do the Malrauvian heroes view an illuminated world. While Vincent's meditation is but dimly lighted by the stars, the essence of Walter's anecdote is shrouded in total darkness.

During the voyage across Switzerland, the third-class compartment occupied by Walter, the dying philosopher, their two companions, some Italian laborers, and a peasant woman became the metaphorical, Pascalian cell in which condemned prisoners were obliged to watch their fellowmen die. Passing through the dark Saint Gotthard tunnel, Nietzsche began to sing his last poem. When the train emerged into the light, Walter thought, in opposition to Pascal's views on the godless man, "The greatest mystery is not that we are thrown by chance between the profusion of matter and of the stars; it is rather that, in this prison, we are able to draw out of ourselves images strong enough to deny our nothingness" (pp. 98–99).

In Walter's mind, the work of art offered the artist a foothold on eternity. In an art created out of an artist's "miserable pile of secrets," he saw an alternative to the quest for salvation associated with Vincent's starry sky. The author could gain a sort of second-hand immortality by turning the raw stuff of his life into a resistant literary monument to his own existence. He would not enjoy the participation in the afterlife promised by Christianity: he would, at least, attain the immortality that the political adventurer seeks, but a somewhat superior immortality for being less exposed to the vicissitudes of history. In the eyes of the German historian viewing man in the framework of Western humanism, only the artist could enjoy a redemption from the oblivion to which death inevitably condemned all others. The introspective writers—the Montaignes, Baudelaires, and Prousts of French literature, and the T. E. Lawrences of English literature—stand the greatest chance for a personal salvation through their confessional works.

Walter's understanding of the personality, as Vincent indicates, is conditioned by his concept of an art which can redeem the personality from disappearance at death. His confidence in a personal salvation through art has led him to reverse cause and effect: according to his nephew, he erroneously conceives of the personality in terms of what art can preserve, whereas he should be defining art in terms of what is preservable—at least so long as art is to retain its eternal qualities, and on this point Vincent and Walter have no quarrel.

Walter's hope for immortality through art has been part of Western culture since the Renaissance, when humanists first encouraged Europeans to doubt the immortality of the soul and artists discovered the immortality of Grecian art.[13] Vincent does not contest his uncle's faith that some sort of personal immortality might come through art. Neither, however, does he find it an acceptable solution to the tragedy of human destiny. While Walter's solution resembles Christian salvation, Vincent seeks an attachment to the eternity of all of mankind. His salvation must come from a sense of participation in a universal history. In the Islamic Orient, he learned that Western respect for the personality prevents such a participation: cultivation of one's own particularity in order to make it the material of art isolates the individual from what is permanent in the universe. Salvation, however, requires a renunciation of the personality. He elaborates his views in the course of the colloquium, which, in spite of its title, gives more attention to what is ephemeral than to what is permanent or even metamorphic in man.

Walter Berger's guests at the Altenburg Abbey debate with Germanic seriousness questions of art and culture. It is the talk of the ethnologist Möllberg, however, that arouses the participants' interest. The other characters are secondary, employed mainly to give some precision to the earlier conversation on the Western concept of the personality. While their debates lend some drama to the abstract subjects, the caricatures of the German and French participants also convey Malraux's criticism of these intellectuals, for whom ideas are born from other ideas rather than from experience. Through one character he makes his point with disarming sympathy. Count Rabaud, who has spent thirty years affecting the appearance of the French poet Mallarmé, earnestly defends the notion of permanance in art. He supports the view that Walter had earlier advanced in the suicide conversation, and in Rabaud's talk, the reversal of cause and effect becomes pathetically evident. Malraux has eliminated from his *Antimemoirs* the discussion stimulated by the talk. Because it slows down the movement of the novel, such editing seems justified, but since the talk and the ensuing debate give Malraux's interpretation of the Christian origins of Western psychology and of the European sense of metaphysical isolation, the discussion does merit some consideration.

Count Rabaud's thesis, evidently a tissue of banalities, is disputed by one participant who identifies the limits of European culture. Rather than teach what is eternal in man and therefore capable of surviving after an individual's death, a certain Thirard contends, Western culture only describes the cultivated European. The European may fail to understand the man of another culture, because he attempts to understand him in terms of the Western psychology. When Vincent Berger finally enters the discussion in support of Thirard, it is to explain the Western concept of the personality as a product of Christianity. The agnostic might have made a more interesting contribution to the discussion by reversing the order. Instead of showing how an attachment to the personality could have been developed by

Christianity, he might have proposed more provocatively that Christianity flourished among a people who already possessed this attachment. Malraux is, however, less interested in determining origins than in identifying our modern concept of the personality with Europe. Since our modern views on the personality unquestionably involve its Christian traditions, it matters little in the novel whether or not a faith in the existence of a soul preceded the religion or grew out of it.

Vincent finds, nonetheless, in the personal struggle for salvation the basis for the European's sense of metaphysical alienation —a sentiment he did not find among the Moslems. But so long as the European Christian remained confident of the immortality of his soul, he was immune to the torments of the absurd. Repeating notions from Malraux's earliest fiction, Vincent observes that only when the European lost faith in God and the soul did he begin to feel his isolation in the universe. To his sorrow, he retained the Christian concept of the personality in its opposition to the world. This antagonism between the Westerner and the world becomes then his "destiny." Feisty old Thirard snorts his disapproval of this expression from the vocabulary of tragedy. The interjection allows Vincent—and the author—to define destiny as the cultural isolation transmitted by Western traditions. It is a notion incorporated in the earlier *The Temptation of the West*, but it lay dormant for some fifteen years. Once it is revived in *The Walnut Trees of Altenburg*, it combines with the absurdist's feeling of cosmic isolation to yield a new definition of post-Christian Europe. Then it can be understood as an essential ingredient of the heritage of Western man and can be combatted.

This refinement in Malraux's thought gives a new direction to the lives of his characters. No longer do they look to the historical evolution of one society for their redemption: starting with Vincent Berger, they seek to transcend the cultural conditioning that prevents them from viewing their lives in terms of a universal "eternity of all mankind." It is during the Altenburg colloquium that Vincent takes the first steps toward discovering how his European destiny prevented him from attaining the religious comforts he sought.

Malraux's Heroes and History

In the framework of his European heritage with its emphasis on the personality, he has already sought and failed to find a personal redemption through political opportunism. Now he rejects the artist's opportunism. Introducing a line of thought which Malraux was to amplify later in *The Voices of Silence*,[14] Berger observes that Western artists have corrupted art to satisfy their own needs for a personal salvation. They have thereby deprived it of its special function of reconstituting the world on a human scale so that man can understand his place in it:

> Our art appears to me to be a rectification of the world, a means of escaping from the human condition. The capital confusion appears to me to come from the idea we have accepted of Greek tragedy—but it's disappearing—that to represent fate was to submit to it. But, how wrong. To represent fate is almost to possess it. The very fact of representing it, of conceiving it releases fate from real destiny, from the implacable divine scale; reduces it to the human scale. Essentially our art [should be] a humanization of the world (p. 128).

This passage constitutes Vincent's second attack on the basic tenets of Western humanism: after first denying the universality of the Western notion of the personality, he now rejects the view of art that nourished it. Art, rather than affording a personal salvation in the face of a tragic human fate, should be a description of that fate. Those who do not recognize this fundamental quality, Vincent's logic implies, are guilty of turning art into a vehicle for a second-hand immortality—an esthetic means of preserving the personality that parallels the historical means pursued by political adventurers. There is a limit, however, to Vincent Berger's iconoclasm, and presumably then to Malraux's. Although the author uses his character to attack political opportunism and immortality *through* art, he never questions the immortality *of* art. What survives this phase of the Altenburg debates on the "Permanence and Metamorphosis of Man" is a confidence in the eternity of art that, according to Malraux, Western man first discovered during the Italian Renaissance.

History Reassessed

Having reached the level of perception required to explain Greek tragedy, Vincent Berger should have been able to bring his intellectual odyssey to a conclusion. It appears that he was well on the way to making the association between art as a representation of fate and as a "possession of destiny." That he did not proceed from there to the deduction that his son makes twenty-seven years later can only be explained by Malraux's desire to dramatize the final discovery. From this peak of enlightenment, Vincent will fall back to a level of relative ignorance, retaining only the hope that he can discover a concept of human existence that will replace personal immortality as a hedge against destiny.

Previously, in *Days of Wrath* and *Man's Hope,* Malraux had proposed a reconciliation of Western and Eastern concepts of man through a Marxist view of history. By identifying with the historical evolution of society, Kassner, Manuel, and Magnin appeared to find an eternal attachment to the universe which allowed for a "virile" expression of the will. During the second part of the colloquium, the assembled intellectuals discuss the possibility of history constituting a redemption from destiny, what Malraux later calls an "antidestiny."[15] Rather than Marx's, however, they consider Hegel's view of the historical dialectic—a view especially cherished by German intellectuals because it placed Germany at the fore in history. The discussion is provoked by the talk of the ethnologist Möllberg whose first publications led the participants to expect a confirmation of Hegel's comprehensive concept of history.

The character Möllberg functions in the novel as a stand-in for Vincent Berger. His reports of his African studies vicariously take Vincent's intellectual adventure beyond the stage where Malraux's European revolutionaries found a metaphysical identification with historical universals. His special function earns him a respect that the other guests at Altenburg do not merit. Only Möllberg is spared Malraux's satire: the German ethnologist is the only intellectual to have tested his ideas empirically. For long years in Africa, he had been doing research for a study to be entitled "Civilization as Conquest and Destiny." His research did

155

not, however, corroborate his original hypothesis. He gave up his work, scattered his manuscript dramatically across North Africa, and espoused a contrary view. Instead of hearing a theory of cultural unity, the Altenburg intellectuals hear an interpretation of cultural fragmentation that appears to preclude any antidestiny.

In order for political commitment to satisfy the Malrauvian hero's need for participation in the dialectic, Hegelian or Marxist, he must determine historical evolution for all society. In the mind of the European, it would matter little whether the dialectic were a translation of the abstract Hegelian Ideal or of the Marxist economic and demographic factors: so long as he retained the confidence that his culture would ultimately dominate and supplant all others, he could consider the evolution of the West as a historical absolute. In Möllberg's terms, this confidence "attached man to the infinite" (p. 140); it permitted the revolutionaries of the two previous novels to find a surrogate religion in history. Möllberg's African research failed, however, to substantiate the view of an all-encompassing historical evolution. Instead, he found only evidence of cultural disunity.

Some years after the period represented here, but long before *The Walnut Trees of Altenburg* was published, Spengler and Leo Frobenius proposed similar theories of cultural fragmentation.[16] Historical analysts more inclined to geopolitics, like Paul Valéry, speculated in the 1920s that Europe might be reduced to little more than a "peninsula of the Eurasian supercontinent."[17] Malraux's fictional ethnologist anticipates the thought of these historical theorists. He continues, then, to demonstrate how national culture, which gives the human animal his grandeur, comes to function as a "destiny" preventing any participation in the universal human community.

Taking the raw, animal material of humanity, the culture gives man a form. While it raises the individual above the animal state, it also imposes upon him a stamp of the cultural particularity of a European or an Oriental, an Alsatian or a Russian. Consequently, according to Möllberg, the traditions that mold peoples prevent them from sharing a common heritage and, at the same time, prevent them from participating in a single cultural evolution. Aware of the independent evolution of alien societies, the European realizes that history cannot be a surrogate religion. It lacks for him the universality necessary to function as an absolute. The culture in which many of the intellectuals assembled at Altenburg had hoped to find immortality is shown to separate them from the rest of mankind.

The author avoids any reference to Marxism. Still, it is clear that, where Hegel's concept of a coherent, dialectical unity of history is rejected, so also is the Marxist interpretation of the dialectic.[18] It is impossible, then, for the individual to find any metaphysical satisfaction in identifying his actions with a society's political evolution. At best, the individual would be espousing the history of his national culture, which is *not* the history of mankind: commitment to a historical, political movement can offer no better metaphysical satisfaction than an adventurer's efforts at political domination. Through Möllberg, Malraux repudiates his communist exemplars, Kassner and the Spanish revolutionaries. Supplanting the Spanish ethnologist who served as Malraux's interpreter of history in *Man's Hope*, the German ethnologist observes that the only universal, permanent human qualities that can be discerned occur in an abject state of ignorance. He concludes his talk by challenging his listeners to resign themselves to the absurdity of their human destiny.

Vincent Berger has been easily convinced by Möllberg's demonstration that history can be no antidestiny. He is spared the necessity of retracing the adventures of Malraux's earlier heroes. Because he benefits from the experience of the German ethnologist, his rebirth after his abortive Turkish adventure does not lead into the political activism of a Kassner. Vincent Berger does not, however, accept Möllberg's resignation to the futility of existence. He refuses to acknowledge that an integration with the eternal is impossible and that man need remain a victim of the tragic absurd. In opposition to the ethnologist's conclusion that the permanence of man lies in animal ignorance, he responds that it lies in the "fundamental." The human instincts which brought civilizations into being can be identified, he suggests, if the individual is observed in a situation where cultural elements do not separate him from the rest of mankind.

157

Malraux's Heroes and History

In response to Vincent Berger's arguments, Möllberg disputes the notion that there is anything fundamental in man. He discredits the idea as a dream of intellectuals and challenges his interlocutor to conjure up a fundamental workman. Offering no opportunity for a response, he continues that, without a civilization to structure life, man is nothing. His opinion betrays his own ethnological prejudices: revealing himself now to be only somewhat better than the tradition-bound participants in the colloquium, he refuses to see anything more fundamental to man than an animal physiology. Skipping over the transition between the animal state and the civilized state of man, he shows himself incapable of understanding that there lies within man an urge to create civilizations, which, in itself, distinguishes man from animal.

Malraux underscores Möllberg's oversight through the image that gives the novel its title. He makes his cynical ethnologist represent the fundamental material of the wooden boat prow and the wooden gothic statues decorating the old abbey as the logs, not the walnut wood from which they are carved. Möllberg sees nothing between the sculptured figures and the biological substance from which they were formed: he is blind to the fact that the figures have not been produced from just any wood, but from walnut. Likewise, he appears blind to the fact that civilizations are the product of not just any animal, but of a special animal with a special concern for his place in the universe. The Mallarmé imitator reminds the speaker that man is distinguished from the rest of the animals by his "aptitude for raising questions about the world." The observation is dismissed with the quip: "Sisyphus is eternal too" (p. 147). Quite by accident, Malraux hit upon the same mythological figure as Camus to typify one response to the absurd. Malraux's intention is quite different, however: his character has chosen Sisyphus in order to denigrate man's futile interrogation of the world as a punishment of the gods rather than as a mark of an enduring human quality. Deeper than the ethnologist wishes to penetrate, however, there is truth in Count Rabaud's remark. But once again, Malraux exercises the writer's prerogative to end the debate. He has succeeded in setting up Möllberg as a straw man to be knocked down by his protagonist.

History Reassessed

Vincent's solitary meditation following the afternoon's deliberations only strengthens his belief in unifying human qualities.

The vehement reaction to Möllberg's closing remarks threatens to disrupt the colloquium. Fearful that the program degenerate into petty bickering, Walter Berger takes the floor to end the discussion. Vincent, who has been silent during the last heated exchanges, strolls out across the fields to a wooded copse. There he discovers some century-old walnut trees. Like the trees in earlier novels, these walnut trees of Altenburg are used to symbolize man's relation to his universe. Previously, in *The Royal Way*, the jungle growth communicated the hostility of the world; then, in *Man's Hope*, the view of the aviators through the embracing limbs of the mountain trees registered the rapport between man and the cosmos; in this last novel, the protagonist again views life through trees. But instead of framing individuals, the gnarled wood of the aged trees frames a landscape of Rhineland vineyards and the distant towers of the Strasbourg Cathedral, a tableau of man's accomplishments.

From the crest overlooking the Rhine valley, Vincent contemplates the signs of man's efforts to deny his nothingness. Leaving the vineyards and the distant cathedral, his glance sweeps upwards to behold the walnut leaves projected against the eternal sky. The scene recalls the sky imagery represented in Vincent's conversation with Walter at Dietrich's deathbed. Then the black, unfathomable night sky stood for man's ignorance about his place in the universe. In this evening setting, there is not enough light to indicate that Malraux's protagonist has attained a better understanding of man's place under the eternal sky, but there is enough for the foliage of the walnut trees, Malraux's symbol of the still undefined, fundamental quality of mankind, to stand out clearly against his symbol of eternity. And his shaman, responding instinctively to the signs before him, understands that there is a redemption from the absurd.

As this lyrical passage points out, Vincent Berger is able—or perhaps is condemned—to live his life on the most elevated of planes. His spiritual adventures are elevated beyond history and beyond cultural boundaries and acquire, thereby, a metaphysical significance that T. E. Lawrence's never attain. He goes beyond

Malraux's Heroes and History

Western humanism to seek eternal, universal human truths. He would concur with Möllberg that a national culture prevents man from understanding the universal value in his acts, but he would not agree that cultural differences prevent man from giving his acts a universal value. He would agree with Walter that the miracle of man is that human life can have an eternal meaning; but he would deny that this eternal meaning comes through a probing of the personality. Vincent's message involves a reconciliation of Möllberg and Walter, not a categorical refutation of their views. Malraux presents and analyzes opposing notions, too often, perhaps, at a very abstract level; then he synthesizes the oppositions. The outbreak of war in 1914 provides the framework for the synthesis.

It has become almost commonplace to observe that Malraux's novels bear all the marks of the violence of his century. Repeatedly, he uses wars, revolutionary or nationalistic, as the background for man's quest for meaning. War appears as a concentration of the forces of destiny, but, for the one-time revolutionary, the great historical cataclysms are not destructive of human values. As men survive wars, so do their fundamental, human qualities, and out of war's violence there emerges the antidestiny which resists the political upheavals that pit one nation or one culture against another.

The war along the eastern front is in its final stages, and the German troops are throwing the Russians back from their positions in what had formerly been Austrian Poland. In spite of Vincent Berger's request for duty in Turkey, the German military staff has assigned him to duty along the Vistula. He is not entirely disappointed. At least he has not been sent to the western front where he would have to face a French enemy: as an Alsatian, he has strong reasons for feeling that French and Germans own a common heritage, and he would resent fighting against soldiers with whom he shared a cultural bond. Russia seems initially quite alien to him, and it should be easier to wage war against a foreign enemy.[19]

Malraux's fictional narrator introduces the last phase of his father's spiritual adventure with this element of Möllberg's principle of cultural disunity. During the gas attack that ensues, it

160

becomes evident that cultural differences do not isolate men. From underneath a cultural veneer, something more fundamental surges forth to unite the German and Russian soldiers. Vincent Berger begins to feel the tug of these bonds long before the battle begins. As an intelligence officer, he has the onerous duty of transcribing his superior's interrogation of a woman suspected of spying. Forced to observe how Captain Wurtz preys on her weaknesses, Vincent feels nothing but shame for the abuse the woman receives. Wurtz's justification, that he is only trying to spare the lives of German soldiers, seems inadequate to explain these indignities; perhaps it only served as a pretext for the pleasure Wurtz felt as he humiliated others. His actions betray the sadism that typifies Malraux's police officers and prison guards. Soon, however, Vincent Berger witnesses his fellow man being subjected to indignities repugnant even to Wurtz.

He and Wurtz have been reassigned to battle duty along the Vistula. There, the first phosgene gas attack is to be launched against the Russians, and the two intelligence officers are to protect the chemist who has developed the lethal gas.[20] The day before the attack, they meet the chemist and his son. During the time he spends with the two, Vincent notes their warped sentimentality: the father is attached only to the family property; the son, only to dogs. Neither appears capable of affection for a human. Vincent is struck, too, by Hoffman's explanation for having developed phosgene: it will save German lives. Old Hoffman repeats Wurtz's justification for having humiliated the spy suspect. Now, however, even Wurtz finds the explanation unsatisfactory—appeal to nationalism or, perhaps, any other idealism appears to justify any enormity of crime. This criticism is only incidental. Malraux is more concerned with how nationalism operates to isolate and dehumanize men and with how it can be transcended.

The soldiers who must occupy the Russian positions after the fatal cloud of phosgene clears resist dehumanization. From his position in the trenches, Vincent Berger overhears their conversations as they await the order to attack. They seem to be only subconsciously aware of the role they are about to play, and their banal conversations divert their attention from the danger they

161

must soon face. Their banter appears to be the unparticularized, eternal voice of the only animal who has learned, although only very badly, that he is going to die. After a moment's distraction, Vincent observes:

> The darkness was again inhabited by voices, voices of indifference and of hundred-year-old dreams, voices of trades—as if the trades alone might have survived under depersonalized and temporary men. The pitch changed, but the tone remained the same, very ancient, clothed in the past like the shadows of that trench—the same resignation, the same false authority, the same absurd knowledge and the same experience, the same inexhaustible gayety, and these discussions could be resolved only by a more and more forceful declaration, as if these voices from the darkness could not even individualize their anger (p. 199).

Underneath its indignation, Vincent's observation conveys an admiration. Perhaps somewhat romantically, he discerns in the soldiers' words evidence of primordial man uncorrupted by a Western culture which insists that individualism be cultivated and respected. In their uncultured way, these peasants and work-ingmen testify to what is permanent and universal in man. Unso-phisticated and unschooled, they are all the more able to demonstrate during the gas attack how the resistance to death unites all mankind, transcending national and cultural barriers.

Once the gas is released, its yellowish haze casts an ethereal pall over the battleground. The battle noises are stilled by the poison, but out of the awesome silence emerges a riderless horse. Everyone's attention is momentarily fixed upon the stupid beast, rushing about in the ominous haze. In this morbid scene, Mal-raux presents the animal's reaction to the threat of death. Lack-ing the intelligence to protect himself, the beast darts aimlessly about. His automatic, animal reaction is suicidal. The spectacle acquires its significance only when the reader recalls Möllberg's contention that universal human qualities exist only at the animal level. Taking this caricature of an animal reaction as a point of departure, Malraux offers his own refutation of Möllberg: man alone displays the urge to protect himself. The threat of a violent death calls forth the expression of the instinct that distinguishes man from animals.

The German soldiers advance across the fields to the Russian positions. Their humanity prevents them, however, from taking advantage of their evil weapon. Instead of following the orders to occupy the enemy positions, the first wave of attackers returns towards its own trenches carrying Russian gas victims. From his position of safety, Vincent Berger observes this drama of man resisting death. But he does not understand it. To get an explanation from the returning German soldiers, Vincent leaves his post. He finds a horse to carry him out into the miasma bathed in an eerie light.[21] When interpreted in the context of Malraux's previous images of light and darkness, the luminescence signals Vincent's approaching insight. The battleground becomes the stage for Vincent's discovery, which combines elements from Kassner's illuminated epiphany in *Days of Wrath* and Ximenez's revelation to Manuel in *Man's Hope.*

Vincent's horse cannot keep its footing, and he is thrown onto the slime to which the gas has reduced all vegetation. The lieutenant drops, literally and symbolically, to the level of the most lowly human fighting against death to give meaning to his life. There he gropes for an explanation of the soldiers' disobedience, an explanation which lies in a human nature obscured by Western culture. Only when Vincent's own cultural veneer is eroded is he able to find the explanation.

Proceeding on foot across the fields, the intelligence officer encounters several German soldiers bearing dying Russians to the German ambulances. To his questions about the attack, their response reveals only their scorn for the officer associated with the apocalypse and their fraternal concern for its victims. Vincent soon realizes that he has become as "mad" as the soldiers and discovers that he too "must find a Russian who hasn't been killed —any one will do, put him on his own shoulders and save him" (p. 233). The instinct to protect his fellowman against the inhuman forces of destruction has effaced national enmities and restored a fundamental human unity. Whatever sense of superiority he felt as he was listening to the banal conversations of the soldiers in the trenches has disappeared, and he acts only on the fraternal impulse to rescue the Russians.

Vincent's sense of brotherhood and that of the German soldiers contrast markedly with that of the revolutionaries in *Man's Hope*. For the Communists in Spain, fraternity united only comrades-in-arms sharing the same political goals. Because they found a redemption from the absurd in their identification with the course of history, they needed a victory: only victors determine the course of history. Their enemies stood between them and victory, and the revolutionaries spared no quarter to achieve it. Vincent understands, however, that history cannot be an antidestiny. He is looking for a different redemption, one which is revealed through human instincts. He allows himself to follow his instinctive sympathy and searches among the silent trenches for a Russian to rescue.

Seeing a group of bodies, he seizes one, aware but unconcerned that it was already dead: "This fraternal corpse . . . protected him like a shield against everything he was fleeing from" (p. 233). The futile gesture only serves to confirm Vincent's humanity. In the tragic world of *Man's Fate*, where there was no hope for human progress, such gestures alone seemed to preserve the dignity of Malraux's heroes. Vincent will not be the victim of tragedy that Kyo Gisors and Katow were. "He opened his arms: the corpse fell. He no longer needed to embrace a dead body in order to fight against inhumanity" (p. 235). He understands that there are more effective ways of denying what Walter Berger earlier called the nothingness of the human condition. Vincent's insight fills him with a sense of satisfaction that, even in the midst of the devastation wrought by the gas, finds an expression in laughter, not words. Then, picking up a living Russian, he joins the reverse "assault of pity" on the German first-aid stations. Back at his own lines, he recalls the vision of the walnut trees at Altenburg. Now, however, he is able to penetrate to the meaning of that lyrical moment.

While out on the battle field, he came to understand the inhuman evil of the cosmos. It appeared as "a mystery which did not reveal its secret, but only its presence, so simple and so despotic that it reduced to nothingness any thought linked to it—as the presence of death undoubtedly does" (p. 244). During the apocalyptic episode, he discovered the human instinct that gives life meaning even in the face of death and destruction. It combines an anguished resistance to death with the fraternity of sharing this anguish. The double instinct unites all men in a common effort to protect humanity against annihilation by an inhuman evil. Because these fundamental qualities transcend cultural boundaries, they constitute human universals. Such, at least, is the conclusion of the final scene of Vincent Berger's drama, a drama which repudiates Möllberg's contention that man is fundamentally undistinguishable from an animal. In the human instincts transmitted across the millenia to the German soldiers, Vincent Berger has discovered what distinguishes man from the animal—or to use the imagery of the title, what distinguishes the noble wood of the walnut trees from any baser wood.

The destruction of battle appears as that fundamental human condition which elicits the fundamental, instinctive response. The instincts that Vincent Berger rediscovers on the Vistula front provide the direction for all human endeavor. Within the framework of man's eternal struggle to rescue his life and that of his fellow man from annihilation, human enterprise can take on an eternal meaning. Aware of the conditions of his life and of the possibility of inscribing his acts into this eternal human struggle, the individual can find the religious comforts of participation in the universal. It can be found, Malraux demonstrates through his protagonist, without any self-delusion, without any act of faith or delusion concerning man's place in history or in the universe.

Participation in the universal life takes many forms, the most basic being the rescue of one's fellowman from destruction. According to Malraux, a comparable expression would be the creation of a culture which multiplies the possible expressions of this eternal struggle. When the most humble of human endeavors are viewed as elements of a culture, even the most humble builders, farmers, tradesmen, and artists should be able to find their place in the collective task of giving meaning to human existence. Such a view seems on the surface most egalitarian; but not all human enterprise shares the universality of an antidestiny. Some acts acquire only the meaning accorded by the civilization in which they are produced and thereby isolate the individual from the universal community of man. One example of such an enterprise would be Germany's role in World War I, inspired by a historical idealism traceable to Hegel, but which unquestionably grew upon the fertile ground of an awakened nineteenth-century German nationalism. Another would be the Communist Revolution predicated on European economic progress.

Malraux's view of antihistory, which has been only slightly modified by his more recent studies of painting and sculpture, takes man out of history, where human progress is possible, and places him in an immutable realm above its vicissitudes or evolution. The Malrauvian hero need no longer be the victim of an irrational flux of events as Garine, Perken and Kyo were; no longer does he look for a surrogate religion in a historical dialectic as Kassner and Manuel did. His lofty view of the human condition precludes any notion of progress or change in the fundamental human condition: man is able to provide only a succession of responses to an unalterable problem. From this perspective, politics loses its importance, and mankind is forever condemned, like Sisyphus, to repeat the same drama. The record of his responses ceases to be the history of successes and failures, but becomes an antihistory where no significant change is possible.[22]

Students and scholars of contemporary French literature have been wont to identify Malraux with the existentialist writers who became fashionable after World War II. It is true that he did, like Sartre, Camus, and others, concern himself with redefining the conditions of human existence in a universe from which God has apparently withdrawn. And like them, he refuses to resign himself to the absurdity of the human condition. But his works bear a metaphysical stamp lacking in the investigations of other agnostic existentialists. He persisted in searching for a basis for attaching human life to an eternal universal. Only when he rejects history in favor of an antihistory does he find a redemption from the senseless existence of the absurd. Since no future generation can progress beyond the state of our generation or any past generation, time will not erode our circumscribed struggles to give meaning to life. Malraux's antidestiny offers, then, not a way out of the tragic absurd, but a way of living with it without being reduced to despair and inaction.

Few people could take encouragement from this view of life. Few, however, feel the need to justify their actions in the name of a universal. Among agnostic philosophers, perhaps the seventeenth-century rationalist, Baruch de Spinoza, best anticipates Malraux's lofty concerns. In his inculcation to view all actions as existing "under a certain form of eternity," Spinoza had hoped to propose a precept that would spare man any spiritual torment. But when the individual judges his acts according to Spinoza's precepts, not only does he find solace for disappointment, but he is also obliged to view his achievements as insignificant. Spinoza's modest accommodation of what the modern European calls the absurd would, however, have sustained Vincent Berger had he survived the war. His exposure to the toxic phosgene appears fatal, but he does not look upon his existence as a vain absurdity, devoid of positive values.

In what can only be interpreted as an incongruous expression of hedonism, his spirit cries out against everything that "prevented him from being happy" (p. 245). Commentators have misunderstood Vincent's reaction: in the 1948 preface, Malraux admitted his intention to convey a psychological reaction to death. The development of the novel permits the careful reader to understand Vincent's reaction in such a light. For however fragile life may be and however shallow its values, Vincent continues to cherish life. His last moments lend an emotional confirmation to the values that he discovered intellectually just before his death.

Vincent Berger is the first Malrauvian exemplar to die since *Man's Fate.*[23] The example of his death contrasts significantly with those of Kyo and Katow, who faced death with stoic resignation. Awaiting their execution, they experienced no anguish, accepting stoically the tragedy of their existence. For them, brotherhood relieved their sense of isolation and provided the only comfort possible in a tragic world. In the face of inevitable execution by Chiang Kai-shek's soldiers, they felt no anguish; their acceptance of tragedy conveyed a message of futility—the opposite of the lesson provided by Vincent's death. As life ebbs

167

from his body, he realizes that there is yet more meaning to give to life. He has discovered the "fundamental," but his discovery only takes on meaning when it is translated into deeds. Still his life is not futile: his son is able to interpret his experience in reconstructing his memoirs. Through this artistic medium, young Berger gives his father's life its ultimate meaning, a meaning which Malraux implies should be superior to that which the individualistic soldier-adventurer, T. E. Lawrence, gave his life in *The Seven Pillars of Wisdom.*

9   BEYOND THE SEVEN
PILLARS OF WISDOM

$\mathcal{C}$OMPLETION of his father's biography does not end the task young Berger undertakes in the Chartres internment camp. He is different from Malraux's previous narrators, the anonymous admirer who registered Pierre Garine's story in *The Conquerors* and Claude Vannec, who reported on Perken's hapless enterprise in *The Royal Way*. They detailed the futile efforts of individualistic adventurers to resist an implacable destiny. The tragedies of Garine and Perken were not intended as exemplary responses to the absurd. Vincent Berger's adventure, on the other hand, brought him to a new understanding of the individual's place in the universe. If the discovery he made on the Vistula battlefield is to have any value, it must serve as an inspiration to the son who understood its significance.

The Conquerors and *The Royal Way* end with the deaths of the protagonists, but young Berger's narrative goes on. In the concluding portion of the novel, he replaces his father as the hero. Vincent Berger's spiritual itinerary is continued by his son, who enjoys the privilege of translating his father's discovery into deeds. It is this young tank commander in World War II who succeeds in drawing a meaning out of what his uncle, Walter Berger, called the "nothingness of human existence." Before that is possible, however, he must relive, some twenty-five years later, his father's First World War experiences. They provide the action in the concluding portion of the novel, the section which reveals how art replaces the Marxist view of history as the individual's link to the eternity of mankind.

The conclusion of *The Walnut Trees of Altenburg* is repeated in *Antimemoirs* (pp. 294–321). Of the first-person narrative attributed to young Berger, Malraux retained everything except

169

Malraux's Heroes and History

the two introductory paragraphs, which provide the transition from the World War I battleground in Poland to the beginnings of World War II in Flanders. He altered one passage of the novel somewhat to make it read more like an autobiography.[1] But otherwise, nothing prevents the reader from interpreting the fictional version as an account of Malraux's own experiences. Repetition of the text almost three decades later stands as a reaffirmation of the views initially attributed to young Berger. Nonetheless, the passage appears in dissimilar contexts, and the meaning it takes on at the conclusion of the novel does not correspond exactly to the meaning it holds within the body of the autobiographical work. Submerged within the *Antimemoirs,* the text clarifies but part of Malraux's life; at the end of the novel, however, it conveys the message of the entire work.

An Alsatian like his father, young Berger became French when his embattled province was restored to France after World War I. Also like his father, he is engaged in a technological war. The situation depicted is not so apocalyptic as the 1915 phosgene attack on the Vistula, but the conditions of battle equally dehumanize the adversary. In the bowels of a tank rumbling across the dark Flemish countryside, the narrator does not think of the enemy as the German soldiers on the other side of the battle lines but as the tank traps and the artillery trained upon them. The author intentionally suppresses the human intelligence behind these machines of destruction: he destroys thereby any impression of harmony between man and his world, depicting rather a world opposed to man and man made painfully aware of this opposition by the conditions of battle:

> Of the old accord between man and earth, nothing remains: this wheat that we're pitching and rolling across is not wheat, but camouflage; there are no cultivated fields, only fields of trenches and mines: and it seems that the tank charges all by itself towards some trap dug all by itself, that future forms of life begin tonight their own combat beyond the realm of human adventure (p. 269).

Malraux has been attacked for dehumanizing the battle by a critic who disregarded Malraux's intention to make war a meta-

Beyond the Seven Pillars of Wisdom

phor of the human condition,[2] a metaphor replacing the Pascalian prison of his earlier Oriental tragedies. Political realities and territorial ambitions have no place in the wars of Vincent Berger and his son. Nor do Malraux's soldiers engage a human enemy in battle. They struggle to give a meaning to life. Man's adversary is not another man, but a mechanical absurd, independent of man, that threatens to destroy him and all human values. And again the confrontation between man and the absurd takes place under the unfathomable darkness of the eternal sky.

Into the nocturnal battle against the inhuman enemy, the narrator leads the tank crew composed of a former pimp, a laborer, and a fire guard from a sleazy Paris nightclub. None of the four had volunteered for service in this war which appears so much more metaphysical than nationalistic. All are conscripts in the battle to wrest from the mechanical absurd a meaning for human existence.

Reflecting on the barracks squabbles of the past months, young Berger's thoughts allow the reader to see into the lives of his undistinguished crewmen. Recollections of their conversation reveal the banality of their concerns. Undifferentiated in their crudeness, they resemble the German soldiers who rescued the Russian phosgene victims along the Vistula front twenty-five years earlier. The French soldiers do not appear so selfless, but their actions confirm Vincent Berger's discovery that the individual is united to all of mankind in a common, instinctive opposition to death.

As they cross the German defenses, the products of their own military technology offer them little protection against the enemy. Their tank seems to be a vehicle of their destruction: it carries them into the enemy tank trap, where an artillery volley could destroy the tank and its crew. In the face of death, the crewmen forget the petty antagonisms that earlier separated them. Without a word of command being spoken, the four men cooperate in the agonizing struggle to bring the tank out of the pit. They then join the column advancing to what must have been one of the rare French victories of the brief 1940 campaign.

This escape from death is young Berger's own reprieve from destiny. It constitutes his rebirth. Like those of Kassner in *Days of Wrath* and of Vincent Berger, his is also accompanied by an illuminated revelation, but it is far more lyrical than either of the previous ones. The light is that of the dawn that awakens the Flemish hamlet where the tank crew has spent the night.

Under the dazzling morning sun, young Berger inventories the farm animals and primitive agricultural tools that attest to the unchanging nature of man. Familiar though this ageless setting may be, he takes in the scene with "the eyes of a foreigner." It is possible to recognize in the sense of alienation Malraux attributes to his spiritually reborn character the preparation for a higher understanding. To the atheistic narrator, this experience takes on the force of a religious revelation. He associates it with the birth of Christ, which, in Christian tradition, marks a new relation between man and the world. The revelation received by young Berger is, however, far more modest than the promise of eternal salvation that Christ holds out to his followers, but it is no less inspiring to Malraux's hero. The difference is signaled by a fleeting reference to the three Wise Men. In 1940, the Magi would not bring a gift; they would simply say that the doors that formerly hid from view any understanding of man's place in the universe are now open; they would reveal no mystery nor announce the consummation of any prophecy. Rather, they would encourage man to discover a new relation between himself and his universe. During this lyrical moment, young Berger appears to accept what he has interpreted as the modern gift of the Magi: in this incongruously tranquil setting, he finds the basis for a new harmony between man and the cosmos. This is what his experience at the beginning of World War II adds to the adventure of his father.

All about him, young Berger finds the stamp of human ingenuity. He sees that man has created tools, houses, and gardens—that he has given form to the chaos of nature. Focusing his attention on human accomplishment, the young tank commander discovers that man has created an accord between himself and his world, an accord he was not aware of the night before as he led his men into battle. In a few hours, he has evolved from the tormented state of the Oriental adventurer to that of the European activist. With his rebirth, he has left the domain of the absurd and entered a realm where man no longer appears as a victim of history's adversity. But unlike Kassner and the heroes of *Man's Hope,* young Berger does not find a redeption from the absurd in the Marxist dialectic or in the exaltation of action: it is through the creation of works which satisfy man's age-old religious yearning for a harmony with his universe that he finds his salvation. The products of one's intelligence, he discovers, permit the artist to restore to man a sense of integration into the eternal, an integration not disrupted by fears of death. The artist is, of course, unable to recreate the harmony offered by Christianity or Eastern religions. But through works of enduring formal beauty, Malraux implies, the artist can inscribe his actions in the universal "eternity of man." He cannot recover the comforts of a personal eternal salvation; but, through his art, he comes as close as possible to reconstituting man's divinely ordained place in the universe, the nostalgic aspiration of Europeans since they lost their faith.

Young Berger does not express Malraux's esthetics in any systematic fashion. This passage is far too lyrical to constitute an explanation of the function of art. It is nonetheless consistent with the judgments Vincent Berger made on art in general and literature more specifically at the Altenburg colloquium.[3] There, his observations were not carried to a climax. They were abruptly terminated as Walter Berger closed the debates. That inconclusive presentation stands, however, as the preparation and explanation of this final scene of the novel. Here young Berger has the privilege of carrying his father's speculations to their conclusion.

For having postponed the resolution of the Altenburg debates to the conclusion of his book, Malraux deserves to be criticized. This fragmentation lends an incoherence to the novel. Perhaps his intention to correct this fault explains his prefatory remark about the extensive revisions he planned but never completed. Still, behind this break in development lies Malraux's intention to give a religious dimension to art. In order for art to be seen as an "antidestiny," it was necessary to take it out of the arid, intellectual atmosphere of the colloquium where "ideas only gave birth to other ideas" and where action has no place. Its force must be demonstrated in circumstances where death poses its awesome menace. So it is that, on the morning following his

surprising escape from the German tank trap, young Berger recalls Pascal's image of the human condition. He refuses to allow
his joyous rebirth to be corrupted by this somber picture of the
death of man without God:

> Perhaps anguish is always the strongest; perhaps it is
> contaminated from the beginning, that joy given to the only
> animal that knows he is not immortal. But this morning, I
> am pure rebirth . . . and, as I saw the night . . . surge forth
> from that pit, there now rises out of that night the
> miraculous revelation of the day (pp. 289–90).

Young Berger's sense of exaltation is explained by his insight
into art as an attachment to the whole of mankind across the ages,
the attachment Malraux's political activists found in the Marxist
concept of history. But instead of restricting the individual to his
own culture and isolating him from other societies, art permits
man to share the unchanging metaphysical or religious concerns
that, for Malraux, are the qualities that define humanity. Through
the example of his last fictional hero, Malraux illustrates the most
effective link between the individual and eternity. With young
Berger, he returns to a theme announced in the early *The Temptation of the West* but then postponed while different sorts of historical redemption from the absurd were being investigated.

The conclusion of *The Walnut Trees of Altenburg* thus resolves
after a delay of two decades the existential problems raised by
Malraux in his first fully developed work of fiction. It illustrates
how art satisfies the European's religious aspirations to give his
life a meaning which cannot be destroyed by death. By postpon-
ing this view of art to the end of his novel, Malraux is able to cast
it in a religious framework. But he also draws a structural advantage out of allowing his narrator to continue Vincent Berger's
spiritual odyssey in the somewhat artificially postponed climax.
Young Berger can be seen to put his insight to work by continuing his own adventure beyond the last pages of the novel.

Like Kassner, who was sent out into the streets of Prague by
his illumination, Malraux's first artist-hero is driven to translate
his understanding into a work of art. He makes his father's adven-

tures and then his own experiences his subject: he writes the novel we have just read, the conclusion of which prepares the prologue, set, at the latest, only a few weeks later in the internment camp at Chartres. Like Proust's *Remembrance of Things Past,* the work takes on a circular quality. To appreciate its meaning fully, Malraux's brief novel must be reread. Because of its density, it is a task worth undertaking—and it is at least as rewarding as a second reading of Proust's massive opus. The second reading of the narrator's prologue reveals, first of all, that once again Malraux is using the prison as a metaphor of the absurd human condition. Young Berger's efforts to tell his story cease, then, to be merely a prison occupation undertaken to while away the hours of boredom. It represents the recourse to art to wrest a meaning out of an existence when all other actions are reduced to futility. His book aims at what is universal in the human experience and receives the author's endorsement for attaching the individual to the whole of mankind across the ages.

To anchor human values in art as Malraux does is elitist in the extreme. Few individuals feel impelled to judge their acts from such a lofty perspective; few could be the artists who might hope for redemption from the absurd. But for all his protestations of brotherhood, Malraux was never egalitarian. Even in his communistic works, the brotherhood that linked men in revolutionary battle afforded only the leaders a redemption from the absurd. Then, in *The Walnut Trees of Altenburg,* Vincent Berger had rejected the equality of men before he discovered the instinct of fraternity. After discussing his uncle's concept of man as a pile of secrets, he remarked, "in the matter of what is secret, men are a little too easily equal" (p. 90). The fraternity that he later discovered on the Polish battlefield bound men together in a mutual struggle, but, as the experience of his son now illustrates, not as equals. There is a hierarchy of responses, the highest being that of the person able to understand the absurd and able to engage in an activity of transcending value. It is impossible to imagine that the consumer of an artist's creation enjoys the same participation in the universal as the artist.

His elitist view of human values notwithstanding, Malraux continues to write of the importance of human fraternity. Its importance in his hierarchy of values is not at once evident. But for the artist's creation to acquire any universal value, he must write, paint, or sculpt as a spokesman for mankind. Consequently it is necessary that he feel a common bond with those less articulate or less understanding than he. While the artist may feel but little sympathy for the ignorant, he is at least able to recognize in their incoherent expressions a shared anxiety to which he is able to give expression.

It is in terms of an abstract, historical human collectivity that Malraux views art. And fraternity is the abstraction in whose name the artist works. It justifies art by conferring upon it a universality. Malraux's fraternal attachment to his fellowman—or more precisely that of his characters—is more of an intellectual deduction than an automatic emotional response. And it cannot be said that he depicts his secondary characters as being interesting in themselves. They are interesting for what they reveal about mankind in general. Curiosity about human nature underlies Malraux's fictional inquiries, but there is in his works little of the sympathy or respect for the individual that characterizes the novels of an Albert Camus. One of the rare exceptions is the almost tender representation of the old couple encountered in the Flemish village.

It is only after having understood how the creation of formal beauty restores harmony with the universe that human beings enter into young Berger's thoughts. Up until then the works that have given meaning to life were the products of "the old race of man," of that abstraction called mankind whose existence is evidenced by such humble inventions as the watering can. Then his vision brings the aged couple into the inventory. Undoubtedly, these old peasants have had their part in imposing a form on this Flemish landscape. But this is not their principal function in the novel: they exemplify for young Berger a calm acceptance of the human condition.

Listening in on a brief conversation between one of his crewmen and the peasants, seemingly unconcerned about the course of the war, he overhears the former laborer Pradé inquire idly, "Well, gramps, you getting warm?" It is the old woman who

responds that she and her husband have nothing left to do but
sun themselves. She adds, "When you're old, there's nothing left
but wearing out" (p. 291). Young Berger interprets this remark
as evidence of her reconciliation to aging and dying, the sort of
placid reconciliation to be enjoyed by the artist and the inventor
confident of their place in the eternity of man. For them, as for
the peasant couple, the world's political events have scant importance. They have placed their lives outside the sphere of history
and in the realm of antihistory. The narrator adds a final lyrical
impression that shows the old woman to be

> . . . propped up against the cosmos like a rock. . . . She
> smiles, nonetheless, a slow, delayed, reflective smile: beyond
> the soccer field with its lonely goals, beyond the turrets of
> the tanks glistening with dew like the branches that
> camouflage them, she appears to look into the distance at
> death with indulgence, and even—oh, mysterious wink; oh,
> sharp shadow from the edge of eyelids—with irony (p. 291).

The narrator's sympathy for the old couple content to sun
themselves in the face of imminent destruction is misleading.
Although he admires the old peasants, he is nonetheless aware
that their "ironic winking at death" falls short of being a redemption from the absurd. They resign themselves too easily to dying.
Still, they confirm young Berger's new hope that a reconciliation
between man and the universe is possible, and they stand thereby
as human counterparts of the symbolic walnut trees of the title.
But where these peasants illustrate only a calm resignation to the
human condition, Malraux's narrator experiences a mystical exaltation. It comes from his discovery of the secret of art, identified
as a divine secret in the concluding lines of the novel:

> I now understand the meaning of the ancient myths of
> beings rescued from the dead. I scarcely remember the
> terror: what I am carrying within myself is the discovery of
> a simple but sacred secret. Perhaps this is how God looked
> at the first man (p. 291).

Malraux's Heroes and History

The young tank commander feels himself elevated above ordinary man by his "secret" insight. In the framework of this post-Christian revelation, the secret is, first, the rediscovered, antihistorical harmony between man and his world and, second, the narrator's own role in translating his insight. While he cannot aspire to the divine function of creating life or even, like the Greek gods, of mediating destiny, he can interpret the meaning of life. He will assume the role of the ancient authors of tragedy, at least insofar as his father defined it during the Altenburg colloquium: he will "possess his destiny," rather than blindly submit to it or delude himself into thinking that he might escape it. He will inscribe his work in the universal tradition of the Greek tragedy and enjoy the first privilege of the artist, that of participation in the universal struggle of man to wrest his life from nothingness by his own creative effort. In an art that restores to man his forgotten sense of harmony with the world, he will find his own antidestiny and satisfy what Malraux has since identified as the intellectual's totalitarian need.[4]

In the last pages of the novel, the resolution of this theme is handicapped not only by Malraux's characteristically elliptical style, but by the additional burdens of a religious lyricism and an intentionally fragmented development. The obscurity of the conclusion led early critics to suppose that the novel was incomplete and that the conclusion lay in the two portions supposedly destroyed by the Gestapo. The circularity revealed by a rereading proves that *The Walnut Trees of Altenburg* is complete.[5] Perhaps it was as much to correct the flaws that gave way to such impressions as to complete the last two portions of his trilogy that Malraux returned to "The Struggle with the Angel." Nothing yet published, however, confirms Malraux's announced intention of carrying his fiction beyond the point of describing the metaphysical force of art. After the Liberation, he devoted his efforts to investigating what is eternal in painting and sculpture: once he had determined through his own fictional art what his place in the universe must be, he set about chronicling the religious quest of the generations of artists that preceded him. What he found in the plastic arts is what the reader can find in Malraux's fiction in general and, in a highly condensed form, in his last novel.

Beyond the Seven Pillars of Wisdom

Had Malraux's public life not become identified with Gaullism during the Fifth Republic, he might have ended his literary career as an art historian. In that case, the story of the Berger family would have been, as one critic indicated, the bridge between the two phases of his career.[6] Now it is possible to see that it has three phases, the third being the period of service as Minister of Culture during Charles de Gaulle's presidency. *The Walnut Trees of Altenburg* remains, nonetheless, the transitional work. It serves a second time in the *Antimemoirs,* Malraux's autobiographical essay dealing principally with his career in politics. The same work leads into his account of service to the state after having first opened onto art. How this is done is worth some attention.

For his autobiography, Malraux has retained those portions of Vincent's story that took place in Alsace in 1913. He has reduced to a fleeting reference the long flashback which recounts Vincent Berger's Turkish adventure. What is retained gains from a regular chronology, but it is impossible to see the similarity between Vincent Berger and T. E. Lawrence—perhaps Malraux wished to do away with the resemblance. What remains is a character searching for a definition of man, but rejecting both the traditional European definitions and Möllberg's resignation to the absurd. Discovery of fundamental, human instincts does not come on the battlefields of World War I. The scene in which Vincent discovers the foundations of an antidestiny and, coincidentally, finds his death is replaced by Malraux's own adventures. The sentence, "Here I expect to meet only art and death" (*Antimemoirs,* p. 51) announces that the figure initially inspired by Lawrence of Arabia gives way to the author himself and that the remaining adventures are no longer fictional. The rest of the book becomes Malraux's own *Seven Pillars of Wisdom,* the autobiography that, unlike Lawrence, he attempted to place out of the reach of time.

In his brief study of *Seven Pillars of Wisdom,*[7] Malraux addresses himself principally to Lawrence's shortcomings—his misconceptions of man's place in history which Malraux sought to rectify through his own conception of Vincent Berger. Specifically, he criticizes Lawrence for believing in an absolute standard of heroism against which he hoped to measure his personal achievement. Consequently, according to Malraux, the British officer counted his failure to create a viable spirit of Arab nationalism as a personal inadequacy. His autobiography then became the record of this disappointment projected against the background of the Arab campaign against the Turks. The book in turn fails, in Malraux's judgment, to attain the stature Lawrence intended for it. For the French novelist, *Seven Pillars of Wisdom* is scarcely more significant than the memoirs that any retired officer might have written. Had Lawrence understood, as did Malraux and Vincent Berger, that his military failure revealed only the absurd emptiness of human experience, his autobiography might have stood as an indictment of the gods: "A man's own lucid self-portrait—if there were in the world a single man lucid enough to recount his own life—would be the most virulent indictment of the gods which could be imagined; as great as the man himself is great" ("Lawrence," p. 527).

Accompanying this criticism is Malraux's admiration for the view of art conveyed by *Seven Pillars of Wisdom,* the view that art is the ally of man in his struggle against his fate. According to Malraux, Lawrence did not believe in history but in art. Lawrence presumably hoped that the literary art of autobiography would confer upon him the immortality that history withheld. Reconstructing his adventures during the composition of his memoirs, Lawrence must have analyzed his deeds in search of an understanding of himself. His quest then would have taken place on a a higher plane than the war. What he contributed to the course of the war or how the war figured into the history of mankind, according to Malraux's own analysis of Lawrence, counts for less than the literary work that it nourished. But, since his autobiography aims at an impossible, personal immortality, Lawrence does not come to grips with the existential problems facing Western man. Consequently, his account of the war in the Middle East fails Malraux's test of the work of art.

Malraux's appreciation of the *Seven Pillars of Wisdom* can be easily contested. It would be generous, for instance, to qualify his assessment of Lawrence's religious background as inaccurate. But it is of but secondary interest to test the validity of Malraux's observations. His brief study on Lawrence is important not for its comments on the British adventurer but for what it reveals about the French novelist's view of history. It stands as confirmation of the less explicit views of antihistory drawn from his fiction. Although he withholds from Lawrence's autobiography the praise due to a true masterpiece, Malraux does endorse the view of art he finds in it. But he differs with the British adventurer over the importance of the work of art to rescue human existence from the absurd. Malraux's criticism of Lawrence for overlooking the absurd stands as the source of *The Walnut Trees of Altenburg*. This novel can be seen as the corrective of Lawrence's "memoirs," a sort of revision clearly based on a character modeled after the British intelligence officer.

The fictional quest of Vincent Berger, then that of his son, is anchored in an absurd disregarded by Lawrence, too characteristically Anglo-Saxon to be tormented by such metaphysical concerns. The portraits of the two Alsatian soldiers thus becomes the "virulent indictment of the gods" that Lawrence failed to produce. Then, by later annexing his own life to that of the character inspired by T. E. Lawrence, he casts his own adventures in that metaphysical dimension that eluded the British adventurer. He avoids anything that limits the scope of his experiences to French politics. Rather than write "memoirs" that, like a destiny, would identify his role with a moment in history, he composes his *Antimemoirs* so that his life can be placed in the realm of antihistory and exemplify an antidestiny. But this effort does not deprive Malraux's life of its adventure. Not only do his adventures appear every bit as romantic as Lawrence's, they also aspire more successfully to that timelessness that, according to Malraux's hopes, should spare them any erosion by history. With his *Antimemoirs*, the French novelist-adventurer-statesman challenges Lawrence's unique place in history.[8] While he certainly warrants a comparable acclaim for his literary accomplishments alone, his participation in antifascist movements, the Spanish Civil War, the Resistance, and the two de Gaulle governments can only reinforce his place among those of us who continue to count history as important.

10 SOULS WITHOUT GOD OR CHRIST

$\mathcal{W}$HETHER it is expressed in fiction, art history, or autobiography, Malraux's thought is characterized, as one scholar has observed, by a "frightening consistency."[1] It was noted first by his early critics, who found throughout his works a literary translation of his own quest for a religion to replace a moribund European Christianity. For them, the change in Malraux's views involved principally an elaboration of metaphysical and esthetic themes announced in his earliest fiction. While it is true that he has repeatedly raised the same questions about man's place in the cosmos, he has found different answers at different moments of his career. What has properly been considered his elaboration of a metaphysics and an esthetics rests on changing concepts of history. His historical concepts have been so divergent that they constitute the major "inconsistency" in what is otherwise a unified literary production.

Some recent critics of Malraux, writing from a political rather than an existentialistic perspective, have observed this evolution. They, however, studied his novels as a view of the individual's role in society, disregarding the metaphysical urge that drove the characters to search for a meaning to life that death could not destroy. The key to understanding Malraux's fiction lies in a combination of the two views. Because each successive step in Malraux's elaboration of his basic themes presents the individual in a different relation to history, a fuller appreciation of his novels requires the understanding of how his heroes satisfy their religious needs in the political action which makes history happen.

By way of recapitulation, it has been possible to observe three distinct views of history in Malraux's seven works of fiction. The tragic concept of history infused the works dating from 1926 to

183

Malraux's Heroes and History

1933. The books of this period, starting with *The Temptation of the West* and going to *Man's Fate,* all deal with Oriental subjects. In them, Malraux represents the feeble attempts of the European to satisfy his yearning for personal glory and immortality. From the perspective of the individual who sets himself against his fellow-man, history has only the direction which, presumably, the conquerors give it. But Malraux's fiction admits no conquerors, only victims. Thus history appears unresponsive to the will of his characters, and historical events have no direction, except that they inevitably turn against the characters and destroy them. At their defeat, the efforts of Malraux's individualistic characters are seen to have been futile. Determined though they may be, they are too frail to turn history to their own ends. History cannot satisfy the spiritual needs the European has inherited from his individualistic culture. Rather than offer a redemption from the absurd, history—or better politics, the level at which the individual participates in history—becomes the instrument by which the tragedy of the human condition is communicated to the European avidly trying to preserve his own soul. Malraux's first two novels, *The Conquerors* and *The Royal Way,* illustrate the tragedy of Western man. In *Man's Fate,* his third and, by all acclaim, his most successful work, he represented a heroic accommodation of tragedy. History remains no less perverse and no less independent of human will, but Malraux's communist revolutionary casts aside the Western urge to dominate. Even in the defeat of the Communists in the 1927 Shanghai uprisings, he finds a satisfaction in virile fraternity. In spite of his defeat, Kyo Gisors draws a comfort from his political activism but only because he does not look for the justification of his life in a success that history still does not permit.

This representation of a broken revolt closed the first cycle of Malraux's fiction. The resignation to failure that it conveyed would not long remain his picture of man in history. Once he began treating European subjects, he showed himself more optimistic about man's ability to influence events. *Days of Wrath,* published in 1935, and *Man's Hope,* which followed two years later, are built largely upon the dialectical concept of history as an organized succession of events fostered by man's will. Al-

184

though rejecting Marxist economic determinism, Malraux accepted the notion of a "metahistory." Within its scope, his revolutionaries found the religious comforts that come from inscribing their actions in a great, unending continuum.

A humanitarian concern for their fellowman brought Kassner, Manuel, and Magnin into the antifascist struggles in Germany and Spain. Like Kyo before them, they fought for a goal higher than the one envisioned by the self-centered individualist. But they gained the victories that historical adversity withheld from Kyo. They are fictional victories to be sure: fascist victories in Germany and Spain in the 1930s show that victory still lay beyond the grasp of the revolutionary. Malraux had, however, become more optimistic about the European's place in history and infused his revolutionary heroes with his optimism. They would not gain the personal conquest that would stand as an indestructible monument to their own existence, but by committing themselves to a collective victory, they discovered that they were able to influence history. In so doing, they sacrificed the individuality that, for Christians, was represented by a personal soul, but they found their place in the eternal collective soul of mankind that aspires to social justice for all. Their discovery was accompanied by what can only be described as a religious exaltation.

With these political novels, Malraux's characters left the world of tragedy and entered a domain where a new view of man's role in history offered a sense of attachment to the only universal value man could know. He did not find there the redemption from death nor the communion with the cosmos that the Christian European once enjoyed, but he did recover the more modest joys of earning through his own willful efforts an attachment to the social evolution that began long before his life and would continue long after his death.

This dialectical view of history did not stand long, however, as a surrogate for Christianity. In the political turmoil that followed the Spanish Civil War and preceded World War II may very well lie the explanation of Malraux's apostasy. Within a few months of the 1940 Franco-German armistice, he was already at work on the novel in which he would repudiate the historical dialectic. He ceased to view it as a link between all mankind across the ages of

Malraux's Heroes and History

history. Societies, he observed through the characters of his last novel, evolve in different directions. Identification with the evolution of one's own society could only lead to an isolation from the rest of humanity. Still, Malraux insisted, there is a universal struggle in which the individual can earn a place in the eternity of mankind. It is the unending fraternal struggle to give meaning to human existence, and it is waged not in the political arena where social evolution is decided but on a loftier plane where life is attacked by an unalterable absurd. Here, it is necessary to note, the conditions of the struggle never change. There can be no progress nor any historical evolution where human endeavor is elevated to a metaphysical domain. With *The Walnut Trees of Altenburg,* Malraux's heroes leave history to enter this static realm of "antihistory." There political events lose their significance, and as Malraux indicates in his last work of fiction, art allows the creative individual to participate in the immutable human condition. Through his craft, the artist expresses what is eternal in man. Because it places his existence out of reach of the ravages of time, art affords the spiritual comforts of an "antidestiny." Even though Malraux's artist does not find the immortality sought by Proust or earlier generations of romantics, even though the satisfaction of influencing history is withheld from him, he finds another comfort in his art: the sense of participation in the eternal that Malraux earlier identified with communist revolutionaries of *Days of Wrath* and *Man's Hope.*

After World War II, Malraux announced several times his intentions to continue the fictional triptych of which *The Walnut Trees of Altenburg* was intended as the first part. Over the past three decades, however, nothing he has published confirms that work on the projected "Struggle with the Angel" has actually progressed very far. It was only in the often controversial studies of painting and sculpture that he gave further development to the metaphysical dimensions of art. In them he identified, a decade after the publication of his last novel, the artist's special redemption from the absurd as an "antidestiny."

Because it permits the artist to recover an Oriental sense of integration with the universe, Malraux's concept of antidestiny draws much from the Confucianist world view sketched in *The*

186

Souls Without God or Christ

Temptation of the West. In that dense epistolary work, the identification with the cosmos was sketched as the religious aspiration not only of the Chinese intellectual but also of his European correspondent. A recent scholar, sensitive to the evolution of Malraux's thought, proposed that with the completion of his last novel he had come full cycle: he resolved the metaphysical problem that underlay all his fiction.[2] And, so far as Malrauvian metaphysics is concerned, this assessment is quite sound. But it fails to take into account the reasons for Malraux's initial rejection of the Oriental concept of the personality dissolved in a vast, undifferentiated flux of time.

Malraux, like so many of his European contemporaries, found that attachment to the personality was far stronger than his religious desire for a spiritual identification with the cosmos. The typically Western yearning to assert one's own personality led Europeans, and Malraux with them, into an absurdist sense of cosmic alienation that, for all its torment, proved preferable to the abdication of the self or its dissolution in the cosmos. But he did not renounce, as did Camus and Sartre, the yearning fostered by Christianity for a reconciliation of the individual and the universe.[3] Malraux translated this hope into his fiction. His novels thus record his investigation of the value of human action. And in the universe from which God had withdrawn—the absurd universe of Malraux's fiction—history replaced religion as the proper domain of human endeavor. His novels record successive definitions of history as his characters act on first one concept of it and then another in their attempts to give their lives a transcending value.

The evolution to which Malraux's fiction attests is not only one of changing concepts of history, but one of the changing role of the individual in history. In each of his three stages of evolution, there is a specific view of what man must do to find a redemption: each view of history yields an ethical code that restores to the hero a religious sense of communion with his fellowman. This continuous inquiry into Gisors's question, "what to do with a soul when there is neither God nor Christ," constitutes an evolution parallel to that of Malraux's views of history. It is this inquiry that inspired the evolution of Malraux's fiction, and because of its importance, his successive responses to Gisors's question serve as a suitable conclusion to a study of Malraux's heroes and history.

Of the three heroes of Malraux's Oriental period, only the third enjoys a redemption from the absurd. The first two protagonists, Garine of *The Conquerors* and Perken of *The Royal Way*, both fall victim to history's adversity. Garine's political authority is wrested from him; without his Pascalian "distraction" from the absurd, he is forced to recognize the emptiness of his life. Perken's anachronistic hope for a history-book immortality is dashed by the progress brought by French colonization and industrialization of Indochina. Even Kyo of *Man's Fate* is defeated by historical forces beyond his control, but through him, Malraux has developed a concept of action which turns political failure into success.

When action is doomed in advance to failure, results alone cannot justify a person's life. Where the goal is out of reach, efforts replace results in weighing human worth. In the foreboding Orient of the 1920s, Kyo's actions offer better testimony to his *being* than any summation of his accomplishments, which he speaks of as his "biography."

One should not suppose that, by substituting *being* for *doing*, Malraux devaluates action. Quite to the contrary, he gives it greater emphasis by making it, rather than the progress it should lead to, the index to human value. It is a case of substituting the means for the goal. Thus, Kyo is spared the necessity of establishing a social order based on dignity and justice. To realize whatever success is permitted by the tragic absurd, it is enough that the individual work in the cause of dignity and justice.

Although such a reorientation of values might be criticized as a defeatism, Malraux successfully avoids that judgment. He poses the moral problems on subjective rather than on social terms. The value of Kyo's action is gauged in terms of his own satisfaction. He is made to look for them first in his wife's love, a love earned through his heroism; then he finds it in the fraternal bonds forged in the struggle he shared with other revolutionaries. His activism is sustained to his death by the personal satisfactions that accompany it. And, until old Gisors casts his judgment on Kyo's death, Malraux introduces no other criterion which might discredit his hero's example. And even Kyo's aged father fails to judge his son on historical terms. At the conclusion of the novel, his fruitless activism stands as a valid compromise with the two forces that threaten the individual, the absurd and the malevolence of history. It appears as the only satisfactory response, short of old Gisors's withdrawl into opium. And, like other responses that Malraux endorses, its final expression is cast in the religious aura that makes it appear to be the most exalted action man can perform.

The grace of political martyrdom could hardly have inspired the European determined to improve the lot of his fellowmen. No Communist could have found compensation for failure in brotherhood. And, although Malraux was to remain outside the party, he nonetheless chose Communists for heroes of the first two novels he set in Europe. For them to be credible, he had to attribute to them an ethics consonant with the Marxist view of history in which they found a redemption from the absurd. If social history was to have a direction, that direction must be imparted by the efforts of those working to change society. But change would only come through a series of victories through which, in Malraux's own words, "the order struggling to be born" gradually replaces the established order.

Like communist ideologues, Malraux came to accept the Marxist notion that defeat lends no direction to history. For Malraux, composing *Days of Wrath* and *Man's Hope* in the optimistic days before the communist defeats, fascism stood as the opposition against which victories must be won. Political or revolutionary success inscribed the efforts of Kassner, Manuel, Garcia, and Magnin in the historical "eternity of mankind," which, in the words of Raymond Aron, became "the opium of the intellectuals." For their political commitment to stand as a surrogate religion, everything had to be sacrificed to victory: the respect for human dignity that attracted Malraux's intellectual heroes to the Revolution had to be suspended in the name of military efficiency. But that sacrifice was easily made by those who sought a justification for their lives in the struggle for fraternity and dignity—far more easily than by those like Kyo for whom the goals of the struggle remained fraternity and dignity.[4]

This view of man's function in history, spelled out by Garcia and illustrated by his communist comrades-in-arms in *Man's Hope*, is only implicit in *Days of Wrath*. In the conclusion of that 1935 novel, Kassner undergoes the religious experience in which his place in history is revealed to him. Malraux's conception of the novel prevented him from investigating fully the implications of the metaphysical discovery made by his German revolutionary. They were not developed until three years later in the longer novel depicting the Spanish phase of the conflict against fascism. *Man's Hope* explains the meaning of the truncated conclusion of the novel that first presented the historical dialectic as a surrogate religion. But to understand Malraux's priorities, it is essential to note that Malraux presented the Marxist view of history as the basis of a personal satisfaction before he derived from it a code of political activism. And although the Communists he projects into the Spanish Civil War begin to act according to the imperatives of victory before discovering the religious force of the dialectic, this discovery climaxes the adventures of Manuel and Magnin, the principal characters of this vast revolutionary fresco.

In each of the first two stages of his evolution, redemption from the absurd comes from an identification with the human condition—the opposite of Perken's resistance to it and something more than Garine's resignation. In his Oriental novels, the human condition was tragedy; in the Communist novels, it was progress. With his last novel, Malraux repudiated the Western notion of progress fostered by human endeavor. He came to see man's fate as the unalterable, common resistance to death. He was faced, then, with the problem of giving human effort a value when no change in the fundamental state of mankind is possible. He determined that the only way to reconcile action and permanence was through the artistic representation of the human condition. Art allowed man's actions to acquire a permanent value: it alone permitted the thinking man to avoid the pitfalls of delusion or inertia that deprived human existence of its meaning.

Souls Without God or Christ

But just as Malraux saw during his Marxist stage that there were meaningless directions to the political activism, so does he suggest that certain modes of artistic expression are inconsequential.[5] He reserves his approval for the artist who comes to grips with man's universal struggle and transposes it into his art. Only such an artist succeeds in conferring upon his actions that "sacred" element that spares him the torment of cosmic alienation.

Malraux interpreted this metaphysical art as the wedding of the human urge—or perhaps, more restrictively, the European urge —to impose one's will on the world and of his religious aspiration to give his existence an eternal value. For the author of *The Walnut Trees of Altenburg,* this marriage of the self and the universe stood as the highest achievement of man abandoned by God and Christ. And with such lofty aspirations, it is understandable that the Malrauvian hero-artist should view his fellowmen more as the means of attaining his own salvation than as partners in a common struggle. In spite of his fictional protestations to the contrary, Malraux's heart goes out to those tormented intellectuals capable of creating their own accord with the universe. Those who sympathized with Clara Malraux's account of her turbulent marriage or with her accusations of misogyny might well have anticipated that André Malraux's urge to greatness was anything but egalitarian or fraternal.

Throughout his career as a novelist, a career limited to a period of two decades, Malraux continually posed the same problems. And, because his novels continually reveal his persistent search for a new secular religion capable of resolving the absurd, his novels do attest to the surprising consistency claimed by the first Malraux scholars. Still, a chronological study of his fiction reveals that salvation came through succession of three religions, each markedly different from the other. Each of the faiths is anchored in a different view of history and of the individual's role in history: while they lead to the same redemption, they involve different codes of historical "morality." The souls who are saved by one historical religion are condemned by the succeeding one. Thus, a Kyo is censured by proxy in *Man's Hope;* Manuel, by *The Walnut*

191

Malraux's Heroes and History

Trees of Altenburg. The art studies of the forties and fifties, however, provided a further endorsement of young Berger's view of the artist's place in history.

So long as Malraux holds that art alone expresses the eternal, his paradise will be restricted to artists such as his last fictional hero and those acknowledged and unknown painters and sculptors praised in *The Voices of Silence* and *The Metamorphosis of the Gods.* But already the first volume of his autobiography points to a fourth stage in his evolution, one in which political service becomes an "antidestiny." The continuation of his *Antimemoirs, Felled Oaks (Les chênes qu'on abat),* [6] accords deGaulle a privileged place in his pantheon, a place as exalted as that of Goya, the anonymous sculptors of the Strasbourg Cathedral portals, or, more recently, Picasso in *The Obsidian Head (La tête d'obsidienne).* [7] If there is to be a fourth stage, it will be detailed only in the subsequent installments of *Antimemoirs* or, as Malraux now prefers, *The Mirror of Limbo.* Their representation of man's place in history will most assuredly be drawn after Malraux's own experiences in politics, war, and literature. Malraux will be his own last hero if, indeed, he has not always been.

NOTES

CHAPTER TWO

1. Clara Malraux, *Memoirs* (New York: Farrar, Straus & Giroux, 1967), pp. 193–94, p. 221, and pp. 343–44.

2. Robert Payne, *A Portrait of André Malraux* (Englewood Cliffs, N.J.: Prentice-Hall, 1970), pp. 12–15.

3. *Lunes en papier* (Paris: Editions de la Galerie Simon, 1921).

4. *Oeuvres complètes* (Geneva: Skira, 1945). The seven volumes of this collection contain, besides the two short tales dating from 1921 and 1928, all of Malraux's novels. The reedition *Oeuvres* (Paris: Gallimard, 1970) does not contain Malraux's 1935 novel *Temps du mépris* nor the 1943 *Noyers de l'Altenburg*. The short fictional works were excluded from a 1951 collection published by Gallimard under the title *Romans*.

5. "Journal d'un pompier du jeu de massacre," in *Signaux de France et de Belgique*, 4 (août 1921); and two extracts of "Ecrit pour une idiole à trompe" were published in *Accords*, 3 (octobre 1924) and 4 (novembre 1924); "Ecrit pour un ours en peluche" was published in the review *900*, 4 (été 1927).

6. *Royaume-farfelu* (Paris: Gallimard, 1928).

7. Walter Langlois, *André Malraux: The Indochina Adventure* (New York: Praeger, 1966). This is the best source for Malraux's early political activity. His view is that Malraux did remain politically active after his return to Paris. Langlois shows, however, that from the time of his return to France to the 1933 publication of *Man's Fate*, Malraux wrote no further political commentaries. Documentation on any other political activity during the period 1926–1933 is sparse and mostly conjectural. See Langlois, pp. 200–201 and p. 213. Jean Lacouture, *André Malraux, une vie dans le siècle* (Paris: Seuil, 1973), seconds my interpretation; see pp. 126–27.

8. To my knowledge, this essay has never been translated. It was first published as "D'une jeunesse européenne," in *Ecrits* (Paris: Grasset, 1927), pp. 129–54. It is available in the U.S. in a slightly abridged form in the anthology edited by Joseph D. Gauthier, S. J., *Douze voix françaises*, 1900–1960 (Englewood Cliffs, N.J.: Prentice-Hall, 1969), pp. 105–12.

9. According to Langlois (*Indochina Adventure*, p. 218), Malraux hoped that *The Temptation of the West* would be recognized as a response to Henri Massis's *La Defense de l'Occident* (Paris: Plon, 1926). Malraux later prepared a more direct response in his review article on Massis's book; see *La Nouvelle Revue Française*, 14 (mai 1927: 813–18; and Langlois, pp. 218–21.

10. *La tentation de l'Occident* (Paris: Grasset, 1951), pp. 65–66. The translations of this and all subsequent quotations from Malraux's works are my own. After the

initial reference giving the bibliographical data for each novel, page numbers of the quotations are identified in parenthesis in the body of the study.

11. Malraux's interpretation is appropriate to Aristotelian, Hellenistic Greece but clashes with the notion of the cosmos, the ordered universe where even man is in his proper place. See especially Plato's explanation of the word "soul" in "Phaedrus," p. 124; "Timaeus," pp. 448–50; Philebus, pp. 618–19; and "Laws," bk. X, pp. 759–69, in *Plato, Great Books of the Western World* (Chicago: Encyclopaedia Britannica, 1952), vol. 7.

12. Victor Brombert, "Malraux: Passion and Intellect," in *The Intellectual Hero* (Chicago: University of Chicago Press, 1960), pp. 178–80.

13. "La psychologie de l'art (fragments)," *Verve,* 1 (dec. 1937): 41–48; "La psychologie des renaissances," *Verve,* 1 (printemps 1938): 21–25; and "De la représentation en Orient et en Occident," *Verve,* 1 (été 1938): 69–72.

14. The letter beginning on p. 137 is mistakenly identified as coming from Paris. The same error was repeated in the 1970 Gallimard collective edition, 1:86.

15. Malraux reiterated his belief in this concept of the artist in 1929, in a discussion of his novel, *Les conquérants,* before the *Union pour la Vérité.* The substance of Malraux's remarks was published as *"La question des Conquérants," Variétés,* 15 Oct. 1929, pp. 429–37.

16. In the place of *strengthened,* the original has the metaphorical expression *armed against itself (armée contre elle-même),* which imparts a belligerence foreign to the logic of the essay. To the contrary, Malraux's conclusion reflects something of the optimism fostered by the 1925 Lacarno treaties, which established a mechanism for peaceful settlement of European disputes.

17. In Albert Camus, *Discours de Suède* (Paris: Gallimard, 1958), pp. 9–21. Camus entitled this speech "The Artist and His Time."

18. In a talk given at the Sorbonne, on 14 November 1946, and published as "L'homme et la culture artistique," *Les conférences de l'U.NESCO* (Paris: Fontaine, 1947), pp. 75–89.

CHAPTER THREE

1. Cited as marginal commentary to Gaëton Picon, *Malraux par lui-même* (Paris: Edition du Seuil, Ecrivains de Toujours, 1967), p. 16.

2. "Laclos" in *Le triangle noir* (Paris: Gallimard, 1970), pp. 21–51. The essay originally appeared in *Tableaux de la litterature francaise,* (Paris: Gallimard, 1939), 2: 417–28.

3. See R. W. B. Lewis's introduction to *Malraux: A Collection of Critical Essays,* R. W. B. Lewis, ed. (Englewood Cliffs, N. J.: Prentice-Hall, Spectrum Books, 1964), esp. pp. 4–5.

4. It is more precisely A.D. who calls European conquerors opportunists, *Tentation,* p. 211.

5. Langlois, *André Malraux: The Indochina Adventure,* details Malraux's newspaper reporting of the 1925 Chinese rebellions in the chapter entitled "The Bol-

Notes

shevik Ghost," pp. 127–44. According to Langlois, Malraux has reproduced his news articles in the novel.

6. Immanuel C. Hsü, *The Rise of Modern China* (New York: Oxford University Press, 1970), pp. 538–630. Also useful is Conrad Brandt, *Stalin's Failure in China, 1924–1927* (Cambridge, Mass.: Harvard University Press, 1958) and Harold R. Isaacs, *The Tragedy of the Chinese Revolution* (Stanford, Calif.: Stanford University Press, 1951).

7. Malraux observes in his *Antimémoirs* (Paris: Gallimard, 1967), p. 492, that there were no Russians in Canton in 1925. He must mean in the city of Canton, for there is ample documentation of the Russians' role in the Cantonese Republic in 1925. Projecting Russians into the city of Canton for the novel is simply a case of literary license.

8. *Les Conquérants* in André Malraux, *Romans*, (Paris: Gallimard, Bibliothèque de la Pléiade, 1947), p. 148.

9. In the postface to *The Conquerors*, Malraux alludes to Borodin's demotion following the Nationalist coup of 1927. He reportedly asked Malraux's intervention in his behalf to get an apartment with a fireplace (*Romans*, p. 163). *Who Was Who in the USSR* (Metuchen, N. J.: Scarecrow Press, 1972), p. 85, indicates that Borodin was promoted from Deputy Director of TASS to Chief of the Soviet Information Bureau in 1934. Possibly fireplaces of the Stalinist bureaucracy were restricted for bureau chiefs and above. Anyhow his situation was better than Malraux supposed.

10. In 1925, Malraux and his collaborator, Paul Monin, were conducting an anti-colonial campaign through their Saigon newspaper, *L'Indochine*, and its successor, *L'Indochine Enchaînée;* see Langlois for a detailed account of this year in Malraux's life. He was certainly well enough informed of political events on mainland China to build a plot of them and project his fictional European adventurer into it, but there is some doubt about whether or not he actually observed them: Clara Malraux claims he did not visit the mainland before 1931; Langlois makes a contrary observation, p. 157; and Malraux himself has only obscured the issue by making the impossible claim that he was a Kuomintang commissar in Canton during the uprising (a letter to Edmund Wilson reprinted in his *Literary Chronicle: 1920 to 1950* (New York: Doubleday Anchor Books, 1956), p. 177.)

11. Two prostitutes appear at the beginning of one scene: the narrator arrives at Garine's apartment at an indiscreet moment (pp. 99–100). Not even Claude Mauriac, who misunderstands and exaggerates the effects of Malraux's eroticism, gives this scene much importance in his study *Malraux ou le mal du héros* (Paris: Grasset, 1946).

12. See Camus's first and most successful play, *Caligula*, originally written in 1938, but revised slightly for the stage in 1944; also Jean-Paul Sartre's *La nausée*, originally published in 1938 by Gallimard.

13. André Malraux, "Fragment inédit des *Conquérants*," *Bifur*, 4 (déc 1929): 5–15.

14. See Leon Trotsky, "The Strangled Revolution" in R. W. B. Lewis, op. cit., pp. 12–19. Malraux was also called to task by a group of Leftist intellectuals, the Union pour la Vérité, on charges of having misrepresented the revolution in *The*

Malraux's Heroes and History

Conquerors; Malraux defended his novel as a metaphysical, not a political work; see André Malraux, "La question des *Conquérants,*" *Variétés,* 15 Oct. 1929, pp. 429–37.

15. The general reading public was far more receptive. A journalistic coterie, Le Cercle Interallié, established the Prix Interallié in 1930 and made its first award to Malraux for *The Royal Way.*

16. *Antimémoirs* pp. 375–473. Mayrena's story is narrated by Baron de Clappique who seems to materialize, with all his speech defects, from the pages of *Man's Fate.*

17. That Indochinese adventure likely contributed to a second novel: the early chapters of Paul Morand's *Bouddha Vivant* (Paris: Grasset, 1927) are built around a character, Renaud d'Ecouen, whose activities in Indochina parallel Malraux's. In the review he prepared for the *Nouvelle Revue Francaise,* 14 (août 1927): 253–55, Malraux singled out Renaud for his praise—very likely with his tongue in his cheek!

18. *La voie royale* (Paris: Grasset, Livre de Poche, 1959), p. 13.

19. The criticism of Mayrena may have been intended to tie Perken's story, Part One of the projected "Forces of the Wilderness," to the part treating his exemplar. Perken's remarks would stand then as an introduction to the portrait of a third adventurer, one drawn somewhat more sympathetically than the reader might expect, if we can judge from the *Antimemoirs.*

20. *La psychologie de l'art: le museé imaginaire* (Geneva: Skira, 1947), 1. The same ideas are presented in a somewhat more accessible form in *Les voix du silence* (Paris: Gallimard, La Galerie de la Pléiade, 1951) in the section entitled "Le musée imaginaire," pp. 11–125. Previously they had been published as fragments in *Verve,* supra.

21. *Memoirs,* p. 246. Like her husband, Clara Malraux also made a novel out of this adventure. In her *Portrait de Grisélidis* (Paris: Colbert, 1945), the jungle appears far less menacing than in *The Royal Way* and, in fact, conducive to joys of romantic love.

22. Clara Malraux leveled this charge against her former husband in a newspaper interview entitled "Je suis tombée sur un mari profondément misogyne," *L'Express,* no. 654 (24 Oct. 1963), pp. 40–41. Also in *Memoirs,* pp. 233, 235–36, and 244; and in the third volume (as yet untranslated), *Le bruit de nos pas:* t. III, *Les combats et les jeux* (Paris: Grasset, 1969), p. 76.

23. *L'amant de Lady Chatterly* (Paris: Gallimard, 1932). At the time of publication, Malraux was an editor at Gallimard.

24. René Girard, "The Role of Eroticism in Malraux's Fiction," *Yale French Studies,* no. 11 (1952), p. 52. Girard draws his remark from Malraux's study of Goya.

CHAPTER FOUR

1. Edgar Snow, *Red Star Over China* (New York: Random House, 1938), pp. 42–49. Snow reports an interview with Chou in which the Chinese premier re-

Notes

counted his early days in the Chinese Communist movement. See also C. P. Fitzgerald, *The Birth of Communist China* (Baltimore: Penguin Books, 1964), p. 67.

2. Goldmann, pp. 154–56.

3. Especially virulent is Ilya Ehernburg's criticism reprinted in *Les Critiques de Notre Temps et Malraux* (Paris: Garnier, 1970), pp. 50–52.

4. Denis Boak, *André Malraux* (Oxford: Clarendon Press, 1969), p. 69, reports having received confirmation from Malraux that Kyo Gisors was modeled after Kiyoshi (Kyo) Komatsu, a Japanese writer who translated for Malraux. In *Antimémoires*, p. 514, Malraux hedges on the question of whether or not Chou contributed anything to the conception of Kyo. It appears safe to identify him as a composite: Chou's accomplishments are attributed to a character who, for his background and personality, more resembles Komatsu.

5. *La condition humaine* in *Romans* (Paris: Gallimard, Bibliothèque de la Pléiade, 1947), p. 228 and p. 281. After his son's death, old Gisors describes Kyo's Marxism as a fatality, p. 428. This description is difficult to reconcile with Kyo's expressed views and his activism, but it expresses, as Gisors admits, the vanquished hope that Marxism could give a metaphysical direction to his life. Now after his son's death, Marxism appears as but another of life's tragic deceptions.

6. Quoted in Gaëton Picon, *André Malraux* (Paris: Gallimard, 1945), p. 81. My translation.

7. Frohock, Wilbur M., *André Malraux and the Tragic Imagination* (Stanford, Calif.: Stanford University Press, 1952), pp. 61–67.

8. I am indebted to Margaret Groves for much of this interpretation. See her fine article, "Malraux's Lyricism and the Death of Kyo," *Modern Language Review* 54 (Jan. 1969): 53–61.

9. Kant's practical imperative reads: "Rational nature exists as an end in itself. . . . The practical imperative will thus be as follows: So act as to treat humanity, whether in your own person or in that of any other, always at the same time as an end, and never merely as a means." Quoted in Frederick Copelston, S. J., *A History of Philosophy*, (Garden City, N.J.: Doubleday, Image Books, 1964), 6, part 2: 120. Simone de Beauvoir relied heavily on it for her explanation of Sartre's political "engagement" in *Pour une morale de l'ambigüité* (Paris: Gallimard, Collection Idées, 1966). It should not be confused with the categorical imperative which Sartre borrowed for his cursory definition of existentialism, "Défense d l'existentialisme" reprinted in Gaëtan Picon, *Panorama de la nouvelle littérature francaise* (Paris: Gallimard, 1960), pp. 660–62.

10. In *La psychologie de l'art*, Malraux notes that "he once told the story of a man who did not recognize a recording of his own voice, and for that reason called the story *La condition humaine*, 3:146–47. This elliptical explanation notwithstanding, the title of the novel and its climactic death scene so reflect Pascal that one cannot avoid reading *Man's Fate* in the light of the *Pensées*, and, it seems, without violating Malraux's suggested interpretation.

11. This is at least the implication of Malraux's text, but the construction of the boiler of a steam locomotive would make such an execution impossible. The

Malraux's Heroes and History

only effective way to execute a man with a locomotive would be, in Frohock's words, "to tie him to the rails and run over him."

12. André Malraux, *La Condition Humaine, Extraits,* ed. A. Boutet de Monvel (Paris: Librairie Larousse, Classiques Larousse, 1955).

13. Critics have often pointed out the resemblances between Tchen, the terrorist of *Man's Fate,* and Hong of *The Conquerors.* Tchen's terrorism involves a European response to the absurd, a response conditioned by his European education. The gratuitous terrorism of Hong, although quite similar in expression, has no such roots. But too little is known of him to permit an analysis.

14. Frohock, pp. 58–61, gives a more detailed explanation of the scene. The episode is based on an attempt against the life of the co-editor of the Saigon newspapers, Paul Monin. Malraux knew it only from the point of view of the victim, which is entirely suppressed in the novel.

15. Haakon Chevalier (*Man's Fate,* New York: Random House, Vintage Books, 1961) gives a more delicate translation of this and other passages that associate Tchen's terrorism with a perverse sexuality: the American reader thus loses the implications of Malraux's choice of words.

16. The adjective *totalitarian* is Malraux's own; it is used by the character Scali in *L'espoir* to describe the intellectual's quest for a justification for action which satisfies both his political and metaphysical aspirations: in *Romans* (Paris: Gallimard, Bibliotèque de la Pléiade, 1947) p. 764.

17. After leaving the gambling house, Clappique became involved in an erotic episode set up for the pleasures of a group of voyeurs, *Marianne,* 13 déc 1933, p. 4. The episode was excluded from the novel because, as Malraux explained, it gave too great a place in the work to Clappique.

18. In this study of Laclos, Malraux makes the devaluation of the mystery of human existence the characteristic of the hero. See *Le Triangle Noir,* pp. 43–44. The expression as well as the concept are appropriate to the heroes of *Man's Fate.*

CHAPTER FIVE

1. "Preface," *Le temps du mépris* (Paris: Gallimard, 1935), pp. 8–11.

2. Art as an antidestiny is the principal theme of these and Malraux's subsequent art studies. Once he had repudiated communism, he adopted an esthetic solution to the human condition that he investigated through painting, sculpture, and literature (in *Les noyers de l'Altenburg*), but never through music, which lends itself less successfully to Malraux's thesis.

3. The account of the expedition is repeated fully in *Antimémoirs* pp. 83–106.

4. *Memoirs,* pp. 233, 235–36, and 244. See also Madeleine Chapsal, "Entretien. Clara Malraux: 'Je suis tombée sur un mari profondément misogyne.'" *L'Express,* no. 645 (24 October 1963), pp. 40–41.

5. Raymond Aron evaluates this line of thinking in *L'opium des intellectuels* (Paris: Gallimard, Collection "Idées," 1968). Aron's only specific references to

Notes

Malraux are to his art studies. The criticism directed against Merleau-Ponty, however, also applies to Malraux's thought of the late nineteen-thirties.

6. In preparing his translation, *Days of Wrath* (New York: Random House, 1936), Haakon Chevalier dressed up the expression *fraternité virile* so that the linguistic clues the author gave for connecting the different phases of the development of his theme are lost in the English version.

7. *Antimémoires*, p. 335. The title of Haakon Chevalier's translation also invites a religious interpretation. It emphasizes the aspects of judgment and atonement associated with the *dies irae*, which are far removed from Malraux's intentions.

CHAPTER SIX

1. Payne, pp. 233–45 and p. 461; and Jean Lacouture, *André Malraux: une vie dans le siècle* (Paris: Seuil, 1973), pp. 225–27.

2. A dissertation on the press reception of the novel is now being prepared by John Romeiser, Vanderbilt University.

3. This is the name used by Malraux. In the Stuart Gilbert–Alastair MacDonald translation (New York: Random House, 1938), the American journalist is identified as Slade. All page references are to the text published in the Pléiade edition entitled *Romans* (Paris: Gallimard, 1947).

4. David Siqueiros, the youngest of the three muralists, served in Spain as a propagandist for the Republicans according to his obituary, *The Chicago Daily News*, 7 January 1974. He may likely have inspired Malraux's character, Lopez. The esthetic observations attributed to him are decidedly Malraux's own, having been first made by Malraux in his speech before the Writers International Association for the Defense of Culture in London, 21 June 1936. The text of the speech, "Sur l'héritage cultural," has been reprinted in *Commune*, 37 (September 1936): 1–9.

5. Frohock especially has leveled this criticism, see pp. 90–125.

6. See Hugh Thomas, *The Spanish Civil War* (London: Eyre and Spottiswoode, 1961), pp. 145–48; and Gabriel Jackson, *The Spanish Republic and the Civil War, 1931–1939* (Princeton: Princeton University Press, 1965), p. 239.

7. In the French text, Malraux contrasts the verb *se battre*, which, in the context, carries the connotation of individual courage in a fight, with *combattre*, connoting coordinated fighting in a vast military conflict.

8. Lucien Goldmann, "Introduction à un étude structurale des romans de Malraux" in *Pour une sociologie du roman* (Paris: Gallimard, Bibliothèque des Idées, 1964), pp. 221–39.

9. History records that it was the Nationalists who deserve credit for the best known gesture of nobility performed at the Alcazar siege: having captured the son of the Nationalist commander of the Alcazar, the Republicans demanded the surrender of the citadel in exchange for the young man's life; Moscardo's reported answer was the advice that his son commend his soul to God—thereupon young Moscardo was executed: Cecil D. Eby, *The Siege of the Alcazar* (New York:

Random House, 1965), pp. 61–63. Omission of the incident can best be explained by Malraux's thesis that the Republicans were not yet so set on victory as to employ such tactics.

10. His response is aphoristic: "Transform into awareness the broadest possible experience" (*Romans*, p. 764).

11. Claude Roy interprets Garcia's remarks as Malraux's criticism of insincere Communists. See "Sur André Malraux," *Les Temps Modernes*, 13ᵉ année, nos. 143–44 (janvier–février 1958), pp. 1443–44. The interpretation comes from the substitution of *Communiste* for what Malraux called *révolutionnaire* in *Man's Hope*. But of more interest to Roy is Malraux's hypocrisy: he accuses Malraux, not without some justification, of looking in all his political undertakings for the sort of self-satisfaction that his character Garcia criticized.

CHAPTER SEVEN

1. Malraux's reference (p. 577) is to Karl von Clausewitz's *On War* (London: Kegan Paul, Trench, Trubner & Co., 1940). Published posthumously by his widow between 1832 and 1837, it constituted until the end of World War I the basic work on military strategy. That it should provide the major part of Manuel's knowledge of war is a testimony to his dilettantism as well as to his inexperience. And since Malraux had practically no military experience before 1936, one wonders how much of his own tactical knowledge came out of Clausewitz.

2. Thomas identifies Malraux's Manuel as Enrique Lister, p. 242, fn.

3. Thomas, pp. 383–87. For the composition of the Republicans' first mixed brigade and Lister's assignment as its commander, see Thomas p. 364.

4. A more elaborate description of the dialectic is given by Jean-Paul Sartre, *Critique de la raison dialectique* (Paris: Gallimard, Bibliothèque des Sciences Humaines, 1959). This unreadably profuse work sets out to correct Marxism by applying existentialistic and modern sociological concepts to it. A summary is contained in Sartre's *Questions de méthode* (Paris: Gallimard, Collection Idées, 1960) and in Wilfred Desan, *The Marxism of Jean-Paul Sartre* (New York: Doubleday, 1965.) For Arnold J. Toynbee's analysis of historical evolution see *The Study of History,* (London: Oxford University Press, 1945), 1:175–81: and *Civilization on Trial,* (New York: Oxford University Press, 1948). This latter work goes far towards making a religion of history as the last chapter, "The Meaning of History for the Soul" (pp. 253–63) indicates. To this list might also be added the eighteenth-century French *philosophes,* at least insofar as their historicism was analyzed by Carl L. Becker. See "The Uses of Posterity" in *The Heavenly City of the Eighteenth-Centruy Philosophers.* (New Haven: Yale University Press, 1932), pp. 119–68.

5. According to Payne, it was Malraux's intention to turn his account of the Spanish Civil War into a long philosophical novel, see p. 247. Interpreting the novel with too much regard for Malraux's politics of the time, numerous critics have exaggerated the novel's communism.

Notes

6. "Whosoever will save his life will lose it . . ." *Mark* 8:35; Luke 9:24. In *Antimémoires*, Malraux expresses the Apostles' admonition with a different orientation: ". . . any faith dissolves life in the eternal . . ." (p. 229).

7. A particularly significant one is the peasants' long parable on the coming of Christ to Spain (*Romans*, pp. 583–85). It can easily be taken as an allegorical outline of *Man's Hope* identifying communism as ". . . a star, never before seen (that) rose above them . . ."

8. Cited in previous chapter, p. 111.

9. For instance, the fraternity he feels while reviewing his troops during a parade more than compensates for any compunction he felt for refusing clemency to the deserters (*Romans*, p. 772).

10 Malraux's movie originally bore the title, *Sierra De Teruel*.

11. The peasant in man will receive more attention in the conclusion of Malraux's last work of fiction, but it is useful to recall that the last section of *Man's Hope* originally bore the title "The Peasants"; this title has been retained in the English translation. The change in title to "Hope" can be explained by the desire to avoid the restrictive interpretation that Magnin's fraternity could bring progress without the drive for military success associated with the character Manuel.

CHAPTER EIGHT

1. Charles de Gaulle, "Technique," in *The Army of the Future* (Philadelphia: Lippincott, 1941), pp. 45–70.

2. Clara Malraux, *Le bruit de nos pas*, vol. III: *Les combats et les jeux* (Paris: Grasset, 1969) pp. 192–93.

3. For one fictional view of this collaboration see Jean-Paul Sartre, "Drôle d'amitié," *Les Temps Modernes*, no. 49 (Nov. 1949), pp. 769–806; and no. 50 (Dec. 1949), pp. 1009–39.

4. Lacouture, p. 274.

5. Lacouture, p. 276–77.

6. Janine Mossuz has reconstructed much of Malraux's Resistance experience; see "André Malraux combattant" in her *André Malraux et le gaullisme;* Cahiers de la Fondation Nationale des Sciences Politiques, no. 177 (Paris: Colin, 1970), pp. 23–31.

7. Translated as "Lawrence and the Demon of the Absolute" in *Hudson Review*, 8 (1956): 519–32; originally published in French as *N'était-ce donc que cela?* (Paris: Editions du Pavois, 1946).

8. Richard D. Robinson, *The First Turkish Republic* (Cambridge, Mass.: Harvard University Press, 1965), pp. 1–26.

9. T. E. Lawrence, *Seven Pillars of Wisdom* (New York: Dell, Laurel Editions, 1962), pp. 654–55.

10. For an interpretation of Malraux's notion of "shamanism" see Frohock, pp. 138–46; also R. W. B. Lewis, *The Picaresque Saint* (Philadelphia: Lippincott,

Malraux's Heroes and History

1959), pp. 293–95: here Lewis draws a parallel between Malraux's shaman and his own existential searcher, which he presents as the modern picaro.

11. Langlois identifies as the source of the Altenburg Colloquium a 1926 colloquium at Pontigny that Malraux attended; op. cit., p. 201. Malraux has undoubtedly added some of the flavor of Hermann Keyserling's Darmstadt seminars, which he would have known only indirectly.

12. *Les noyers de l'Altenburg* (Paris: Gallimard, 1948), pp. 89–90.

13. Malraux outlines the estheticism he attributes to Walter Berger in *La Métramorphose des dieux* (Paris: Gallimard, Galerie de la Pléiade, 1951), pp. 24–28.

14. *Les voix du silence,* pp. 70–74.

15. Ibid., p. 637.

16. Armand Hoog, "Malraux, Möllberg and Frobenius," in *Malraux: A Collection of Critical Essays,* pp. 86–95.

17. Paul Valéry, "Notes sur la grandeur et décadence de l'Europe," in *Oeuvres,* vol. 2, (Paris: Gallimard, Bibliothèque de la Pléiade, 1960), pp. 929–34.

18. Lucien Goldmann also observes that this novel carries Malraux's repudiation of communism. His observation is based on a symbolic interpretation of Turanism rather than the notion of historical fragmentation that Malraux attributes to Möllberg. See Goldmann, pp. 252–56. In his analysis, Goldmann mistakenly identifies the hero as Victor, not Vincent Berger.

19. In the context of the novel, Malraux's suggestion that Russia has a non-European heritage appears as something of a literary license. If one recalls that he identifies European traditions with *Roman* Catholicism, Russia can more credibly be taken to have a Byzantine heritage. Malraux repeated this view in his 5 March 1948 political address at the Paris concert hall, Salle Pleyel. He later used this talk, with but negligible changes, as the "Postface" to the Pléiade edition of *The Conquerors* (*Romans,* pp. 163–78).

20. To create this scene, Malraux took some liberties with history. Sir James Edmonds gives in his *Short History of World War I* (London: Oxford University Press, 1951; p. 144) the probable date for the first use of phosgene as 19 Dec. 1915, and the place, Ypres. The *Encyclopedia of Chemical Technology,* vol. 10 (New York: Interscience Encyclopedia, Inc., 1953), corroborates Sir James's date but does not identify the place. To fit the needs of his novel, Malraux appears to have shifted the introduction of the lethal phosgene gas from Flanders to Poland and has advanced the date by at least three months to a time when Germany's eastern front was still active.

21. The etymology of *phosgene* (*phos*=light; *gene*=to make) also suggests a luminescence. The name comes not from a light given off, however, but from the early methods of synthesizing CO and CI_2 gases by exposing them to the sun. Hence *phosgene* is *made by* light.

22. My use of "anthihistory" bears no relation to Bruce Louis Jay's, " 'Antihistory' and the Historical Method of Salammbo," *Romanic Review,* 63 (Feb. 1972): pp. 20–33. Professor Jay describes the novel as antihistorical because Flaubert's events lose all historical perspective as his "artistic imagination works to transform history into a vehicle of spectacle," p. 30.

Notes

23. Although Vincent's death is not depicted, he loses consciousness and everything points to death from gas inhalation. Avril Goldberger, in his *Visions of a Hero* (Paris: Minard, Lettres Modernes, 1965), pp. 231–32, speculates that Vincent did not die on the Vistula battleground. While survival logically accounts for the narrator's insights into Vincent's war experiences, it flies in the face of the poetic logic of Malraux's narrative—and the great majority of critical interpretations.

CHAPTER NINE

1. Malraux has replaced, for instance, the generalization "Comme celui qui rencontre l'Inde pour la première fois . . ." (p. 287), by the more personal "comme lorsque j'avais rencontré l'Asie pour la première fois . . ." *Antimémoires*, p. 318. Malraux has more recently explained that this entire tank episode is invented. Lacouture reports that Malraux never saw service in the tanks and was captured 16 May 1940 "à mi-distance à peu près de Provins et de Sens . . . ," p. 271.

2. Boak, pp. 153–55.

3. Vincent's remarks at the Altenburg colloquium are discussed in "History Reassessed", pp. 195–97.

4. Madeleine Rousseau Raaphorst goes beyond this point to show how the theme of *The Walnut Trees of Altenburg* fits into the structure of *Antimémoires:* see "Rôle et importance des *Noyers de l'Altenburg* dans les *Antimémoires* de Malraux," *Rice University Studies*, 57, No. 2 (1971): 73–87.

5. Frohock devotes the first pages of his chapter on *The Walnut Trees of Altenburg* to make this point; see pp. 126–28.

6. Rima Drell Reck, "Malraux's Transitional Novel: *Les Noyers de l'Altenburg*," *French Review*, 34 (May 1961): 537–44.

7. It is evident that Malraux read *Seven Pillars of Wisdom* and not *Revolt in the Desert*, specifically a military account published by Lawrence to correct Lowell Thomas' romanticized reports: only Lawrence's definitive autobiography, translated into French by Charles Mauron and published in 1936 by Payot, contains the meditations on art that Malraux refers to.

8. With the publication of *La tête d'obsidienne* in 1974, Malraux announced a new title for the autobiographical series. The series is now entitled *Le miroir des limbes* ("The Mirror of Limbo"). *Antimemoirs* is Part One of the series: Part Two is *Métamorphose* ("Metamorphosis") and is now composed of *Les chênes qu'on abat* and *La Tête d'obsidienne*, with other installments promised.

CHAPTER TEN

1. The expression is used by Rima Drell Reck in "*The Antimémoires:* Malraux's Ultimate Form," *Kentucky Romance Quarterly*, 16, no. 2 (1969): 156.

Malraux's Heroes and History

2. The cyclical nature of Malraux's works is the theme of Violet Horvath's study *André Malraux: The Human Adventure*, (New York: Gotham Library, New York University Press), 1969.

3. Here I am thinking particularly of the attitude he attributes to the "absurd man" in *Le mythe de Sisyphe* (Paris: Gallimard, Collection Idées, 1967) pp. 118–22, of his notion of "création sans lendemain," pp. 151–57 and of his portrait of the absurd man, especially in the last pages of *L'Etranger* (New York: Appleton, Century, Crofts, 1955), pp. 125–38. Sartre's refusal to allow death to mediate the value of life is expressed in the subchapter "Ma mort," *L'être et le néant* (Paris: Gallimard, Bibliothèque des idées, 1943), pp. 615–38.

4. This is the view that comes out of Simone de Beauvoir's exegesis of Sartrian *engagement, Pour une moralité de l'ambiguïté,* and from Albert Camus's long essay on the ethics of revolution, *L'homme révolté* (Paris: Gallimard, 1951).

5. Malraux was much more explicit in *Les voix du silence,* pp. 589–600.

6. Paris: Gallimard, 1971.

7. Paris: Gallimard, 1974. The most recent installment, *Lazare* (Paris: Gallimard, 1974), is a meditation based on the temporary paralysis that hospitalized Malraux in 1973.

BIBLIOGRAPHY

$\mathcal{T}$HE following books and articles have contributed directly to *Malraux's Heroes and History:*

Aron, Raymond. *L'opium des intellectuels.* Paris: Gallimard, Collection Idées, 1968.

Beauvoir, Simone de. *Pour une morale de l'ambiguïté.* Paris: Gallimard, Collection Idées, 1966.

Becker, Carl L. *The Heavenly City of the Eighteenth-Century Philosophers.* New Haven: Yale University Press, 1932.

Berl, Emmanuel. *La culture en péril.* Paris: La Table Ronde, 1948.

Bernard, Jean-Pierre. "André Malraux ou le communisme considéré comme action fraternelle," in his *Le parti communiste français et la question littéraire 1921–1939.* Grenoble: Presses Universitaires de Grenoble, 1972, pp. 177–90.

Blend, Charles D. *André Malraux, Tragic Humanist.* Columbus, Ohio: Ohio State University Press, 1963.

Blumenthal, Gerda. *André Malraux; the Conquest of Dread.* Baltimore: Johns Hopkins University Press, 1960.

Boak, Denis. *André Malraux.* Oxford: Clarendon Press, 1969.

Boisdeffre, Pierre de. *André Malraux.* Paris: Classiques du XXᵉ Siècle, Editions Universitaires, 1955.

Brandt, Conrad. *Stalin's Failure in China, 1924–1927.* Cambridge, Mass.: Harvard University Press, 1958.

Brombert, Victor. "Malraux, Passion and Intellect," in his *The Intellectual Hero.* Chicago: University of Chicago Press, 1960, pp. 165–80.

Carduner, Jean. "Les *Antimémoires* dans l'oeuvre de Malraux," *Kentucky Romance Quarterly,* 16, no. 1 (1969): 3–21.

Casey, Bill. "André Malraux's Heart of Darkness," *Twentieth Century Literature,* 5 (1959): 21–26.

Caute, David. *Communism and the French Intellectuals.* New York: MacMillan, 1964. Especially chapter entitled "André Malraux," pp. 242–47.

Chua, C. L. "Nature and Art in the Esthetics of Malraux's *L'espoir,*" *Symposium,* 26 (Spring 1972): 114–27.

Malraux's Heroes and History

Cruickshank, John, ed. *The Novelist as Philosopher: Studies in French Fiction, 1935–1960.* London: Oxford University Press, 1962.

Daniels, Graham. "The Sense of the Past in the Novels of Malraux," *Studies in Modern French Literature Presented to P. Mansell Jones.* Edited by L. J. Austin, Garnet Rees, and Eugene Vinaver. Manchester: Manchester University Press, 1961, pp. 71–86.

Delhomme, Jeane. *Temps et destin: essai sur Malraux.* Paris: Gallimard, série "Les essais," 1955.

Dorenlot, F. E. *Malraux ou l'unité de pensée.* Paris: Gallimard, 1970.

Fitch, Brian T. "Splendeurs et misères du monstre incomparable—les deux univers romanesques d'André Malraux" in his *Le Sentiment d'étrangeté.* Paris: Minard, Les Lettres Modernes, 1964, pp. 15–92.

Fitzgerald, C. P. *The Birth of Communist China.* Baltimore: Penguin, 1964.

Frohock, Wilbur M. *André Malraux and the Tragic Imagination.* Stanford, Calif.: Stanford University Press, 1952.

————. "Malraux and the Poem of the Walnuts," in his *Style and Temper.* New York: Oxford, 1967.

Gaillard, Pol, ed. *Les critiques de notre temps et Malraux.* Paris: Garnier Frères, 1970.

Girard, René. "The Role of Eroticism in Malraux's Fiction," *Yale French Studies,* no. 11 (1952), pp. 49–58.

————. "L'homme et le cosmos dans *L'espoir* et *Les noyers de l'Altenburg* d'André Malraux, *PMLA,* 68 (Mar. 1953): 49–55.

Goldenberger, Avriel. "André Malraux's World of Heroes," in his *Visions of a New Hero.* Paris: Minard, Les Lettres Modernes, 1965, pp. 145–243.

Goldmann, Lucien. "Introduction à une étude structurale des romans de Malraux," in his *Pour une sociologie du roman.* Paris: Gallimard, Collection Idées, 1964, pp. 59–277.

Gross, Harvey. "André Malraux" in his *The Contrived Corridor: History and Fatality in Modern Literature.* Ann Arbor: University of Michigan Press, 1971, pp. 124–54.

Groves, Marguerite. "Malraux's Lyricism and the Death of Kyo," *Modern Language Review,* 64 (Jan. 1969): 53–61.

Hartman, Geoffrey H. "Camus and Malraux: The Common Ground," *Yale French Studies,* no. 25 (Spring 1960), pp. 105–10.

————. *Malraux.* New York: Hillary House, Studies in Modern European Literature and Thought, 1960.

Hoffmann, Joseph. *L'humanisme de Malraux.* Paris: Klincksieck, 1963.

Horvath, Violet. *André Malraux: The Human Adventure,* New York: New York University Press, Gotham Library, 1969.

Bibliography

Hsü, Immanuel C. *The Rise of Modern China.* New York: Oxford University Press, 1970.

Hughes, H. Stuart. *The Obstructed Path: French Social Thought in the Years of Desperation, 1930–1960.* New York: Harper & Row, 1969.

Isaacs, Harold R. *The Tragedy of the Chinese Revolution.* Stanford, Calif.: Stanford University Press, 1951.

Jackson, Gabriel. *The Spanish Republic and the Civil War, 1931–1939.* Princeton: Princeton University Press, 1965.

Jenkins, Cecil. *Malraux.* New York: Twayne World Author Series, 1972.

Kline, Thomas Jefferson. *André Malraux and the Metamorphosis of Death.* New York: Columbia University Press, 1973.

Knight, Everett W. *Literature Considered as Philosophy: The French Example.* London: Routledge and Kegan Paul, 1957.

Lacouture, Jean. *André Malraux: une vie dans le siècle.* Paris: Seuil, 1973.

Langlois, Walter G. "The Debut of André Malraux, Editor (Kra, 1920–1922)," *PMLA,* 80 (March 1965): 111–22.

_____. *André Malraux: The Indochina Adventure.* New York: Praeger, 1966.

_____. "Malraux and the Greek Ideal" in Langois, ed., *The Persistent Voice: Essays on Hellenism in French Literature Since the Eighteenth Century in Honor of Professeur Henri M. Peyre.* New York: New York University Press, 1971, pp. 195–212.

_____. ed. *André Malraux I: Du farfelu aux Antimémoires.* Paris, Les Lettres Modernes, nos. 304–7, 1972.

Lawrence, T[homas] E. *Seven Pillars of Wisdom.* New York: Dell, Laurel Editions, 1962.

Lewis R[ichard] W[arrington] B[aldwin], ed. *Malraux: A Collection of Critical Essays.* Englewood Cliffs, N.J.: Prentice-Hall, 1964.

_____. "Epilogue. The Shared Reality: The Shadow of André Malraux," in his *The Picaresque Saint: Representative Figures in Contemporary Fiction.* Philadelphia: Lippincott, 1959, pp. 275–95.

Malraux, André. *La tentation de l'Occident.* Paris: Grasset, 1926.

_____. "André Malraux et l'Orient," *Les Nouvelles Littéraires,* no. 198 (31 juillet 1926), p. 2.

_____. "*Defense de l'Occident* par Henri Massis," *La Nouvelle Revue Française,* 14 (mai 1927): 813–18.

_____. "*Bouddha vivant* par Paul Morand," *La Nouvelle Revue Française,* 14 (août 1927): 253–55.

_____. "D'une jeunesse européenne," in *Ecrits.* Paris: Grasset, 1927.

_____. "*Journal de voyage d'un philosophe* par Hermann Keyserling," *La Nouvelle Revue Française,* 16 (juin 1929): 884–86.

_____. "La question des *Conquérants,*" *Variétés,* 2 (oct 1929): 429–37.

Malraux's Heroes and History

_____. "*Les conquérants*, fragments inédits," *Bifur*, 4 (31 dec 1929): 5–15.

_____. "André Malraux nous parle de son oeuvre," *Monde*, no. 124 (18 oct 1930), p. 4.

_____. "Response à Trotsky," *La Nouvelle Revue Française*, 19 (avril 1931): 501–7.

_____. "Jeune Chine," *La Nouvelle Revue Française*, 20 (janvier 1932): 5–6.

_____. "Préface" to D. H. Lawrence, *L'Amant de Lady Chatterly*. Translated by Roger Cornaz. Paris: Gallimard, 1932.

_____. "A l'hôtel des sensations inédites," *Marianne*, 13 déc 1933, p. 4.

_____. "L'art est une conquête," *Commune*, 13–14 (sept–oct 1934): 68–71.

_____. "L'attitude de l'artiste," *Commune*, 15 (nov 1934): 166–74.

_____. "Préface" to Andrée Viollis, *Indochina SOS*. Paris: Gallimard, 1935.

_____. "L'oeuvre d'art," *Commune*, 23 (juillet 1935): 1264–66.

_____. "Interview with Malraux," *New Republic*, 24 June 1936, pp. 218–19.

_____. "Sur l'héritage culturel," *Commune*, 37 (sept 1936): 1–9.

_____. "Forging Man's Fate in Spain," *The Nation*, 20 March 1937, pp. 315–16.

_____. "La psychologie de l'art" (fragments), *Verve*, 1 (déc 1937): 41–48.

_____. "La psychologie des renaissances," *Verve*, 1 (printemps 1938): 21–25.

_____. "De la représentation en Orient et en Occident," *Verve*, 1 (été 1938): 69–72.

_____. "L'homme et la culture artistique," *Les Conférences de l'UNESCO*. Paris: Fontaine, 1947, pp. 75–89.

_____. *La psychologie de l'art*, 2 vols. Geneva: Skira, 1947.

_____. *Romans: Les conquérants, La condition humaine, L'espoir*. Paris: Gallimard, Bibliothèque de la Pléiade, 1947.

_____. *Les voix du silence*. Paris: Gallimard, La Galerie de la Pléiade, 1951.

_____. *La condition humaine, extraits*. Edited by A. Boutet de Monvel. Paris: Librairie Larousse, 1955.

_____. "Lawrence and the Demon of the Absolute," *Hudson Review*, 8 (1956): 519–32.

_____. *La métamorphose des dieux*. Paris: Gallimard, 1957.

_____. *La voie royale*. Paris: Grasset, Livre de Poche, 1959.

_____. *Antimémoires*. Paris: Gallimard, 1967.

_____. *Le triangle noir*. Paris: Gallimard, 1970.

Bibliography

_____. *Les chênes qu'on abat.* Paris, Gallimard, 1971.

_____. *La tête d'obsidienne.* Paris: Gallimard, 1974.

_____. *L'irréel.* Paris: Gallimard, 1974. Volume two of *La métamorphose des dieux.*

_____. *Lazare.* Paris: Gallimard, 1974.

Malraux, Clara Goldschmidt. *Memoirs.* Translated by Patrick O'Brian. New York: Farrar, Strauss and Giroux, 1967 (First two parts of her autobiography originally published under collective title *Le bruit de nos pas;* volume one is subtitled "Apprendre à vivre"; volume two, "Nos vingt ans").

_____. *Le bruit de nos pas: Les combats et les jeux.* Paris: Grasset, 1969 (volume three of her autobiography).

_____. *Portrait de Griselidis.* Paris: Editions Colbert, 1945.

Massis, Henri. *Defense of the West.* Translated by S. S. Flint. New York: Harcourt, Brace and Company, 1928.

Mauriac, Claude. *Malraux ou le mal du héros.* Paris: Grasset, 1946.

Morand, Paul. *Bouddha vivant.* Paris: Grasset, 1927.

Mossuz, Janine. *André Malraux et le gaullisme.* Cahiers de la Fondation Nationale des Sciences Politiques, no. 177. Paris: Colin, 1970.

Mounier, Emmanuel. "André Malraux, le conquérant aveugle" in his *Malraux, Camus, Sartre, Bernanos: l'espoir des désespérés.* Paris: Seuil, Collection "Les Points," 1953, pp. 11–63.

Orwell, George. *Homage to Catalonia and Looking Back on the Spanish Civil War.* Hammondworth, England: Penquin Books, 1966.

Payne, Robert. *A Portrait of André Malraux.* Englewood Cliffs, N.J.: Prentice-Hall, 1970.

Payne, Stanley. *The Spanish Revolution.* New York: Norton, 1970.

Picon, Gaëton. *André Malraux.* Paris: Gallimard, 1945.

_____. *Malraux par lui-même.* Paris: Editions du Seuil, Ecrivains de Toujours, 1967.

Raaphorst, Madeleine Rousseau. "Rôle et importance des *Noyers de l'Altenburg* dans les Antimémoires de Malraux," *Rice University Studies,* 55, no. 2 (1971): 73–87.

Reck, Rima Drell. "Malraux's Heroes: Activists and Aesthetes," *University of Kansas City Review* 28, no. 1 (Autumn 1961): 39–46 and 28, no. 2 (winter, 1961): 151–57.

_____. "Malraux's Transitional Novel: *Les noyers de l'Altenburg,*" *French Review,* 34 (May 1961): 537–44.

_____. "Malraux's Cerebral Eroticism," *Forum,* 11 (1962): 44–46.

_____. "The *Antimémoires:* Malraux's Ultimate Form," *Kentucky Romance Quarterly,* 16, no. 2 (1969):155–62.

Malraux's Heroes and History

Robinson, Richard D. *The First Turkish Republic: A Case Study in National Development.* Cambridge, Mass.: Harvard University Press, 1965.

Roy, Claude. "Sur André Malraux," *Les Temps Modernes,* 13e année, nos. 143–44 (janvier-février 1958), pp. 1436–52.

Sabourin, Pascal. *La réflexion sur l'art d'André Malraux.* Paris: Klincksieck, 1972.

Savage, Catherine. "Malraux and the Political Novel" in her *Malraux, Sartre, and Aragon as Political Novelists.* Gainesville, Fla.: University of Florida Press, University of Florida Monographs—Humanities, no. 17, 1964, pp. 6–16.

Sartre, Jean-Paul. *Questions de Méthode.* Paris: Gallimard, Collection Idees, 1960.

————. *Critique de la raison dialectique.* Paris: Gallimard, Bibliothèque des Sciences Humaines, 1959.

Simon, Pierre-Henri. "André Malraux et le sacré" in his *Témoins de l'homme.* Paris: Armand Colin, 1952, pp. 135–53.

Stephane, Roger. *Portrait de l'aventurier.* Paris: Sagittaire, 1950.

Snow, Edgar. *Red Star over China.* New York: Random House, 1938.

Sonnenfeld, Albert. "Malraux and the Tyranny of Time: The Circle and the Gesture," *Romanic Review,* 14, no. 3 (1963): 198–212.

Spengler, Oswald. *Decline of the West,* two vols. New York: Alfred Knopf, 1928.

Thomas, Hugh. *The Spanish Civil War.* London: Eyre and Spottiswoode, 1961.

Toynbee, Arnold. *The Study of History.* London: Oxford University Press, 1945.

————. *Civilization on Trial.* New York: Oxford University Press, 1948.

Vandegans, André. *La jeunesse littéraire d'André Malraux.* Paris: Pauvert, 1964.

Werth, Alexandre. *France 1940–1955.* New York: Holt, 1956.

Wilkinson, David. *Malraux: An Essay in Political Criticism.* Cambridge, Mass.: Harvard University Press, 1967.

Passion and the Intellect or André Malraux, Yale French Studies, no. 18. New Haven, 1957. Entire number devoted to Malraux.

This bibliography is hardly exhaustive. Works that fall into a general philosophical domain, such as Marx's *Capital* and Hegel's *Philosophy of Right,* have been omitted, as have works that have contributed only secondarily to *Malraux's Heroes and History.* Readers interested in more extensive, general Malraux bibliographies can profitably consult these compilations:

Bibliography

"Selection bibliographique." In *Les critiques de notre temps et Malraux*, edited by Pol Gaillard. Cited above, pp. 177–89.

Kline, Thomas Jefferson. "Selected Bibliography," in his *André Malraux and the Metamorphosis of Death*. Cited above, pp. 181–94.

Langlois, Walter G. *Malraux Criticism in English: essai de bibliographie des études en langue anglaise*. Paris: Minard Les Lettres Modernes, 1972.

Mossuz, Janine. "Bibliographie" (an especially detailed listing of Malraux's works and speeches in "Oeuvres de Malraux") in her *André Malraux et le gaullisme*. Cited above, pp. 291–313.

Sabourin, Pascal. "Bibliographie" in his *La réflexion sur l'art d'André Malraux*. Cited above, pp. 223–38.

Wilkinson, David. "Selected Bibliography" in his *Malraux: An Essay in Political Criticism*. cited above, pp. 202–16.

INDEX

213

Malraux's Heroes and History

214

Index

Malraux's Heroes and History

Index

Index

Index

WITHDRAWN